Developing and Managing Your School Guidance Program

Norman C. Gysbers

and

Patricia Henderson

American Association for Counseling and Development
5999 Stevenson Avenue, Alexandria, Virginia 22304 703/823-9800

Serving the counseling,
guidance and human
development professions
since 1952.

Copyright 1988 © by the American Association for Counseling and Development

All rights reserved.

American Association for Counseling and Development
5999 Stevenson Avenue
Alexandria, Virginia 22304

Library of Congress Cataloging-in-Publication Data

Gysbers, Norman C.
    Developing and managing your school guidance program.

    Bibliography: p.
    Includes index.
    1. Personnel service in education—United States.
I. Henderson, Patricia. II. Title.
LB1027.5.G929   1988   371.4′0973   88-3508
ISBN 1-55620-043-9

(Fourth Printing) Printed in the United States of America

To School Counselors

Contents

Appendices

Preface

Society is changing and the changes continue to accelerate. The changing labor market, extended life expectancy, the expectation of lifelong learning, divorce, single-parent families, blended families, teenage suicide, substance abuse, sexual experimentation, and peer and family pressure are not abstract issues. They are real and have a substantial impact on students and their personal, social, career, and educational development. (The Iowa K–12 Career Guidance Curriculum Guide for Student Development, 1987).

Educational Reform

To respond to changes such as these, education is being challenged. Education is in the midst of reform as it probably will be into the forseeable future. Numerous reports have been issued that speak to educational reform (Gardner, 1983; Boyer, 1983), but, unfortunately, most reports have said very little about the contributions of guidance (Herr, 1984). This is a serious omission because as Herr pointed out:

> Effective functioning in the schooling process and in the work force requires attention to emotional values and decision-making components that school counselors and guidance processes contribute to the overall educational mission. Students cannot choose opportunities that they do not know about and they cannot compete effectively when they are unsure or unaware of their own aptitudes and interests or preoccupied with their changing and perhaps neglectful family situations or chemical dependency. Intellectual effort and educational excellence frequently rest on resolution of such matters. They are affected by student feelings of security and self-esteem that simply cannot be ignored if children or youths are to develop the diverse competencies to become fully functioning adults and future workers of quality. (p. 219)

Reconceptualization of Guidance

To be responsive to continuing societal and individual changes as well as to calls for reform, education must look to reforming the entire educational enterprize, including guidance in the schools. Guidance reform will require a reconceptualization of guidance from an ancillary, crisis-oriented service to a comprehensive program firmly grounded on principles of human growth and development. Such a reconceptualization of guidance will require that the guidance program become an equal partner with the instructional program—with the concern for the intellectual development of individuals. Traditionally, however, guidance was not conceptualized and implemented in this manner, because, as Aubrey (1973) suggested, guidance was seen as a support service lacking a content base of its own. Sprinthall (1971) made this same point when he stated that there is little content in the practice of guidance and that guidance textbooks usually avoid discussion of a subject-matter base for guidance programs.

If guidance is to become an equal partner in education and meet the increasingly complex needs of individuals and society, it is our opinion that a content base for guidance is required. The call for this is not new; many early guidance pioneers issued the same call. But the call was not loud enough during the early years so that by the 1920s guidance had become essentially process- or technique-oriented. The need and the call continued to emerge occasionally thereafter, however, but it wasn't until the late 1960s and early 1970s that it reemerged and became visible once more in the form of developmental guidance.

That is not to say that developmental guidance was not present before the late 1960s. What it does mean, however, is that by the late 1960s the need for attention to aspects of human development other than "the time-honored cognitive aspect of learning-subject matter mastery" (Cottingham 1973, p. 341) again had become apparent. Cottingham characterized these other aspects of human development as "personal adequacy learning" (p. 342). Kehas (1973) pointed to this same need by stating that an individual should have opportunities "to develop intelligence about his self—his personal, unique, idiosyncratic, individual self" (p. 110).

It seems clear then that the next step in the evolution of guidance was to establish guidance as a comprehensive program—a program that is an integral part of the educational process with a content base of its own. In response to this need Gysbers and Moore (1981) published a book titled *Improving Guidance Programs*. It presented a content-based, K–12 comprehensive guidance program model and described the steps to implement the model. This current book uses the model and implementation steps presented in *Improving Guidance Programs* as a base, but expands and extends the model and implementation steps substantially.

Four Phases of Program Improvement

The four phases of developing and implementing a comprehensive guidance program as described by Mitchell and Gysbers (1978) are used as the organizers for this book. The four phases are planning, designing, implementing, and evaluating. Chapters 1–4 address planning, chapters 5 and 6, designing, chapters 7 and 8, implementing, and chapter 9, evaluating.

Planning

Chapter 1 traces the evolution of guidance in the schools from the turn of the century. The changing influences, emphases, and structures from then until now are described and discussed in detail. The recent emergence of developmental comprehensive guidance programs is highlighted. To have an understanding of the evolution of guidance in the schools and the emergence of developmental comprehensive programs is the first step in improving your school's guidance program.

Based on this understanding, we turn to the specifics of the planning phase. Chapter 2 focuses on the issues and concerns in planning and organizing guidance program improvement. Next, chapter 3 presents a model guidance program based on the concept of life career development; it is organized around three structural components and four program components. Chapter 4, the last chapter on the planning phase, discusses in detail the steps involved in finding out how well your current program is working and where improvement is needed.

Designing

Chapter 5 begins the designing phase of the program improvement process, focusing on designing the program of your choice. Issues and steps in selecting the desired program structure for your comprehensive program are presented. Next in the designing phase, chapter 6 describes in detail the steps necessary to make the transition to a comprehensive school guidance program.

Implementing

Chapter 7 describes the steps in actually making the transition to your comprehensive school guidance program. It describes transition activities required at the district and building level. Chapter 8 focuses on how to ensure that school counselors have the necessary competency to develop and manage a comprehensive school guidance program. Counselor supervision procedures are highlighted.

Evaluating

Comprehensive school guidance program evaluation is discussed in detail in chapter 9. Program evaluation, student outcome evaluation, and professional personnel evaluation are featured. Special attention is given to evaluation procedures in each.

Concluding Thoughts

The chapter organization may lead some readers to think that guidance program improvement activities follow one another in a linear fashion. Although there is a progression involved, some of the activities described in chapters 1 through 9 may be carried on concurrently. This is true particularly for the evaluation procedures described in chapter 9. Some of these procedures are carried out from the beginning of the program improvement process throughout the life of the program. Also, some readers may misinterpret what has been written and think that guidance program improvement is a simple task requiring little staff time and few resources. This is not true. Although substantial work can be completed during 1 year, at least 2 to 3 years with the necessary resources available to ensure successful implementation are required.

Finally, a word about who the book is for. It is written to inform and involve all members of the guidance staff about the development and management of comprehensive school guidance programs. Although specific parts are highlighted for guidance program leaders (central or building level directors, supervisors, coordinators, department heads) and school administrators, the information provided is important for all. Also, the book is designed for practitioners already on-the-job as well as for counselors-in-training and administrators-in-training. It can and should be used in preservice education as well as inservice education.

References

Aubrey, R. F. (1973). Organizational victimization of school counselors. *School Counselor, 20*, 346–354.

Boyer, E. (1983). *High school: A report on secondary education in America.* New York: Harper & Row.

Cottingham, H. F. (1973). Psychological education, the guidance function, and the school counselor. *School Counselor, 20*, 340–345.

Gardner, D. (1983). *A nation at risk: The imperative for educational reform.* Washington, DC: U.S. Department of Education.

Gysbers, N. C., & Moore, E. J. (1981). *Improving guidance programs.* Englewood Cliffs, NJ: Prentice-Hall.

Herr, E. L. (1984). The national reports on reform in schooling: Some missing ingredients. *Journal of Counseling and Development, 63*(4), 217–220.

The Iowa K–12 career guidance curriculum guide for student development (1987). Des Moines, IA: Department of Education, Guidance Services.

Kehas, C. D. (1973). Guidance and the process of schooling: Curriculum and career education. *School Counselor, 20*, 109–115.

Mitchell, A., & Gysbers, N. C. (1978). Comprehensive school guidance programs. In *The status of guidance and counseling in the nation's schools* (pp. 23–39). Washington, DC: American Personnel and Guidance Association.

Sprinthall, N. A. (1971). *Guidance for human growth.* New York: Van Nostrand Reinhold.

Acknowledgments

We wish to express our indebtedness to the late Earl J. Moore for his work on the early version of the current comprehensive guidance program model used in this book. He was our friend and colleague. We are particularly grateful to H. B. Gelatt for his encouragement and support. His key insights, derived from his extensive experience with school guidance programs and practices, improved the book immeasurably.

We wish to thank the school counselors from Missouri who participated in the Missouri Comprehensive Guidance Project, and Bob Larivee and Marion Starr, from the Missouri Department of Elementary and Secondary Education, who are providing continued leadership for the project. We also wish to thank Mark Hargens and the St. Joseph Missouri District school counselors.

In addition, we want to recognize especially the school counselors from Northside Independent School District in San Antonio, Texas, who have demonstrated the leadership and professionalism of school counselors at their best. The counselors on the Northside Guidance Steering Committee are Vance Baldwin, Kay Barrows, Mary Lou Fisher, Lupita Garcia, Yvette Lucchelli, Joan Ponfick, and Judy Rath. The additional members of the Guidance Leadership Team were Marjorie Bolt, LaVerne Britt, Don Hardy-Holley, Martha Mahaffey, and Maureen Pisano. Northside's successful transition to a comprehensive, developmentally based guidance program would not have happened without the understanding and support of Mr. J. E. Rawlinson, Associate Superintendent for Instruction.

Finally, thanks to Tirza Kroeker, Tammy Oliver, and Elaine Himmelberg for their invaluable assistance in typing parts of the manuscript for the book.

About the Authors

Norman C. Gysbers is a professor in the Department of Educational and Counseling Psychology, University of Missouri-Columbia. Patricia Henderson is Director of Guidance and Counseling at the Northside Independent School District, San Antonio, Texas.

PART 1—Planning

CHAPTER 1

THE EVOLUTION OF COMPREHENSIVE GUIDANCE PROGRAMS IN THE SCHOOLS

By the beginning of the 20th century, the United States was deeply involved in the Industrial Revolution. It was a period of rapid industrial growth, social protest, social reform, and utopian idealism. Social protest and social reform were being carried out under the banner of the Progressive Movement, a movement that sought to change negative social conditions associated with industrial growth.

> These conditions were the unanticipated effects of industrial growth. They included: the emergence of cities with slums and immigrant-filled ghettos, the decline of puritan morality, the eclipse of the individual by organizations, corrupt political bossism, and the demise of the apprenticeship method of learning a vocation. (Stephens, 1970, pp. 148–149)

The Early Years

Guidance was born during the height of the Progressive Movement as "but one manifestation of the broader movement of progressive reform which occurred in this country in the late nineteenth and early twentieth centuries" (Stephens, 1970, p. 5). Its beginnings can be traced to the work of a number of individuals and social institutions. People such as Frank Parson, Meyer Bloomfield, Jessie Davis, Anna Reed, Eli Weaver, and David Hill, working through a number of organizations and movements such as the settlement house movement, the National Society for the Promotion of Industrial Education (NSPIE), and schools in Grand Rapids, Seattle, New York, and New Orleans were instrumental in formulating and implementing early conceptions of guidance.

The implementation of one of the first systematic conceptions of guidance in the country took place in Civic Service House, Boston, Massachusetts, when the Boston Vocation Bureau was established in January, 1908, by Mrs. Quincy Agassiz Shaw, based on plans drawn up by Frank Parsons. The establishment of the Vocation Bureau was an outgrowth of Parsons's work with individuals at Civic Service House. According to Davis (1969, p. 113), Parsons issued his first report of the Bureau on May 1, 1908. "This was an important report because the term 'vocational guidance' apparently appeared for the first time in print as the designation of an organized service." It also was an important report because it emphasized that vocational guidance should be provided by trained experts and become part of every public school system.

Parsons's conception of guidance stressed the scientific approach to choosing an occupation. The first paragraph in the first chapter of his book, *Choosing A Vocation* (1909), illustrates his concern.

> No step in life, unless it may be the choice of a husband or wife, is more important than the choice of a vocation. The wise selection of the business, profession, trade, or occupation to which one's life is to be devoted and the development of full efficiency in the chosen field are matters of deepest movement to young men and to the public. These vital problems should be solved in a careful, scientific way, with due regard to each person's aptitudes, abilities, ambitions, resources, and limitations, and the relations of these elements to the conditions of success in different industries. (p. 3)

The basis for Parsons's conceptualization of guidance stressing the scientific approach was his concern about society's general lack of attention to the development of human resources. "It trains its horses, as a rule, better than men. It spends unlimited money to perfect the inanimate machinery of production but pays very little attention to the business of perfecting the human machinery, though it is by far the most important in production" (Parsons, 1909, p. 160). He also was concerned about assisting young people in making the transition from school to work. "Yet there is no part of life where the need for guidance is more emphatic than in the transition from school to work—the choice of a vocation, adequate preparation for it, and the attainment of efficiency and success" (Parsons, p. 4).

The work of Frank Parsons and the Vocation Bureau soon became known across the country. Out of it grew the first National Conference on Vocational Guidance, held in Boston in 1910, followed by a similar conference in New York in 1912 and the formation of the National Vocational Guidance Association in Grand Rapids in 1913 (Ryan, 1919). It also had a direct impact on the Boston public schools because in 1909, the Boston School Committee asked personnel in the Vocation Bureau to outline a program of vocational guidance for the public schools of Boston. On June 7, 1909, the Boston School Committee approved the bureau's suggestion and "instructed the Superintendent of Schools to appoint a committee of six to work with the director" (Bloomfield, 1915, p. 34).

The report of this committee, the Committee on Vocational Direction, is interesting because it pointed out that a vocational counselor already had been appointed in every high school and all but one elementary school, and that a vocational record card for every elementary school graduate also had been completed, ready to be forwarded to the high school. The committee, in its report, spelled out three primary aims of vocational guidance.

> Three aims have stood out above all others: first, to secure thoughtful consideration, on the part of parents, pupils, and teachers, of the importance of a life-career motive; second, to assist in every way possible in placing pupils in some remunerative work on leaving school; and third, to keep in touch with and help them thereafter, suggesting means of improvement and watching the advancement of those who need such aid. (Bloomfield, 1915, p. 36)

These aims were to be implemented by a central office staff and by appointed counselors in each school. The central office functioned in an advisory capacity only, however, and in most schools the counselors were teachers with some time allowed for counseling students. Nevertheless, according to Brewer (1922), the work in Boston was commendable and promising.

At about the same time that the Boston schools were establishing a vocational guidance program, a group of New York City teachers, the Student Aid Committee of the High School Teachers' Association, under the leadership of E.W. Weaver, was active in establishing a program in the New York City schools. A report issued in 1909 by the committee indicated they had passed the experimental stage and were ready to request that:

> (1) the vocational officers of the large high schools be allowed at least one extra period of unassigned time to attend to this work; (2) that they be provided with facilities for keeping records of students and employment; and (3) that they have opportunities for holding conferences with students and employers. (Ryan, 1919, p. 25)

In Grand Rapids, vocational guidance began first in the classroom and then was organized in a central office. Jessie B. Davis (1914) inaugurated a plan of teaching vocational guidance through the English curriculum. The following general topics were to be covered in each of the grades:

Seventh grade:	Vocational ambition
Eighth grade:	The value of education
Ninth grade:	The elements of character that make for success
Tenth grade:	The world's work—a call to service
Eleventh grade:	Choosing a vocation
Twelfth grade:	Preparation for one's life work

The Grand Rapids approach suffered from some of the same problems that had plagued guidance efforts in Boston and New York, however. In fact, Brewer

(1922, p. 39) commented that no large city had "succeeded in spreading the interest widely enough and in securing adequate funds to bring about what could be called a complete, city-wide plan for vocational guidance." For the most part, vocational guidance was being carried out on a voluntary, permissive basis in Grand Rapids and elsewhere.

Vocational guidance was being introduced also into the public schools in other parts of the country. In Chicago, it first took the form of a central office to serve students applying for employment certificates and for placement, and it also published vocational bulletins. In other cities such as Buffalo; Los Angeles; Rochester; New York; DeKalb, Illinois; Cincinnati; Milwaukee; Philadelphia; and San Jose, California, vocational guidance took several different forms but relied mostly on disseminating occupational information and on conducting occupational surveys, placement activities, and life-career classes. For example, Newton, Massachusetts, organized an Educational-Vocational Guidance Department with the following three responsibilities:

(1) The change of all school-attendance records including the school census and the enforcement of school attendance laws;
(2) The granting of work certificates; and
(3) Educational-Vocational Guidance work.
     (Bloomfield, 1915, p. 53–54)

According to Ryan (1919, p. 26) "by April 1914, approximately 100 public high schools, representing some 40 cities, were reported to the Bureau of Education as having definitely organized conscious plans of vocational guidance, through vocation bureaus, consultation committees, trial vocational courses, or regular courses in vocations." (It is interesting to note the titles of some of the offices. For example, in Minneapolis, the Divisionof Attendance and Vocational Guidance was established.) This expansion continued throughout the next 4 years so that by 1918, 10 years after the establishment of the Vocation Bureau in Boston, "932 four-year high schools reported vocation bureaus, employment departments, or similar devices for placing pupils" (Ryan, 1919, p. 36).

Changes in Theory and Practice

As the vocational guidance movement expanded in the 1920s, a number of visible shifts began to occur in its theory and practice. Up until about 1920, vocational guidance was

bound up with vocational training, prevocational education, continuation school work, the cooperative plan of half-time work, the Gary Plan, and the junior high school, and, like most of these it presupposes a complete remaking of education on the basis of occupational demands. (Ryan, 1919, p. 98)

From 1920 on, however, there was less emphasis on guidance for vocation and more on education as guidance. This shift apparently was a natural outgrowth of a change that was taking place in education itself. With the advent of the Seven Cardinal Principles in 1917, education, at least philosophically, began to shift from preparation for college alone to education for total life.

> This was a life to be characterized by an integration of health with command of fundamental processes, worthy home membership, vocational competence, civic responsibility, worthy use of leisure time and ethical character...Given these Seven Cardinal Principles, all education now appeared equally vocationally relevant—from this one could construe that all of education is guidance into later vocational living. (Johnson, 1972, p. 27–28)

This shift occurred partly because the leadership of guidance, particularly on the part of people like John Brewer, increasingly was more educationally oriented. It also occurred, according to Stephens (1970), because the National Education Association's Commission on the Reorganization of Secondary Education "had so broadened the definition of vocation as to soften it, if not to virtually eliminate it as a cardinal principle of secondary education" (p. 113). This move by the Commission on the Reorganization of Secondary Education, together with the more educationally oriented leadership of guidance, served to separate the twin reform movements of education, vocational education and vocational guidance, as Stephens called them, leaving vocational guidance to struggle with its own identity. This point is made in a similar way by Johnson (1972).

> The 1918 report of the NEA's Commission on the Reorganization of Secondary Education construed almost all of education as training for efficient vocational and avocational life. No element in the curriculum appeared salient after the CRSE report. This was no less true of vocational education. Thus, as a "cardinal principle" vocational education was virtually eliminated. The once correlated responsibility of vocational guidance lost its historical anchorage to vocational education and was set adrift in the public school system to be redefined by the logic of the education subculture. (p. 204)

What was the direction of this new identity? It was clear that by the 1920s less attention was being focused on the social, industrial, and national-political aspects of individuals whereas considerably more attention was being given to the personal, educational, and statistically measurable aspects of individuals. More specifically, at least within the school setting, there apparently was a "displacement of the traditional vocational, socioeconomic and political concerns from the culture at large to the student of the educational subculture whose vocational socialization problems were reinterpreted as educational and psychological problems of personal adjustment." (Johnson, 1972, p. 221)

The Clinical-Services Model Emerges

This shift in emphasis in the theory and practice of vocational guidance was related to a number of influences in education in the 1920s. These included the continued growth of the mental hygiene and measurement movements, developmental studies of children, the introduction of cumulative records, and progressive education. In effect, "Vocational guidance was taking on the new vocabulary present in the culture at large and in the educational sub-culture; the language of mental health, progressive education, child development and measurement theory" (Johnson, 1972, p. 160).

As a result of these new influences, a new model of vocational guidance began to emerge—one that was clinical in nature. Vocational guidance theory and practice began to emphasize a more personal, diagnostic, and clinical orientation to the student, with an increasing emphasis on psychological measurement.

> Content to explore with yet greater precision the psychological dimensions of the student, and guaranteed a demand for testing services in the public school system, the guidance movement defined its professional role to meet the expectations of its institutional colleagues. Thus, there developed a mutual role expectation that requires analysis and synthesis (gathering and organizing personal data), diagnosis (comparing personal data to test norms, and occupational or professional profiles), prognosis (indicating available career choices), counseling (or treating, to effect desired adjustment then or in the future). This formed the basis for the clinical model. Testing had created the demand for a unique technical skill around which the clinical model could develop, and around which vocational guidance had established a professional claim. (Johnson, 1972, p. 138)

Further evidence of this can be seen in the 1921 and 1924 statements of the Principles of Vocational Guidance of the National Vocational Guidance Association (Allen, 1927). These principles stressed testing, the use of an extensive cumulative record system, information, the study of occupations, counseling, and case studies. Between 1925 and 1930, as the clinical model of vocational guidance emerged, counseling became of primary concern. "Vocational guidance became problem oriented, centering on adjustable psychological, personal problems—not social, moral, religious, ethical or political problems" (Johnson, 1972, p. 201).

As the 1920s continued to unfold, the main ingredients of the new model of vocational guidance began to appear. There was continued stress on occupational information, placement, and follow-up, as had been true between 1908–1920. In addition, however, counseling from a more psychological perspective and testing emerged. In fact, to some, these latter two elements began to assume preeminance and became the basis for the emerging clinical model. It also seems clear that the foundation for the present-day conception called the services model of guidance was laid during the 1920s—those services in present-day language being orientation, assessment, information, counseling, placement, and follow-up. Only orientation as a service did not seem to be discussed at length during the 1920s. As evidence of this, Payne (1925, pp. 237–240) listed the following functions and responsibilities of the vocational guidance advisor:

   I. Tests and Technique—A guidance advisor should be thoroughly familiar with, and specifically trained in, the technique of giving all kinds of tests, such as intelligence, achievement, prognosis, aptitude, character, psychiatric, and vocational tests.

  II. Records and Reports—The vocational guidance advisor should maintain complete and up-to-date records and make reports as called for concerning (1) classes, programs, registration, syllabi, and tests; (2) student data...; (3) vocational data on opportunities for full-time work, part-time work, vocation work, apprenticeship, follow-up and supervision data; (4) education and training...

  III. Courses of Study—The guidance advisor should supervise or conduct courses of study in vocational information...Collect and disseminate vocational information...

  IV. Cooperation—The guidance advisor should at all times be ready to cooperate with various agencies...

  V. Placement—The guidance advisor should maintain and develop contacts with all forms of placement agencies.

  VI. Follow-up and Employment Supervision—The guidance advisor should record, check, and follow up the results of all advice given...

  VII. Statistics and Research—The guidance advisor should make statistical studies...

Among the functions and responsibilities for vocational guidance advisors listed by Payne was the keeping of records. The keeping of such records in schools has had a long evolutionary history, beginning with the adoption of the school register in the 1830s. It wasn't until the early 1900s, however, that the pupil attendance record—the school register—was supplemented by various kinds of individual record systems. One of the first such systems was developed in 1909 by Charles M. Lamprey, the Director of the Boston Model School. His system was adopted in the Boston public schools in 1910.

The first modern cumulative record card did not become available until 1928. It was designed primarily as a guidance instrument by its authors, Ben D. Wood of Columbia University and E.L. Clark of Northwestern University. It was published by the American Council on Education. According to Humphreys and Traxler (1954), its publication "constituted a landmark in the history of individual guidance in the United States" (p. 96).

As vocational guidance was becoming institutionalized in schools and in the process being defined and implemented by its leadership, the expectations of other educational personnel concerning vocational guidance also were being shaped. This seemed to be particularly true for school administrators. Johnson (1972) underlined this when he pointed out that administrative obligations were a substantial part of the new professional responsibilities. In fact, many suggested vocational guidance responsibilities delineated by the profession became administrative obligations when incorporated into the school settings. (See Payne's listing of seven suggested functions and responsibilities for evidence of this.) "Professional responsibilities became in fact administrative obligations for which guidance would be held accountable not to professionally determined values but values of the education subculture interpreted through its administrative structure" (Johnson, p. 191).

By the beginning of the 1930s, as a result of the work of A. Gesell, the mental health movement, and the emerging clinical model of counseling, personal counseling began to dominate professional theory and practice.

> Up to 1930,...not much progress had been made in differentiating this function (personal counseling) from the preexisting programs of vocational and educational guidance. After that date, more and more of a separation appeared as guidance workers in the high schools became aware of increasingly large numbers of students who were troubled by personal problems involving hostility to authority, sex relationships, unfortunate home situations, and financial stringencies. (Rudy, 1965, p. 25)

It was clear too that by the 1930s, the term *guidance* was seen as an all-inclusive term including "problems of adjustment to health, religion, recreation, to family and friends, to school and to work" (Campbell, 1932, p. 4). *Vocational guidance*, on the other hand, was defined as "the process of assisting the individual to choose an occupation, prepare for it, enter upon and progress in it. As preparation for an occupation involves decisions in the choice of studies, choice of curriculums, and the choice of schools and colleges, it becomes evident that vocational guidance cannot be separated from educational guidance" (Campbell, 1932, p. 4).

It also is interesting to note that vocational guidance was seen as a process that helped individuals examine all occupations, not just those for which vocational education provided training.

> As vocational guidance and vocational education are linked together in many minds, a statement of this relationship may clarify the situation. Vocational education is the giving of training to persons who desire to work in a specific occupation. Vocational guidance offers information and assistance which leads to the choice of an occupation and the training which precedes it. It does not give such training. The term vocational refers to any occupation, be it medicine, law, carpentry, or nursing. Preparation for many occupations and professions must be planned in the secondary school and in college by taking numerous courses which are not usually known as vocational. Vocational guidance concerns itself, therefore, with pupils in

the academic courses in high school or students of the liberal arts in college, as well as with the pupils in the trade and commercial courses which have become known as vocational education. (Campbell, 1932, p. 4)

This distinction is important because during the 1960s, 1970s, and 1980s this was a point of contention in the development and implementation of guidance in vocational education legislation. Some individuals contended that vocational guidance was guidance for vocational education only, and that if money were made available it should be spent only for vocational education students.

Finally, it is clear that by the beginning of the 1930s the terms *counseling, testing, information, placement,* and *follow-up* were being used widely to describe the components of guidance. These components, or services, as they were later called, were implemented in schools through a list of duties to be performed by counselors including counseling pupils, changing courses, dealing with failures and problem pupils, providing transcripts and personnel records, and cooperating with other agencies (Campbell, 1932, pp. 335–340).

Education as Guidance

As guidance became more firmly incorporated into the schools during the 1930s, efforts were made to interpret much, if not all, of education as guidance. From this perspective, guidance was seen by some as an emphasis on the individual during the educational process.

...in the late 1920's and through the 1930's guidance was in danger of being so absorbed into curriculum revision in particular and into the educational effort in general, that even a congressional investigating committee would not be able to recognize it as a function existing in its own right. (Miller, 1971, p. 6)

The guidance-as-education view was advocated particularly by Jones and Hand (1938). They felt that guidance was an inseparable part of education. They emphasized the point that teaching involved both guidance and instruction and that neither could be delegated to separate personnel (Jones & Hand, pp. 24–25). They did not suggest that specialists were not needed—in fact they pointed out the need for more specialists. They did emphasize, however, that it was impossible to separate guidance and instruction. "It distinctly does mean, however, that the tasks of guiding and instructing cannot legitimately be made the respective responsibilities of separate groups of educational workers" (p.25).

This meant, in their minds, that classroom teachers were in a unique position to deliver guidance and could do so more effectively than could specialists. As a result, they advocated the use of teacher counselors who would serve as guides, instructors, and directors of instruction for small groups of from 30 to 40 students.

During the 1930s, then, it was apparent that a major effort was under way to make guidance an integral part of the instructional program. The homeroom approach frequently was talked about as a valuable guidance device.

> The home room, argued one enthusiast, would do away with the excessively "artificial," intellectual emphasis of earlier times and give needed attention to the "all-around" needs and adjustment of the average pupil in the new era of mass education. (Rudy, 1965, p. 25)

Several other themes also began to emerge during the 1930s. Personal counseling, with its emphasis on adjustment that emerged in the 1920s, became even stronger in the 1930s. Bell (1939), in a book on personal counseling, stated that the goal of counseling was student adjustment through personal contact between counselor and student. Adjustment in his thinking included all phases of an individual's life: school, health, occupational, motor and mechanical, social, home, emotional, and religious phases.

Federal Initiatives Begin

Although the personal adjustment theme for guidance continued to play a dominant role in guidance theory and practice in the schools during the 1930s, the occupational emphasis continued to show strength. In February, 1933, the National Occupational Conference, funded by a Carnegie grant, opened its doors. The activities of the National Occupational Conference included studies and research related to the problems of occupational adjustment, the publication of a number of books, and the development of a service that provided information and consultation about vocational guidance activities. The National Occupational Conference for a time also provided joint support for *Occupations*, the official journal of the National Vocational Guidance Association.

In 1938, a national advisory committee on education, orginally appointed in 1936 by the President, issued a report that pointed to the need for an occupational information service at the national level as well as for guidance and placement services as a part of a sound program of vocational education. As a result of these recommendations and the George Dean Act, the Occupational Information and Guidance Service was established in 1938 in the Vocational Division of the U.S. Office of Education. Richard Allen served for a few months as the chief of the unit before Harry Jager assumed the post (Wellman, 1978). Although the service was established in the Vocational Division, it was not designed to be exclusively vocational in nature. This point was made clear in a document, *Principles Underlying the Organization and Administration of the Occupational Information and Guidance Service*, issued by the U.S. Office of Education in 1940.

The functions to be performed by the Occupational Information and Guidance Service are to be as broad and complete as it is practicable for the Office to provide for at any given time within the limits of funds, cooperative assistance from various organizations, both within the government and outside, and other assets. The activities in which the service will be interested will include such phases of guidance as vocational guidance, personal guidance, educational guidance, and placement. While, with respect to personnel, no service in the Office can now be said to be complete, the various divisions or services go as far as possible in their respective fields in meeting needs or requests for service. Thus, for example, in the field of education for exceptional children, a service which would require fifteen or twenty professional workers in the office if it were even to approximate "completeness" in numbers and types of persons needed, we have only one specialist. Yet this specialist is responsible for representing the Office in handling all problems and service in this particular field. (Smith, 1951, p. 66)

Of particular importance in this statement are the words "The activities in which the Service will be interested will include such phases of guidance as vocational guidance, personal guidance, educational guidance, and placement." Not only did the statement clearly outline the broad mission of the service, and, as a result, of guidance in the schools, but it also described a currently popular way of describing guidance as having three phases—vocational, personal, and educational. Once the Occupational Information and Guidance Service was established at the federal level, it also became possible to establish guidance offices in state departments of education. Such funds could be used only for state offices, however.

Reimbursement was provided for State Supervision under the George Dean Act and the number of States with a State Guidance Supervisor increased from two to twenty-eight between 1938 and 1942. The Occupational Information and Guidance Service was instrumental in initiating conferences of State Supervisors to consider issues in the field. This group subsequently became the NAGS (National Association of Guidance Supervisors), then NAGCT (National Association of Guidance Supervisors and Counselor Trainers), and finally the current ACES (Association for Counselor Education and Supervision). (Wellman, 1978, p. 92)

A Growing Interest in Psychotherapy

As the 1930s ended, the clinical-services model of guidance and counseling was continuing to evolve, assisted by a growing interest in psychotherapy. Of particular importance to guidance and counseling in the schools was the work of Carl Rogers, beginning with the publication of his book *Counseling and Psychotherapy* in 1942. "The years following its publication in 1942 saw a growth in interest in psychotherapeutic procedures which soon became even greater than interest in psychometrics. This movement, and the numerous research and theoretical contributions which have accompanied it, has had its impact on vocational guidance'' (Super, 1955, p. 5). Aubrey (1982) used the expression ''steamroller impact'' to describe the impact that this book as well as the later works of Rogers had on guidance and counseling in the schools.

The impact of psychotherapy on vocational guidance and the testing movement precipitated a new field, the field of counseling psychology. This, in turn, had a substantial impact on the professional development of school guidance and the school counselor in the 1950s, 1960s, and 1970s, particularly in terms of the training counselors received and the role models and literature available to them.

> An important outcome of the merger of the vocational orientation, psychometric, and personality development movements has been a changed concept of the function and training of the person who does the counseling. He was first either a teacher who helped people explore the world of work or a psychologist who gave and interpreted tests. The he, who might or might not have been a psychologist, was a user of community resources, of occupational information, and of psychological tests. He has now emerged as a psychologist who uses varying combinations of exploratory experiences, psychometric techniques, and psychotherapeutic interviewing to assist people to grow and to develop. This is the counseling psychologist. (American Psychological Association, 1956, p. 284)

The George-Barden Act

In 1946, an event occurred that was to have substantial impact on the growth and development of guidance in the schools. The event was the passage of the George-Barden Act. As a result of the act, funds could be used to support guidance activities in a variety of settings and situations. More specifically, the U.S. Commissioner ruled that federal funds could be used for the following four purposes:

1. The maintenance of a State program of supervision;
2. Reimbursement of salaries of counselor-trainers;
3. Research in the field of guidance; and
4. Reimbursement of salaries of local guidance supervisors and counselors. (Smith, 1951, pp. 67–68)

For the first time, because of the ruling of the U.S. Commissioner concerning the George-Barden Act, guidance received material, leadership, and financial support. The result of such support was a rapid growth of guidance at state and local levels. It also signaled to all concerned the need for attention to the preparation of counselors. This problem had been of concern for some time but had not been given extensive consideration. The passage of the George-Barden Act, which made it possible to use state funds to reimburse counselor training, made the constantly reoccurring question, ''What should constitute a counselor training program?'' of extreme importance. How this question was answered set the pattern for the practice of guidance in the schools for years to come.

In the spring of 1948 the Occupational Information and Guidance Service staff called a meeting of state guidance supervisors and counselor trainers in cooperation with the Division of Higher Education of the U.S. Office of Education. The question was: What should be the preparation of counselors? Eight major subtopics were identified and subcommittees were established to study each subtopic. A report was presented for consideration at the National Conference of State Supervisors of Guidance Services and Counselor Trainers held in Washington, DC on September 13–18, 1948. These reports were revised with others participating in the work. Six of the seven were then published between 1949 to 1950 by the Federal Security Agency, Office of Education. The titles and dates of the six published reports and the one not published are:

1. *Duties, Standards, and Qualifications for Counselors*, February, 1949, Co-Chairpersons, Eleanor Zeis and Dolph Camp
2. *The Basic Course* (never published)
3. *Counselor Competencies in Occupational Information*, March, 1949, Chairperson, Edward C. Roeber
4. *Counselor Competencies in the Analysis of the Individual*, July 1949, Chairperson, Ralph C. Bedell
5. *Counselor Competencies in Counseling Techniques*, July, 1949, Chairperson, Stanley R. Ostrom
6. *Administrative Relationships of the Guidance Program*, July, 1949, Chairperson, Glenn Smith
7. *In-Service Preparation for Guidance Duties, Parts One and Two*, May, 1950, Chairperson, John G. Odgers

A report had been issued on supervised practice at the 8th National Conference but was referred back to committee. After revision it was considered at the 9th National Conference in Ames, Iowa, September 11–15, 1950, and with subsequent revision was released as the eighth report in the series.

8. *Supervised Practice in Counselor Preparation*, April, 1952, Chairperson, Roy Bryan

All seven published reports were edited by Clifford P. Froehlich, Specialist for the Training of Guidance Personnel, under the general direction of Harry A. Jager, Chief, Guidance and Personnel Services Branch.

During the early and middle 1950s, a major change occurred in the organizational structure of guidance at the federal level. On May 16, 1952, the Guidance and Personnel Branch of the U.S. Office of Education was discontinued under the Division of Vocational Education. On October 27, 1953, a Pupil Personnel Services Section was established in the Division of State and Local School

Systems with Harry Jager designated as chief. This work was halted with the death of Harry Jager the following year. However, in 1955, a Guidance and Personnel Services Section was once again established. Frank L. Sievers was the first chief of this new section (Miller, 1971).

These changes reflected the shift that was taking place in the schools—a shift from guidance as vocational to guidance as a part of pupil personnel services. As we will see later, the pupil personnel services movement, which had its origins in the 1930s, particularly at the college level, was to become a dominant theme in school guidance in the late 1950s and in the 1960s.

The National Defense Education Act

In 1958, another important influence on guidance in the schools emerged— an influence that continued throughout the 1960s and interacted with the pupil personnel services movement to further conceptualize and institutionalize school guidance as a collection of services related to other psychological services in the schools. This influence appeared in the form of federal legislation, the National Defense Education Act of 1958—Public Law 85–864. Under Title V, the guidance title in the act, funds were provided for two major programs. The first part, Part A, provided funds in the form of grants to states to establish statewide testing programs. The second part, Part B, provided funds for training institutes to prepare individuals to be counselors in secondary schools. In the 1960s, the provisions were expanded to include support for guidance programs, testing, and training at the elementary and junior high school levels as well.

It is not our purpose here fully to report on the impact of the NDEA of 1958 and its many modifications that occurred later. Rather, our attention will focus briefly on the act's impact on how school guidance was further conceptualized and institutionalized as a result of its implementation. Of particular importance is the nature of training the participants received and the major professional issues addressed during the courses of training for institute participants.

Pierson (1965) discussed five issues that seemed to be central to the training of school counselors during NDEA institutes.

1. Determinism and a free society;
2. Mental health and individual responsibility;
3. Basic science and supervised practice;
4. Teaching and counseling; and
5. The role of the school counselor.

Of these, issues 4 and 5 related most directly to how counselors function in schools. The teaching-counseling issue was resolved according to Pierson by counselor educators who promoted the position "That the services of the high school counselor are adjunct to the services of the classroom teacher" (p. 40).

The role definition issue was handled by saying that the role of the counselor cannot be predetermined. Lists of duties were downplayed. Counselors were to develop their own role definition. "The adequately trained school counselor develops his own role, a role that tends to be unique with him and unique to the situation in which the role is developed" (p. 39).

Another aspect of the counselor role dilemma was identified by Tyler (1960) in her review of the first 50 institutes. She describes it as follows.

> Before one can really define the role of the counselor, it will be necessary to clarify the roles of all workers who make up guidance staffs. It may be desirable to replace the ambiguous word "guidance" with the clearer term "pupil personnel work." (p. 77)

Further analysis of NDEA institutes also makes it clear that there was a heavy emphasis on individual and group counseling through counseling practica and group procedures courses. Placement and traditional educational and occupational information procedures (collecting, classifying, and using information) as well as philosophy and principles received relatively less attention. Pierson (1965) summarized curriculum offerings in institutes by pointing out that:

> the curriculum in regular session institutes has placed great stress upon practicum; about one-third of an enrollee's time has been spent in supervised practice in counseling. At the same time, institutes have strengthened their instruction in psychology, particularly in the areas of personality, learning, growth and development, and mental health. (p. 46)

Pupil Personnel Services Model

Concurrent with the influence of NDEA on the development of guidance in the schools was the influence of the pupil personnel services movement in the 1960s. What began in the 1930s and was nurtured in the 1940s and 1950s finally matured in the 1960s. What were those services? The Council of Chief State School Officers stated in 1960 that pupil personnel services included the following: "guidance, health, psychological services, school social work, and attendance" (p. 3). Thus, guidance was seen as one of the services that sought to "facilitate pupil learning through an interdisciplinary approach" (Stoughton, McKenna, & Cook, 1969, p. 1).

Of particular importance to the development of the pupil personnel services concept was the creation in 1962 of the Interprofessional Research Commission on Pupil Personnel Services (IRCOPPS). IRCOPPS was initiated and fostered by the U.S. Office of Education and was financed by the National Institutes of Mental Health. It was composed of 16 professional member associations. The aims of the Commission were threefold:

1. to provide through research a body of knowledge that will increase the effectiveness of all professions and services collaborating to provide the total learning experience;
2. to demonstate efficient programs of pupil personnel services for various sizes and types of communities; and
3. to carry on and stimulate research on preventative mental hygiene related to the schools. (Eckerson & Smith, 1966, p. 4)

In the IRCOPPS conception of pupil personnel services, guidance was viewed "as a lifetime service, from preschool to retirement, with the goal of increasing each individual's capacity for self-direction" (Eckerson & Smith, p. 24).

As the 1960s continued to unfold, the impact of the pupil personnel services movement on guidance became increasingly apparent. Many state departments of education and local school districts placed guidance and counseling administratively under the pupil personnel services umbrella. Also, textbooks written in the 1960s on the organization and administration of guidance adopted the pupil personnel services model as the way to organize guidance in the schools. This fit nicely with the service model of guidance that had been evolving since the 1920s. As a result, guidance became a subset of services to be delivered within the broader framework of pupil personnel services. The number of these guidance services varied depending upon the authority quoted, but usually there were six, including orientation, individual inventory or appraisal, counseling, information, placement, and follow-up. Also, as a result of the clinical model of guidance and the focus on personal adjustment discussed earlier in this chapter, the counseling service emerged as the central service of guidance.

Stripling and Lane (1966) stressed the centrality of counseling—both individual and group. A second priority area was consultation with parents and teachers. Other traditional guidance functions such as appraisal, placement, and evaluation were seen as supplementary and supportive to counseling, group procedures, and consultation. Ferguson (1963) emphasized the same theme of counseling as the core service: "No longer is it viewed merely as a technique and limited to vocational and educational matters; counseling is regarded as the central service in the guidance program" (p. 40).

The emphasis on counseling during the 1960s had deep historical roots. It began to emerge in the 1920s under the clinical model name and the intense interest in personal adjustment that followed. It was reinforced further, however, according to Hoyt (1974) by the NDEA Title V–B Training Institutes whose enrollees by law were either counselors or teachers and by the standards used by the U.S.O.E. to judge whether or not a proposal from a training institution was acceptable for funding. These factors, Hoyt suggested, led the training institutes to place " . . . a heavy emphasis on the counseling function . . . The emphasis was on counseling and counselors, not on guidance and guidance programs . . . (p. 504).

School Counselor Model

The services model for guidance was not the only model being advocated for guidance in the 1960s, however. As increasing numbers of counselors entered the schools, less emphasis was given to guidance programs and more to the role and functions of school counselors. In fact, to many individuals, what school counselors did became the guidance program. Hence, literally hundreds of articles were written (and are still written today) about the role and functions of school counselors. The need for such statements was heightened considerably by competition from other pupil personnel workers as they too sought to establish themselves and their roles in the schools, particularly when the Commission on Guidance in American Schools proposed that:

> . . . the confusing term guidance services be abandoned and that pupil personnel services be seen as the activities of the school counselor, the school psychologist, the school social worker, the school health officer, and the school attendance officer. Pupil personnel services thus became broader than any so-called guidance services and yet a central function of such services is the work of the school counselor. (Wrenn, 1962, p. 142)

Wrenn (1962), in his landmark work, *The Counselor in a Changing World*, also emphasized the work of the counselor. He delineated four major functions for the school counselor.

> It is recommended: that the professional job description of a school counselor specify that he perform four major functions: (a) counsel with students; (b) consult with teachers, administrators, and parents as they in turn deal with students; (c) study the changing facts about the student population and interpret what is found to school committees and administrators; (d) coordinate counseling resources in school and between school and community. From two-thirds to three-fourths of the counselor's time, in either elementary or high school, should be committed to the first two of these functions. (p. 137)

In a similar fashion, Roeber (1963) outlined proposed school counselors' functions. He suggested that counselors engage in helping relationships including individual counseling, group procedures, and consulting. In addition, the counselor would have supporting responsibilities including pupil-environment studies, program development, and personal development. This emphasis on the counselor during the 1960s came at a time when some individuals were calling for "the abandonment of the term *guidance* as it is associated with services provided by a counselor" (Roeber, p. 22).

Elementary Guidance and Counseling Emerges

Finally, the 1960s witnessed the birth of elementary school guidance, culminating a gestation period of over 50 years. Professional literature indicated that elementary counselors were employed as early as 1910 in the Boston schools. Apparently, however, the secondary school emphasis was so strong during the early years that little attention was paid to work in the elementary school. What attention there was proved to be heavily occupational in nature. Witness the publication of a book by McCracken and Lamb titled *Occupational Information in the Elementary School* published in 1923.

Faust (1968) divided the emergence of elementary school counselors into three time periods. The first period he titled traditional. It stretched from the beginnings of the guidance movement in 1908 through 1940s. During this period, elementary guidance borrowed methods and techniques extensively from secondary school guidance practice. For the next 15 years, from 1950 to 1965, elementary guidance began to change. Faust called it the neotraditionalist period characterized by a deemphasis on traditional secondary methods coupled with more emphasis on group counseling and learning climates. Finally, in the middle 1960s, the developmentalist period emerged. According to Faust, elementary school counselors had arrived with an identity of their own. The emphasis now was developmental, not crisis-centered. Individual and group work were stressed.

The developmental emphasis was reinforced by a preliminary report of the Joint ACES-ASCA Committee on the Elementary School Counselor that appeared in the February, 1966, issue of the *Personnel and Guidance Journal*. Its central focus was "on the child and teacher in the educative process" (Faust, 1968, p. 74). Effective learning climates were to be central.

The Call To Change

Beginning in the 1960s but particularly in the 1970s the concept of guidance for development emerged. The call came to reorient guidance from what had become an ancillary, crisis-oriented service to a comprehensive program. The call for reorientation came from diverse sources, including a renewed interest in vocational-career guidance and its theoretical base of career development, concern about the efficacy of the prevailing approach to guidance in the schools, concern about accountability and evaluation, and a renewed interest in developmental guidance.

Vocational-Career Guidance

The resurgence of interest in vocational-career guidance that began in the 1960s was aided, in part, by a series of national conferences on the topic. These conferences were funded through the Vocational Education Act of 1963 and later the Vocational Amendments of 1968. It is clear from Hoyt's (1974) account of these conferences that they contributed substantially to the renewed interest in the term *guidance* and its practice in the schools.

In addition, the resurgence of interest in vocational-career guidance also was aided by a number of career guidance projects begun in the 1960s. Among them was the Developmental Career Guidance Project, begun in 1964 in Detroit to provide career guidance for disadvantaged youth. It was one of the early developmental career guidance programs, one that accumulated sufficient evaluative data to support the further development of comprehensive guidance programming in schools (Leonard & Vriend, 1975).

Concern About the Prevailing Approach

Paralleling the resurgence of interest in vocational-career guidance was a growing concern about the efficacy of the counselor-clinical-services approach in schools. Particular concern was expressed about an overemphasis on the one-to-one relationship model of counseling and the tendency of counselors to focus mainly on crises and problems.

> The traditional one-to-one relationship in counseling which we have cherished and perhaps overvalued will, of course, continue. But it is quite likely that the conception of the counselor as a roombound agent of behavior change must be critically reappraised. The counselor of the future will likely serve as a social catalyst, interacting in a two-person relationship with the counselee part of the time, but also serving as a facilitator of the environmental and human conditions which are known to promote the counselee's total psychological development, including vocational development. (Borow, 1965, p.88)

This same issue was discussed from a slightly different perspective in an exchange between Brammer (1968) and Felix (1968). Brammer proposed the abandonment of the guidance model for counselors and the adoption of a counseling psychologist model in its place. Felix, in a reply to Brammer, sharply disagreed with Brammer's recommendation, pointing out that the counseling psychologist model was not valid for a school setting. Felix instead recommended an educational model for guidance. Similarly Aubrey (1969) recommended an educational model as opposed to a therapy model by pointing out that the therapy model was at odds or even frequently incongruent with educational objectives.

During the 1960s there were also expressions of concern about the potency of the guidance services concept and the need for more meaningful reconceptualizations for guidance, if guidance were to reach higher levels of development (Roeber, Walz, & Smith, 1969). This same theme was echoed by Sprinthall (1971).

> It is probably not an understatement to say that the service concept has so dominated guidance and counseling that more basic and significant questions are not even acknowledged, let alone answered. Instead, the counselor assumes a service orientation that limits and defines his role to minor administrative procedures. (p. 20)

The Accountability Movement

The call for change in guidance was reinforced by the accountability movement in education, which had begun during the 1960s. As education was being held accountable for its outcomes, so too was guidance. It was apparent that it would be necessary for counselors to state guidance goals and objectives in measurable outcome terms and show how these goals and objectives were related to the general goals of education. Dickinson (1969–70) made this point when he stated that "counselors must turn their attention to setting specific goals if we are to remain a major force in education. This is going to be a difficult task, and we must begin now" (p. 16).

Wellman and Twiford (1961) also stressed this point when they stated that the one appropriate measure of the value of a guidance program was its impact on students. Later in the 1960s personnel of the National Study of Guidance under the direction of Wellman (1968) developed a systems model for evaluation. A taxonomy of guidance objectives classified in three domains of educational, vocational, and social development accompanied the model. Wellman's model and its companion taxonomy of objectives served as a basis for a number of evaluation models that began appearing in the late 1960s and early 1970s. *A Process Guide for the Development of Objectives*, originally published by the California State Department of Education in 1970 and later published by the California Personnel and Guidance Association (Sullivan & O'Hare, 1971), is an example of one such model.

The accountability movement, with its focus on measurable outcomes, presented a real problem for counselors, however. The traditional service approach emphasized *techniques* of guidance rather than *purpose* of guidance (Sprinthall, 1971). As a result, counselors were known for the techniques they used, not for the outcomes these techniques produced in individuals. This perspective was supported by counselor education programs because the focus of such programs tended to be mainly on counselors and techniques and not as much on guidance program outcomes. Apparently, it was assumed that guidance techniques, particularly individual counseling, were difficult to learn and, therefore, a majority of training time needed to be devoted to them. Learning how to develop and manage a guidance program with an emphasis on measurable outcomes, it was felt, need not be stressed as much, because such things could be learned on the job (Gysbers, 1969a).

Developmental Guidance

Finally, in the 1960s, the term *developmental guidance* was heard with increasing frequency. Mathewson (1962), in discussing future trends for guidance, suggested that although adjustive guidance was popular, a long-term movement toward developmental forms of guidance would probably prevail.

In spite of present tendencies, a long-term movement toward educative and developmental forms of guidance in schools may yet prevail for these reasons: the need to develop all human potentialities, the persistence and power of human individuality, the effects of dynamic educative experience, the necessity for educational adaptability, the comparative costs, and the urge to preserve human freedom. (p. 375)

Similarly, Zaccaria (1966) stressed the importance of and need for developmental guidance. He pointed out that developmental guidance was a concept in transition, that it was in tune with the times but still largely untried in practice.

Developmental Programs Emerge

In the early 1970s the accountability movement intensified. It was joined by increasing interest in career development theory, research, and practice and their educational manifestations, in career guidance, and in career education. Other educational movements such as psychological education, moral education, and process education also emerged. In addition, interest in the development of comprehensive systematic approaches to guidance program development and management continued to increase. The convergence of these movements in the early 1970s served as a stimulus to continue the task of defining guidance developmentally in measurable individual outcome terms—as a program in its own right rather than as services ancillary to other programs.

By 1970 a substantial amount of preliminary work had been done in developing basic ideas, vocabulary, and constructs to define guidance in comprehensive-developmental-outcome terms. As early as 1961 Glanz identified and described four basic models for organizing guidance because of his concern about the lack of discernible patterns for implementing guidance in the schools. Tiedeman and Field (1962) issued a call to make guidance an integral part of the educational process. They also stressed the need for a developmental, liberating perspective of guidance. Zaccaria (1965) stressed the need to examine developmental tasks as a basis for determining the goals of guidance. Shaw and Tuel (1966) developed a model for a guidance program designed to serve all students. At the elementary level Dinkmeyer (1966) emphasized the need for developmental counseling by describing pertinent child development research that supported a developmental perspective.

Paralleling the preliminary work on ideas, vocabulary, and constructs was the application of systems thinking to guidance. Based on a nationwide survey of vocational guidance in 1968, a systems model for vocational guidance was developed at the Center for Vocational and Technical Education in Columbus, Ohio. The model focused on student behavioral objectives, alternative activities, program evaluation, and implementation strategies (Campbell, Dworkin, Jackson, Hoeltzel, Parsons, & Lacey, 1971). Ryan (1969), Thoresen (1969), and

Hosford and Ryan (1970) also proposed the use of systems theory and systems techniques for the development and improvement of comprehensive guidance programs.

On the West Coast McDaniel (1970) proposed a model for guidance called Youth Guidance Systems. It was organized around goals, objectives, programs, implementation plans, and designs for evaluation. The primary student outcome in this model was considered to be decision making. Closely related to this model was the Comprehensive Career Guidance System (CCGS) developed by personnel at the American Institutes for Research (Jones, Nelson, Ganschow, & Hamilton, 1971; Jones, Hamilton, Ganschow, Helliwell, & Wolff, 1972). The CCGS was designed to plan, implement, and evaluate guidance programs systematically. Systems thinking also undergirded Ryan and Zeran's (1972) approach to the organization and administration of guidance services. They stressed the need for a systems approach to guidance in order to ensure the development and implementation of an accountable program. Finally, a systematic approach to guidance was advocated in the PLAN (Program of Learning in Accordance with Needs) System of Individualized Education (Dunn, 1972). Guidance was seen as a major component of PLAN and was treated as an integral part of the regular instructional program.

The task of defining guidance in comprehensive-developmental-outcome terms received substantial support from these approaches that applied systems thinking to guidance. Additional support was provided by the development in a number of states in the early 1970s of state guides for integrating career development into the school curriculum. One such guide was developed in August 1970 by the State of Wisconsin (Drier, 1971), closely followed by the development of the California Model for Career Development in the summer of 1971 (California State Department of Education, 1971).

The idea of implementing career development through the curriculum did not, of course, originate with these models. As early as 1914 Davis had outlined such a curriculum. Of more immediate interest, however, is the work of Tennyson, Soldahl, and Mueller (1965) entitled *The Teacher's Role in Career Development* and the Airlie House Conference in May 1966 on the topic "Implementing Career Development Theory and Research through the Curriculum," sponsored by the National Vocational Guidance Association (Ashcraft, 1966). Later in the 1960s and early 1970s came the work of such theorists and practitioners as Gysbers (1969b), Herr (1969), Hansen (1970), and Tennyson and Hansen (1971), all of whom spoke to the need to integrate career development concepts into the curriculum. Through these efforts and others like them, career development concepts began to be translated into individual outcomes and the resulting goals and objectives arranged sequentially, K–12.

Concurrent with these efforts, a national effort was begun to assist the states in developing and implementing state models or guides for career guidance, counseling, and placement. On July 1, 1971, the University of Missouri-Columbia was awarded a U.S. Office of Education grant to assist each state, the District of Columbia, and Puerto Rico in developing models or guides for implementing career guidance, counseling, and placement programs in local schools. This project was the next step in a program of work begun as a result of a previous project at the university, a project that conducted a national conference on career guidance, counseling, and placement in October 1969 and regional conferences across the country during the spring of 1970. All 50 states, the District of Columbia, and Puerto Rico were involved in the 1971 project, and by the time the project ended in 1974, 44 states had developed some type of guide or model for career guidance, counseling, and placement. As a part of the assistance provided to the states, project staff conducted a national conference in January 1972 and developed a manual (Gysbers & Moore, 1974) to be used by the states as they developed their own guides.

By the early 1970s it was clear that the movement toward developing and implementing comprehensive, developmental guidance programs was well under way. Influenced by career development theory and research, the accountability-evaluation movement, and systems thinking, the earlier promise of guidance for development began to take on form and substance. Career development theory and research offered the content and objectives (Herr & Cramer, 1972; Walz, Smith, & Benjamin, 1974; Tennyson, Hansen, Klaurens, & Anholz, 1975); the emphasis on accountability-evaluation provided the impetus, knowledge, and methods to plan, structure, implement and judge guidance programs (O'Hare & Lasser, 1971; Mease & Benson, 1973; Wellman & Moore, 1975); and systems thinking provided a way to systematically organize evaluation (Ryan, 1969; Thoresen, 1969; Hosford & Ryan, 1970; McDaniel, 1970; Jones, Nelson, Ganschow, & Hamilton, 1971; Jones, Hamilton, Ganschow, Helliwell, & Wolff, 1972; Ryan & Zeran, 1972).

As the 1970s continued to unfold, professional literature devoted to the why and how of developing and implementing systematic accountable guidance programs continued to be written. Humes (1972) urged consideration of applying the planning, programming, budgeting system (PPBS) to guidance programs. Hays (1972) stressed the need for guidance programs to be accountable. Pulvino and Sanborn (1972) underlined the same point, and then described a communications system for planning and carrying out guidance and counseling activities. Koch (1974) issued a more cautious call to accountability through behavioral objectives. He outlined possible negative side effects and then listed conditions through which behavioral objective writing for guidance could come to fruition. In a similar manner Gubser (1974) stressed the point that for counselor accountability to take place the school system must also be accountable. One cannot be accountable independently of the other.

As the movement toward planning and implementing systematic developmental and accountable guidance programs in the early 1970s became more sophisticated, theoretical models began to be translated into practical, workable models to be implemented in the schools. One vehicle used in this translation process was an expanded conception of career guidance. An example effort in this regard began in 1972 in Mesa, Arizona (McKinnon & Jones, 1975). The guidance staff in Mesa felt the need to reorient their guidance program to make it more accountable. The vehicle they chose to do this was a comprehensive career guidance program that included needs assessment, goals and objectives development, and related guidance activities. In cooperation with the American Institutes for Research, competency-based training packages were written to train staff in program development and implementation methods and procedures.

A similar example effort was begun at the Grossmont Union High School District in the state of California in 1974 (Jacobson & Mitchell, 1975). Guidance personnel in the district chose the California Model for Career Development (California State Department of Education, 1971) to supply the content of the program and then proceeded to lay out a systematic, developmental career guidance program. Another example occurred in Georgia when the Georgia State Department of Education initiated a project funded by the U.S. Office of Education to coordinate the efforts of several Georgia school systems in planning and implementing comprehensive career guidance programs. The goal of the project was to develop a career guidance system based on student needs, focusing on a team approach and curriculum-based strategies (Dagley, 1974).

On July 1, 1974, the American Institutes for Research began work on bringing together program planning efforts previously undertaken by the Pupil Personnel Division of the California State Department of Education and their own Youth Development Research Program in Mesa, Arizona, and elsewhere (Jones, Helliwell, & Ganschow, 1975). This resulted in the development of 12 competency-based staff development modules on developing comprehensive career guidance programs K–12. As a part of the project, the modules were field-tested in two school districts in California in the summer of 1975 and in a preservice class of guidance and counseling majors at the University of Missouri-Columbia in the fall of 1975. A final report of this project was issued by the American Institutes for Research in January 1976 (Dayton, 1976). Later Jones, Dayton, and Gelatt (1977) used the 12 modules as a point of departure to suggest a systematic approach in planning and evaluating human service programs.

The work that began in the early 1970s on guidance program models was continued and expanded as the 1970s unfolded. In May 1975 a special issue of the *Personnel and Guidance Journal* entitled "Career Development: Guidance and Education," edited by Hansen and Gysbers (1975), was published. In it a number of articles described program models and examples of programs in operation. In 1976 the American College Testing Program published a programmatic model for guidance. It was titled *River City High School Guidance Services: A Conceptual Model* (American College Testing Program, 1976).

The systems approach to program development, first emphasized in the late 1960s, continued to receive important emphasis in the later part of the 1970s.

Ewens, Dobson, and Seals (1976) described and discussed a systems approach to career guidance K–12 and beyond. In a similar fashion, although using the traditional services model, Ryan (1978) presented a systems approach to the organization and adminsitration of guidance services.

By the later part of the 1970s an increasing number of articles, monographs, and books were being published on various aspects of comprehensive guidance programming. Brown (1977) discussed the organization and evaluation of elementary school guidance services using the three-C's approach of counseling, consulting, and coordinating. Upton, Lowrey, Mitchell, Varenhorst, and Benvenuti (1978) described procedures for developing a career guidance curriculum and presented leadership strategies to teach the procedures to those who would implement the curriculum. Ballast and Shoemaker (1978) outlined and described a step-by-step approach to developing a comprehensive K–12 guidance program. Campbell, Rodebaugh, and Shaltry (1978) edited a handbook that presented numerous examples of career guidance programs, practices, and models. Herr and Cramer (1979) described and discussed a systematic planning approach for career guidance, delineating goals, objectives, and activities for elementary, junior, and high schools as well as for higher and adult education. And finally, Hilton (1979) provided a conceptual framework for career guidance in the secondary school.

In an article in the handbook by Campbell, Rodebaugh, and Shaltry, Gysbers (1978) listed and described a number of systematic approaches to comprehensive guidance programming, including the Career Planning Support System (Campbell, 1977) and the Cooperative Rural Guidance System (Drier, 1976), both developed at the National Center for Research in Vocational Education, Columbus, Ohio. Another similar approach developed during the later 1970s was the Programmatic Approach to Guidance Excellence: PAGE 2 (Peterson & Treichel, 1978). Finally, articles by Mitchell (1978) and Mitchell and Gysbers (1978) described the need for comprehensive guidance programs and provided recommendations for how to develop and implement such programs, and a publication by Halasz-Salster and Peterson (1979) presented descriptions of different guidance planning models.

The later half of the 1970s also witnessed increasing legislative activity to mandate comprehensive, developmental guidance programming in schools. For example, developmental elementary school guidance was identified as a critical area of education in the state of Oklahoma. The 1978 state legislature appropriated $1.72 million to be distributed to schools on the basis of $5,000 per program (Fisher, 1978). Grants are made to eligible schools provided the schools meet these minimum criteria: statement of philosphy; needs assessment; program goals; objectives; activities; evaluation of objectives; program evaluation, review, and modification; personnel; student ratio; physical facilities; materials and equipment; budget; cross-level program articulation, and professional growth and development. Similar mandating efforts were undertaken by a task force of guidance professionals in California in 1977 (Hooper, 1977). In addition, on September 28, 1979, a bill, H.R. 5477, titled "Elementary School Guidance and Counseling Incentive Act of 1979," was introduced in the U.S. House of Representatives. The purpose of this bill was to "assure the accessibility of developmental guidance and counseling to all children of elementary school age by providing funds for comprehensive elementary school guidance and counseling programs."

At the same time that attention was being given to state and federal legislation and mandates, some states were developing planning models for guidance. For example, personnel at Marshall University undertook a project to develop a planning model and a state plan for improving comprehensive systems of career guidance in West Virginia. The plan includes offering community-based guidance services, upgrading guidance services personnel, and evaluating guidance services programs for students, out-of-school youth, and adults (West Virginia Department of Education, 1979).

Comprehensive Guidance Programs: Putting the Idea Into Practice in the 1980s and 1990s

As the 1970s drew to a close, it was clear that traditional patterns of organizing and managing guidance and counseling in the nation's schools were being reexamined and that new patterns were being recommended (Herr, 1979). The counselor-clinical-services model of the previous decade was gradually being encompassed conceptually if not yet in practice by the idea of developmentally based comprehensive guidance programs. The American School Counselor Association had endorsed this change in a position statement entitled "The School Counselor and the Guidance and Counseling Program" in 1974. It was reviewed and reaffirmed in 1980. In 1978 the association also had adopted a position statement entitled "The School Counselor and Developmental Guidance." It too was reviewed and revised in 1984. Shaw and Goodyear (1984) endorsed this change by stressing the need for guidance specialists to "make concrete, written, and reasonable proposals for the delivery of primary preventive services so that some of their less professional and highly scattered responsibilities can be diminished" (p. 446).

Thus, the work of putting comprehensive guidance programs into place in the schools continued in the 1980s. Gysbers and Moore (1981) published a book entitled *Improving Guidance Programs*. It provided a theoretical base and a step-by-step process to develop and implement comprehensive school guidance programs. It was based, in part, on their earlier work in directing the University of Missouri project in the 1970s to assist the states in developing and implementing state models or guides for career guidance, counseling, and placement (Gysbers & Moore, 1974).

In a document entitled *Guidance 1984*, the Ministry of Education of Ontario, Canada, stated that "each school shall have on file a written guidance program . . ." (p. 4). The Ministry also stated that "The aims of the guidance program shall be achieved through guidance instruction and counseling. Both are essential components of a complete guidance program. A balance shall be maintained in the time allotted to each" (p. 4). Also in 1984, Hargens and Gysbers presented a case study of how one school district had remodeled and revitalized its school guidance program so that it was developmental and comprehensive.

In 1986, the state of Missouri published a draft version of "Missouri Comprehensive Guidance" (1986). It presented Missouri's plan to help school districts to develop, implement, and evaluate comprehensive, systematic school guidance programs that had begun during the 1984–85 school year. Also, Wisconsin published *School Counseling Programs: A Resource and Planning Guide* (Wilson, 1986). This document was the result of work begun in 1984 to reexamine the school counselor's role. Also, in 1986, the National School Boards Association passed a resolution that supported comprehensive programs of guidance and counseling in the schools. (National School Boards Association, 1986). The College Entrance Examination Board issued a report in 1986 that has direct relevance to comprehensive guidance programs in the schools. It was entitled *Keeping the Options Open: Recommendations*. It was based on the work of the Commission on Precollege Guidance and Counseling begun in 1984. In its recommendations the board urged that schools establish comprehensive and developmental guidance programs, kindergarten through the 12th grade.

Henderson (1987), in her article, "A Comprehensive School Guidance Program at Work," described how a comprehensive guidance program was designed and was being implemented in a large school district in Texas. She described the content of a comprehensive program as well as the process used to implement it. Also, the School Climate and Student Support Services Unit of the California State Department of Education (1987) proposed the establishment of quality standards for a model guidance program. These standards identify four broad student outcomes and four program elements. They are as follows:

1. Students acquire regular and timely information to enable them to make informed decisions.
2. Students develop self-management and planning skills.
3. Students are assisted in overcoming disabling educational/personal/social problems.
4. Students experience a supportive and rewarding learning environment.
5. There is a written, publicized program that reflects needs according to priority.

6. Leadership roles within guidance and counseling are evident.
7. The guidance program is comprehensive and provides for staff development.
8. The program is reviewed continually and renewed annually.

Concluding Thoughts

What began at the turn of the century in the schools under the term *vocational guidance*, with a selection and placement focus, and then shifted in the 1920s, 1930s, 1940s, and 1950s to a focus on personal adjustment organized around a counselor-clinical-services model, has now assumed a developmental focus organized around the concept of a comprehensive program. Selection, placement, and adjustment remain, but are incorporated in the concept of development. Organizationally the concept of a comprehensive program has encompassed the counselor-clinical-services model and is now beginning to become a major way of organizing and managing guidance in the schools.

Why is the history of the evolution of guidance in the schools presented in chapter 1 important? It is important because it helps us understand why and how current organization and management structures for guidance evolved. It also is important because it helps us understand why and how the concept of comprehensive guidance programs emerged in response to dissatisfaction with these current structures.

Why are the terms *comprehensive* and *program* important? They are important because they call attention to the following premises that do and will undergird the organization and management of guidance in the schools in the 1980s and 1990s.

First, guidance is a program. As a program it has characteristics similar to other programs in education, including:

1. student outcomes (student competencies);
2. activities and processes to assist students in achieving these outcomes;
3. professionally recognized personnel; and
4. materials and resources.

Second, guidance programs are developmental and comprehensive. They are developmental in that guidance activities are conducted on a regular and planned basis to assist students to achieve specified competencies. Although immediate and crisis needs of students are to be met, a major focus of a developmental program is to provide all students with experiences to help them grow and develop. Guidance programs are comprehensive in that a full range of activities and services such as assessment, information, consultation, counseling, referral, placement, follow-up, and follow-through are provided.

Third, guidance programs feature a team approach. A comprehensive, developmental program of guidance is based on the assumption that all school staff are involved. At the same time, it is understood that professionally certified school counselors are central to the program. School counselors provide direct services to students as well as work in consultative and collaborative relations with other members of the guidance team, members of the school staff, parents, and members of the community.

Based on the understanding we have gained from a review of how guidance has been conceptualized and institutionalized in the schools over the years, we are ready to examine a new organization and management structure for guidance. The chapters that follow provide the theoretical and practical specifics about how to organize and manage guidance, using the concept of a comprehensive program. The issues involved, the procedures and methods to be used, and the resources and personnel required are presented in detail.

References

Allen, F. J. (1927). *Principles and problems in vocational guidance.* New York: McGraw-Hill.

American College Testing Program (1976). *River City High School guidance services: A conceptual model.* Iowa City, IA: Author.

American Psychological Association. Division of Counseling Psychology. Committee on Definition. (1956). Counseling psychology as a specialty. *American Psychologist, 11,* 282–285.

Ashcraft, K. B. (1966). *A report of the invitational conference in implementing career development theory.* Washington, DC: National Vocational Guidance Association.

Aubrey R. F. (1969). Misapplication of therapy models to school counseling. *Personnel and Guidance Journal, 48,* 273–278.

Aubrey, R. F. (1982). A house divided: Guidance and counseling in 20th century America. *Personnel and Guidance Journal, 61,* 198–204.

Ballast, D. L., & Shoemaker, R. L. (1978). *Guidance program development.* Springfield, IL: Charles C Thomas.

Bell, H. M. (1939). *Theory and practice of personal counseling.* Stanford, CA: Stanford University Press.

Bloomfield, M. (1915). *Readings in vocational guidance.* Boston: Athenaeum Press.

Borow, H. (1966). Research in vocational development: Implications for the vocational aspects of counselor education. In C. McDaniels, (Ed.), *Vocational aspects of counselor education* (pp. 70–92). Washington, DC: George Washington University.

Brammer, L. M. (1968). The counselor is a psychologist. *Personnel and Guidance Journal, 47,* 4–9.

Brewer, J. M. (1922). *The vocational-guidance movement.* New York: MacMillan.

Brown, J. A. (1977). *Organizing and evaluating elementary school guidance services: Why, what, and how.* Monterey, CA: Brooks/Cole.

California State Department of Education. (1971). *Career guidance: A California model for career development K-adult.* Sacramento, CA: Author.

California State Department of Education. School Climate and Student Support Services Unit. (1987). *Program quality review for counseling and guidance: Abstract.* Sacramento, CA: State Department of Education.

Campbell, M E. (1932). Vocational guidance-committee on vocational guidance and child labor, section III: Education and training. White House Conference on Child Health and Protection. New York: Century.

Campbell, R. E. (1977). *The career planning support system.* Columbus, OH: National Center for Research in Vocational Education.

Campbell, R. E., Dworkin, E. P., Jackson, D. P., Hoeltzel, K. E., Parsons, G. E., & Lacey, D. W. (1971). *The systems approach: An emerging behavioral model for career guidance.* Columbus, OH: Center for Vocational and Technical Education.

Campbell, R. E., Rodebaugh, H. D., & Shaltry, P. E. (1978). *Building comprehensive career guidance programs for secondary schools.* Columbus, OH: National Center for Research in Vocational Education.

College Entrance Examination Board (1986). *Keeping the options open: Recommendations.* New York: Author.

Council of Chief State School Officers. (1960). *Responsibilities of state departments of education for pupil personnel services.* Washington, DC: Author.

Dagley, J. C. (1974, December). *Georgia career guidance project newsletter.* Athens: University of Georgia.

Davis, J. B. (1914). *Vocational and moral guidance.* Boston: Ginn.

Davis, H. V. (1969). *Frank Parsons: Prophet, innovator, counselor.* Carbondale: Southern Illinois University Press.

Dayton, C. A. (1976). *A validated program development model and staff development prototype for comprehensive career guidance, counseling, placement and follow-up.* Final Report, Grant no. OEG–0–74–1721. Palo Alto, CA: American Institutes for Research.

Dickinson, D. J. (1969–70). Improving guidance with behavioral objectives. *CPGA Journal, 2,* 12–17.

Dinkmeyer, D. (1966). Developmental counseling in the elementary school. *Personnel and Guidance Journal, 45,* 262–66.

Drier, H. N. (1976). *Cooperative rural guidance system.* Columbus, OH: National Center for Research in Vocational Education.

Drier, H. N. (Ed.). (1971). *Guide to the integration of career development into local curriculum-grades K–12.* Madison: Wisconsin Department of Public Instruction.

Dunn, J. A. (1972). *The guidance program in the plan system of individualized education.* Palo Alto, CA: American Institutes for Research.

Eckerson, L. O., & Smith, H. M. (Eds.). (1966). *Scope of pupil personnel services.* Washington, DC: U.S. Government Printing Office.

Ewens, W. P., Dobson, J. S., & Seals, J. M. (1976). *Career guidance: A systems approach.* Dubuque, IA: Kenddall-Hunt.

Faust, V. (1968). *History of elementary school counseling: Overview and critique.* Boston: Houghton Mifflin.

Felix, J. L. (1968). Who decided that? *Personnel and Guidance Journal, 47,* 9–11.

Ferguson, D. G. (1963). *Pupil personnel services.* Washington, DC: Center for Applied Research in Education.

Fisher, L. (1978, May 15). Letter to the superintendents of schools in Oklahoma.

Glanz, E. C. (1961). Emerging concepts and patterns of guidance in American education. *Personnel and Guidance Journal, 40,* 259–65.

Gubser, M. M. (1974). Performance-based counseling: Accountability or liability. *School Counselor, 21,* 296–302.

Guidance, 1984. (1984). Ontario, Canada: Ministry of Education.

Gysbers, N. C. (1969a). Educating school counselors, *Contemporary Education,* November supplement.

Gysbers, N. C. (1969b). *Elements of a model for promoting career development in elementary and junior high school.* Paper presented at the National Conference on Exemplary Programs and Projects, 1968 Amendments to the Vocational Education Act (ED045860), Atlanta, GA.

Gysbers, N. C. (1978). Comprehensive career guidance programs. In R. E. Campbell, H. D. Rodebaugh, & P. E. Shaltry (Eds.), *Building comprehensive career guidance programs for secondary schools* (pp. 3–24). Columbus, OH: National Center for Research in Vocational Education.

Gysbers, N. C., & Moore, E. J. (Eds.), (1974). *Career guidance counseling and placement: Elements of an illustrative program guide.* Columbia: University of Missouri.

Gysbers, N. C., & Moore, E. J. (1981). *Improving guidance programs.* Englewood Cliffs, NJ: Prentice-Hall.

Halasz-Salster, I., & Peterson, M. (1979). *Planning comprehensive career guidance programs: A catalog of alternatives.* Columbus, OH: National Center for Research in Vocational Education.

Hansen, L. S. (1970). *Career guidance practices in school and community.* Washington, DC: National Vocational Guidance Association.

Hansen, L. S., & Gysbers, N. C. (Eds.). (1975). Career development: Guidance and education (special issue). *Personnel and Guidance Journal, 53.*

Hargens, M., & Gysbers, N. C. (1984). How to remodel a guidance program while living in it: A case study. *School Counselor, 32,* 119–125.

Hays, D. G. (1972). Counselor—What are you worth? *School Counselor, 19,* 309–312.

Henderson, P. H. (1987). A comprehensive school guidance program at work. *Texas Association for Counseling and Development Journal, 10,* 25–37.

Herr, E. L. (1969). *Unifying an entire system of education around a career development theme.* Paper presented at the National Conference on Exemplary Programs and Projects, 1968 Amendments to the Vocational Education Act (ED045860), Atlanta, GA.

Herr, E. L. (1979). *Guidance and counseling in the schools: The past, present, and future.* Washington, DC: American Personnel and Guidance Association.

Herr, E. L., & Cramer, S. H. (1972). *Vocational guidance and career development in the schools: Toward a systems approach.* Boston: Houghton Mifflin.

Herr, E. L., & Cramer, S. H. (1979). *Career guidance through the life span*. Boston: Little, Brown.

Hilton, T. L. (1979). *Confronting the future: A conceptual framework for secondary school career guidance*. New York: College Entrance Examination Board.

Hooper, P. (1977). Memo dated September 14.

Hosford, R. E., & Ryan, A. T. (1970). Systems design in the development of counseling and guidance programs, *Personnel and Guidance Journal, 49*, 221–230.

Hoyt, K. B. (1974). Professional preparation for vocational guidance. In E. L. Herr (Ed.), *Vocational guidance and human development* (pp. 502–527). Boston: Houghton Mifflin.

Humes, C. W., Jr. (1972). Program budgeting in guidance. *School Counselor, 19*, 313–318.

Humphreys, J. A., & Traxler, A. E. (1954). *Guidance services*. Chicago: Science Research Associates.

Jacobson, T. J., & Mitchell, A. M. (1975). *Master plan for career guidance and counseling*. Final Report, Pupil, Personnel Services. Grossmont, CA: Grossmont Union High School District.

Johnson, A. H. (1972). Changing conceptions of vocational guidance and concomitant value-orientations 1920–1930. *Dissertation Abstracts International, 33*, 3292A. (University Microfilms No. 72–31, 933)

Jones, A. J., & Hand, H. C. (1938). Guidance and purposive living. In G. M. Whipple (Ed.), *Yearbook of the National Society for the study of Education, Part 1* (pp. 3–29). Bloomington, IL: Public School Publishing Co.

Jones, G. B., Dayton, C., & Gelatt, H. B. (1977). *New methods for delivering human services*. New York: Human Services Press.

Jones, G. B., Hamilton, J. A., Ganschow, L. H., Helliwell, C. B., & Wolff, J. M. (1972). *Planning, developing, and field testing career guidance programs: A manual and report*. Palo Alto, CA: American Institutes for Research.

Jones, G. B., Helliwell, C. B., & Ganschow, L. H. (1975). A planning model for career guidance. *Vocational Guidance Quarterly, 23*, 220–226.

Jones, G. B., Nelson, D. E., Ganschow, L. H., & Hamilton, J. A. (1971). *Development and evaluation of a comprehensive career guidance system*. Palo Alto, CA: American Institutes for Research.

Koch, J. H. (1974). Riding the behavioral objective bandwagon. *School Counselor, 21*, 196–202.

Leonard, G. E., & Vriend, T. J. (1975). Update: The developmental career guidance project. *Personnel and Guidance Journal, 53*, 668–671.

McCracken, T. C., & Lamb, H. E. (1923). *Occupational information in the elementary school*. Boston: Houghton Mifflin.

McDaniel, H. B. (1970). *Youth guidance systems*. Palo Alto, CA: College Entrance Examination Board.

McKinnon, B. E., & Jones, G. B. (1975). Field testing a comprehensive career guidance program, K–12. *Personnel and Guidance Journal, 53*, 663–667.

Mathewson, R. H. (1962). *Guidance policy and practice* (3rd ed.). New York: Harper & Row.

Mease, W. P., & Benson, L. L. (1973). *Outcome management applied to pupil personnel services*. St. Paul: Minnesota Department of Education.

Miller, C. H. (1971). *Foundations of guidance*. New York: Harper & Row.

Missouri comprehensive guidance. (1986). *The Counseling Interviewer, 18*(4), 6–17.

Mitchell, A. M. (1978). The design, development and evaluation of systematic guidance programs. In G. Walz & L. Benjamin (Eds.), *New imperatives for guidance* (pp. 113–148). Ann Arbor, MI: ERIC Counseling and Personnel Services Clearinghouse.

Mitchell, A. M., & Gysbers, N. C. (1978). Comprehensive school guidance programs. In *The status of guidance and counseling in the nation's schools* (pp. 23–39). Washington, DC: American Personnel and Guidance Association.

National School Boards Association. (1986). *Resolution on guidance and counseling*. Adopted by the National School Boards Associative Delegate Assembly, April 4, 5, and 7.

O'Hare, R. W., & Lasser, B. (1971). *Evaluating pupil personnel programs*. Fullerton, CA: California Personnel and Guidance Association.

Parsons, F. (1909). *Choosing a vocation*. Boston: Houghton Mifflin.

Payne, A. F. (1925). *Organization of vocational guidance*. New York: McGraw-Hill.

Peterson, M., & Treichel, J. (1978). *Programmatic approach to guidance excellence, PAGE 2* (Rev. ed.). McComb, IL: Curriculum Publishing Clearinghouse, Western Illinois University.

Pierson, G. A. (1965). *An evaluation—counselor education in regular session institutes*. Washington, DC: U.S. Department of Health, Education, and Welfare, Office of Education, U.S. Government Printing Office.

Pulvino, C. J., & Sanborn, M. P. (1972). Feedback and accountability. *Personnel and Guidance Journal, 51*, 15–20.

Roeber, E C. (1963). *The school counselor*. Washington, DC: Center for Applied Research in Education.

Roeber, E. C., Walz, G. R., & Smith, G. E. (1969). *A strategy for guidance*. New York: Macmillan.

Rogers, C. R. (1942). *Counseling and psychotherapy*. Boston: Houghton Mifflin.

Rudy, W. S. (1965). *Schools in an age of mass culture*. Englewood Cliffs, NJ: Prentice-Hall.

Ryan, T. A. (1969). Systems techniques for programs of counseling and counselor education. *Educational Technology, 9*, 7–17.

Ryan, T. A. (1978). *Guidance services*. Danville, IL: Interstate Printers & Publishers.

Ryan, T. A., & Zeran, F. R. (1972). *Organization and administration of guidance services*. Danville, IL: Interstate Printers & Publishers.

Ryan, W. C., Jr. (1919). *Vocational guidance and the public schools*. Washington, DC: Department of the Interior, Bureau of Education, Bulletin, 1918, No. 24, Government Printing Office.

Shaw, M. C., & Goodyear, R. K. (1984). Prologue to primary prevention in schools. *Personnel and Guidance Journal, 62*, 446–447.

Shaw, M. C., & Tuel, J. K. (1966). A focus for public school guidance programs: A model and proposal. *Personnel and Guidance Journal, 44*, 824–830.

Smith, G. E. (1951). *Principles and practices of the guidance program.* New York: Macmillan.

Sprinthall, N. A. (1971). *Guidance for human growth.* New York: Van Nostrand Reinhold.

Stephens, W. R. (1970). *Social reform and the origins of vocational guidance.* Washington, DC: National Vocational Guidance Association.

Stoughton, R. W., McKenna, J. W., & Cook, R. P. (1969). *Pupil personnel services: A position statement.* National Association of Pupil Personnel Administrators.

Stripling, R. O., & Lane, D. (1966). Guidance services. In L. O. Eckerson & H. M. Smith (Eds.), *Scope of pupil personnel services* (pp. 25–35). Washington, DC: U.S. Government Printing Office.

Sullivan, H. J., & O'Hare, R. W. (1971). *A process guide for the development of objectives.* Fullerton: California personnel and Guidance Association.

Super, D. E. (1955). Transition: From vocational guidance to counseling psychology. *Journal of Counseling Psychology, 2,* 3–9.

Tennyson, W. W., & Hansen, L. S. (1971). Guidance through the curriculum. In L. C. Deighton (Ed.), *The encyclopedia of education, No. 4* (pp. 248–254). New York: Macmillan.

Tennyson, W. W., Hansen, L. S., Klaurens, M. K., & Anholz, M. B. (1975). *Educating for career development.* St. Paul: Minnesota Department of Education.

Tennyson, W. W., Soldahl, T. A., & Mueller, C. (1965). *The teacher's role in career development.* Washington, DC: National Vocational Guidance Association.

Thoresen, C. E. (1969). The systems approach and counselor education: Basic features and implicatons. *Counselor Education and Supervision, 9,* 3–17.

Tiedeman, D. V., & Field, F. C. (1962). Guidance: The science of purposeful action applied through education. *Harvard Educational Review, 32,* 483–501.

Tyler, L. E. (1960). *The vocational defense counseling and guidance training institutes program: A report of the first 50 institutes.* Washington, DC: U.S. Department of Health, Education, and Welfare, Office of Education, U.S. Government printing Office.

Upton, A., Lowery, B., Mitchell, A.M., Varenhorst, B., & Benvenuti, J. (1978). *A planning model for developing career guidance curriculum.* Fullerton: California Personnel and Guidance Association.

Walz, G. R., Smith, R. L., & Benjamin, L. (1974). *A comprehensive view of career development.* Washington, DC: American Personnel and Guidance Association.

Wellman, F. E. (1968). *Contractor's report, Phase I, National Study of Guidance.* Contract OEG 3–6–001147–1147. Washington, DC: U.S. Department of Health, Education, and Welfare, Office of Education.

Wellman, F. E. (1978). U.S. Office of Education Administrative Unit: Past, present, and future. In *Report, current state of the art, guidance and counseling services, U.S. Office of Education, Region Seven.* Developed under the auspices of the Division of Pupil Personnel Services, Missouri State Department of Elementary and Secondary Education, American Personnel and Guidance Association, and the U.S. Office of Education. Columbia, MO.

Wellman, F. E., & Moore, E. J. (1975). *Pupil personnel services: A handbook for program development and evaluation.* Columbia: Missouri Evaluation Projects.

Wellman, F. E., & Twiford, D. D. (1961). *Guidance, counseling and testing: Program evaluation.* Washington, DC: U.S. Department of Health, Education, and Welfare.

West Virginia Department of Education. (1979). *A planning model for the formulation of state and local career and vocational guidance plans: Part IV, Program narrative.* Charleston, WV: Author.

Wilson, P. J. (1986). *School counseling programs: A resource and planning guide.* Madison: Wisconsin Department of Public Instruction.

Wrenn, C. G. (1962). *The counselor in a changing world.* Washington, DC: American Personnel and Guidance Association.

Zaccaria, J. S. (1965). Developmental tasks: Implications for the goals of guidance. *Personnel and Guidance Journal, 44,* 372–375.

Zaccaria, J. S. (1966). Developmental guidance: A concept in transition. *School Counselor, 13,* 226–229.

CHAPTER 2

A COMPREHENSIVE SCHOOL GUIDANCE PROGRAM: GETTING ORGANIZED TO GET THERE FROM WHERE YOU ARE

Traditional patterns of organizing guidance in the schools are giving way to the comprehensive program concept. This major trend was brought into sharp focus in chapter 1 as the evolution of guidance in the schools was described. Although it is a major trend, it is not yet a reality.

This trend is not yet a reality because school counselors are still expected to fulfill multiple, often conflicting roles. They are expected to work in the curriculum; conduct placement, follow-up, and follow-through activities; and do community outreach. In addition, they are expected to continue such guidance functions as crisis counseling and teacher and parent consultation as well as testing, scheduling, and other administrative-clerical duties. School counselors want to respond to new needs and expectations but often find that the press of their existing duties interferes with or actually prevents them from doing so. As a result, school counselors find themselves in a quandary, and, hence, role conflict often is prevalent.

> The range of counselor responsibilities and functions vary not only among school districts but among schools in the same district. The school principal is predominant in determining the daily routine of counselors and, while citing the support their principals provide them, many counselors bemoaned the plethora of administrative tasks they are called upon to perform. Without standard position descriptions, counselors "fill vacuums" with the result that counselors are expected to do "too much for too many." (Commission on Precollege Guidance and Counseling, 1986, p. 38.)

One reason for this dilemma is that current organizational patterns of guidance in many schools are still based on an ancillary services concept loosely grouped

39

around broad role and function statements. It is an undefined program. As a result, school counselors continue to find themselves in mainly supportive, remedial roles, roles that are not seen as mainstream by most people. And, what is worse, this concept reinforces the practice of having counselors do many inappropriate tasks because such tasks can be justified as being of service to someone. The following list is typical.

- Counselors register and schedule all new students;
- Counselors are responsible for giving ability and achievement tests;
- Counselors talk to new students concerning school rules;
- Counselors change students' schedules;
- Counselors are responsible for signing excuses for students who are tardy or absent;
- Counselors teach classes when teachers are absent;
- Counselors do senior grade checks;
- Counselors are assigned lunchroom duty;
- Counselors arrange class schedules for students;
- Students are sent to the counselor for disciplinary action;
- Counselors send students home who are not appropriately dressed;
- Counselors compute grade-point averages;
- Counselors fill out student reports and records;
- Counselors are in charge of student records;
- Counselors supervise study halls; and
- Counselors assist with duties in the principal's office.

Another reason for this jumble of duties is that some counselors are unwilling to see others playing a role in the delivery of the guidance program. They feel that it is their job to carry out the total program. In addition, some counselors take their occupational title literally. They do counseling only (particularly one-to-one), and, as a result are reluctant to take on new competencies to carry out the broader functions of a comprehensive guidance program.

Given this situation, the challenge that we face as school counselors and guidance program leaders is how to make the transition from the ancillary services concept of guidance, with a wide variety of tasks involved, to a comprehensive program, a program that is an equal partner with other programs in education. How do we take an undefined program, improve it, and make it a defined program?

Making the transition is complex and difficult. It means carrying out duties provided by the current organizational plan at the same time as planning and trying out new duties derived from a new organizational plan. It can be done, but it is difficult, time-consuming, and often frustrating.

A number of issues and conditions need to be considered in planning the process of change that are prerequisite to making the transition to a comprehensive school guidance program. Thus, attention in chapter 2 is first given to what is involved in making the all-important decision to change. Then, necessary conditions for change are discussed. Next, the topics of expecting resistance and appreciating the challenges involved in the change process are presented. This is followed by discussion of the need to develop trust among staff so that changes can occur smoothly. Finally, chapter 2 describes how to form groups to participate in the change process such as a steering committee, an advisory committee, and work groups.

Decide That You Want To Change

The initial stimulus to move to a comprehensive guidance program may come from counselors, or it may come from parents, students, school administration, the school board, or community organizations. No matter where the initial stimulus comes from, however, the total K–12 guidance staff must be involved in responding to it with administration involvement and support. The decision to change, we believe, must be made jointly by the school counselors and administrators involved. Because this is a key decision that will change how guidance and counseling are delivered in the schools, it requires time.

In one school district the guidance staff met several times with the full endorsement of administration to assess the need to change. They compared and contrasted activities they thought they should be providing with those they actually were providing. Based on this comparison they decided to take a detailed look at their program. "In retrospect, this was a key decision because it was at this point that the staff decided to take charge of their own destiny rather than leave it to fate or for others to decide." (Hargens & Gysbers, 1984, p. 121). Once consensus was obtained among the guidance staff, the decision was shared with the administration, and its support was obtained to proceed.

When the issue of changing has been fully discussed, consensus must be reached on how to respond. School counselors and administrators may decide to maintain the program as it is and not to change. Or, as in the school district cited above, the decision to change may be made jointly. If the decision to change is made, it is imperative that a majority of staff (counselors and administrators) agree to be involved fully in whatever it takes to change their guidance program, to make it comprehensive, K–12.

Understand the Necessary Conditions for Effective Change

As changes are being contemplated concerning how guidance activities should be organized and implemented, it is important to understand that certain organizational, structural, and political conditions must be addressed during the organizational phase if successful change is to occur. What are some of these conditions? How should they be addressed during this phase of the planning process?

General Conditions to Consider

The guidance staff of the Los Alamos, New Mexico, public schools found that six conditions were important to them as they considered the change process. These included (1) counselors committed to program improvement; (2) counselors committed to change, if change is needed; (3) counselors committed to formulating specific goals; (4) support for the guidance program leader from administration and counselors; (5) funding for inservice training, and (6) backing from the local school board in the initial stages as well as throughout the program improvement process (Engel, Castille, & Neely, 1978).

Mitchell and Gysbers (1978) provided a similar list of conditions that they felt were prerequisite for successful transition to a comprehensive guidance program.

1. All staff members are involved.
2. All staff members are committed to the common objective: total integrated development of individual students.
3. The administration is committed to the comprehensive approach and is willing to negotiate (trade off), helping staff members identify current activities that do not contribute to priority outcomes and supporting staff members' abandonment of such activities in favor of those that do contribute to priority outcomes.
4. All staff members see the comprehensive systematic counseling and guidance program as a function of the total staff rather than the exclusive responsibility of the counselors.
5. Counselors are willing to give up such "security blankets" as writing lengthy reports of their contacts with counselees or seeing counselees individually on matters better addressed in a group.
6. Counselors are interested in acquiring competencies.
7. Staff development activities to help staff members acquire competencies needed for successful implementation of a comprehensive program are provided.
8. Time is made available for planning and designing the program and the evaluation, with all interested groups participating (students, parents, teachers, counselors, administrators, and community).
9. Program developers design an incremental transition rather than abrupt transition that ignores the need for continuing many current activities and thrusts. (p. 36)

Making the transition from guidance as an ancillary service to guidance as a comprehensive program is not easy, automatic, or rapid. It involves changing the behavior patterns of students, parents, the teaching staff, the community, and the guidance staff. Because of this, Mitchell and Gysbers (1978) pointed out that although all nine conditions are important, none is more important than the last. "Abrupt change is difficult and anxiety-producing; it tends to cause participants in the change to build barriers against it" (p. 36).

Visions of Desired Programs

Because modifying an existing school guidance program or planning and implementing a new program is complex and time-consuming, it is important to establish in the beginning a vision of the desired program. This involves having an idea of the content and structure of a comprehensive program that will make sense in your school district. It also involves knowing the change processes to use, the timelines involved in making the transition, and the materials and resources that may be required.

A number of writers have described a variety of ways of going about the change process. They have outlined and described what may be involved in the program planning and implementing process. Ballast and Shoemaker (1978, p. 7) defined program development as a systematic process that includes the following components and sequence: identifying guidance department needs, generating support for program development, establishing departmental leadership, preparing the proposal for leadership development, involving key decision makers, identifying current services and activities, developing tools for the assessment of student needs, administering needs surveys, tabulating the results of needs surveys, identifying priority items of needs surveys, interpreting the results of the needs surveys, developing student outcome statements, determining counselor activities designed to attain student outcomes and integrating these with current activities and services, identifying timelines and materials, developing a guidance calendar including individual counselor responsibilities, and organizing the guidance program handbook.

Mitchell and Gysbers (1978) described the change process that leads to a comprehensive guidance program model as having four major phases: planning, designing, implementing, and evaluating. Each of the phases contains specific tasks to be completed. The phases and tasks they described are as follows:

Planning
1. Statement of values;
2. Selection of a curriculum model;
3. Selection of program goals;
4. Determination of desired student outcomes;
5. Assessment of current program; and
6. Establishment of priorities.

Designing
1. Development of program objectives;
2. Selection of program strategies;
3. Assignment of program components;
4. Analysis of staff competencies; and
5. Provision of staff development.

Implementing
1. Administration of measurement instruments;
2. Installation of program; and
3. Modification based on evaluation data.

Evaluating
1. Formulation of the questions to be answered by the evaluation;
2. Selection of evaluation design;
3. Selection of measurement instruments;
4. Development of procedures for data collection;
5. Establishment of a monitoring system;
6. Performance of data reduction, summary, and analysis tasks; and
7. Preparation of reports.

In addition, a number of other writers and organizations have developed guidance program planning and implementation models. Ryan (1978) developed a model for the management of guidance in which she identified and described three major management functions, including planning, implementing, and evaluating. Jones, Dayton, and Gelatt (1977) described a program planning model developed at the American Institutes for Research. They outlined the steps involved from the initial planning activities to the writing of evaluation reports. Similarly, Ewens, Dobson, and Seals (1976) outlined the steps involved in developing and implementing a systematic guidance program. Finally, two planning models complete with procedural guides, audiovisual materials, survey instruments, and staff training manuals have been developed at the National Center for Research in Vocational Education in Columbus, Ohio. The Career Planning Support System was developed under the leadership of Robert Campbell (1980), and the Cooperative Rural Career Guidance System was developed under the leadership of Harry Drier (1979).

More recently, the State of Wisconsin published a guide, *School Counseling Programs: A Resource and Planning Guide* (Wilson, 1986), which provides a framework for contemporary, developmental guidance programs. Wisconsin's vision of a program contains student competencies to be gained from the program. In addition it shows how to incorporate a variety of personnel into the guidance delivery system. Attention also is given to guidance resource organization and management.

The school counselors of Northside Independent School District, San Antonio, Texas, envision that a comprehensive guidance program should involve the following characteristics if it is to be implemented:

- Assists all students (developmental, preventive, remedial);
- Enhances development in all guidance content areas (personal, social, career, educational);

- Has defined all seven (7) program components (rationale, assumptions, definition, curriculum, individual planning, responsive services, system support);
- Is articulated across all levels;
- Is integrated with all other programs;
- Utilizes all staff in roles appropriate to their training and competence; and
- Is developed through taking all steps in the educational program development process (planning-designing-implementation-evaluation).

A process package called "Program Quality Reviews for Guidance and Counseling" is being developed by the School Climate and Student Support Services Unit of the California State Department of Education (1987) in cooperation with counseling professionals in California. It is designed to encourage and assist schools and districts to begin the process of guidance program renewal. The process package includes a process abstract, a procedures manual, and renewal references. In the procedures manual three steps for change are described.

Program Quality Review for Guidance and Counseling
The Three Process Steps

Step 1. Develop the Climate for Change

- **Getting the school and people ready to review and renew.**
  Successful change is founded on a positive and supportive environment. This includes commitment and support from the school board, superintendent, school administration and staff, students, parents, and community. The following instruments or checklists are provided:
  a. Survey of School Climate. Checking your own perceptions.
  b. Building a Collaborative Team. Establishing and enhancing a supportive political climate.
  c. The Anatomy of a Philosophy. Developing a program philosophy.

Step 2. Analyze the Program

- **Relating what you have to what could be.**
  Change requires an understanding of the difference between what is and what could be. This includes the perceptions of users and providers, empirical data about outcomes, and a vision of the future. The following instruments or checklists are provided:
  a. Provider Survey. Comparing your program to a future model.
  b. User Survey. Collecting current data from program users.

    c. **Audit Procedures.** Collecting other program data.

    d. **Prioritizing Grid.** Determining desired program elements/services.

Step 3. Design the Renewed Program

- **Deciding what you want the new program to be.**

    A successful program requires a well-developed plan. The plan must integrate content, methods, resources, marketing, and evaluation. The following instruments or checklists are provided:

    a. **Counseling Resources.** Determining how much you have.

    b. **Other Possible Resources.** Determining what is available.

    c. **Possible Delivery Methods.** Surveying "how-to-do-it."

    d. **Services, Resources, and Methods.** Combining 2d, 3a, 3b, and 3c.

    e. **Program Description.** Putting it together into a plan.

    f. **Staff Development Design.** Providing skills and knowledge as needed.

    g. **Program Promotion.** Telling others what the program is and does.

    h. **Continuous Evaluation.** Reviewing and renewing again and again.

    i. **The Guidance Program Calendar.** The visual display of what and when.

Major Features of Desired Programs

One major feature of these visions of comprehensive guidance programs is the focus on *student outcomes* (*competencies*); students' achievement of these outcomes is the responsibility of the program. Knowledge and skills to be learned by individuals as a result of the program are variously grouped as (a) personal, social, career, and educational; (b) knowledge of self and others, career planning and exploration, and educational and vocational development; or (c) learning, personal/social, and career/vocational. These categories serve to identify domain or content areas of human growth and development from which student competencies are drawn. Guidance activities and resources designed to assist students achieve these competencies are organized accordingly.

Other features of these visions include a definition of guidance, rationale statements to support the definition, and assumptions about human growth and development and about guidance that give shape and direction to the program.

In addition, most plans describe the ways in which guidance activities and resources are organized to reach agreed-upon student outcomes. They also include a curriculum component incorporating guidance goals, objectives, and activities into such disciplines as English, social studies, and science, or using minicourses, special classes, or special guidance learning packages. Also, most visions of desired programs provide for placement, follow-up, and follow-through activities to assist students in their next step educationally and occupationally. In addition, direct delivery of counseling and other guidance activities on a demand basis is a part of most of these visions of desired guidance programs. This element is included because there may be a need for direct immediate services to students while they are in school.

Expect Resistance to Change

A new conceptualization of guidance such as the comprehensive program is not always accepted enthusiastically by those involved, as Mitchell and Gysbers (1978) pointed out. Comprehensive guidance program proponents suggest that the guidance staff should be performing different tasks from those they are currently doing, whereas some of the staff may feel they have already made commitments and their present investment of time and resources can be justified. Their feelings are often expressed in such statements as:

- Comprehensive guidance is a passing fad!
- Look at what success we have had and are continuing to have with our present program!
- We should wait until it really is better developed!
- We are busy 100% of the time now!
- We could do it if our counselor-student ratio were lower!
- It cannot be added on to what is already being done!

Behind these statements may lie fears of those faced with change. This human condition of some members of the guidance staff must be understood. The failure of some staff members to embrace a programmatic approach can be appreciated if their original justification for existence and their current functions and operational patterns are understood. Many counselors maintain they are trapped and can react only minimally to change; they are victims of school rigidity and bureaucracy that place them in quasi-administrative and services functions that impede them from achieving guidance objectives (Aubrey, 1973).

Appreciate the Challenges Involved

The failure of some members of guidance staffs to readily embrace a programmatic, comprehensive approach to guidance also can be better understood if the challenges that such an approach presents are known. Here are some of these challenges:

- Guidance programs are based on student competencies;
- Guidance programs are accountable for these competencies;
- Guidance programs are developmental;

- Guidance programs are responsive to changing student-school-community needs;
- Counselors need to develop new competencies;
- Counselors need to consider differential staffing;
- Counselors need to be involved in the community; and
- Counselors need to be involved in the curriculum.

Why do some members of guidance staffs consider these factors challenges? They are challenges because they require counselors to change their work behavior. They also may require some counselors to acquire new skills to fulfill the responsibilities of new program emphases. In addition, some counselors fear the potential loss of status and power they enjoy from being associated with the authority of the principal. Involvement within the community and new relationships with teachers and students may make some counselors uncomfortable. New demands and the need for new competencies threaten others. The most difficult challenge most counselors face, however, may be the prospect of accepting responsibility for helping students achieve specific competencies. Can counselors, working in a comprehensive program, deliver what they propose?

Another challenge counselors face in considering change is balancing the "costs" involved (the personal and professional time involved, the changes in day-by-day work behavior) with the benefits to be gained. Will the benefits outweigh the costs involved in working through the transition? One school district faced this challenge and found that the hard work involved paid off in the following ways:

> As a result of the remodeling activities, the school counselors have generated substantial support for their program from their board of education, administrators, teachers, and the public. Over the past 3 years, three elementary counselors were added to the school district's guidance staff. There were none before. High school career centers and many guidance resources were added to the program. In addition, the counselors established their own counselor-student ratios that were accepted by the board of education. These new ratios are lower than those recommended by the State of Missouri and North Central Association.
>
> In addition to these changes, more clerical staff were added to support the guidance staff. The middle school counselors were removed from lunch duty and thus were freed from an activity that consumed over 1 hour of their time each day. The counselors developed learning activity packets (structured group activites) to be used by all counselors. The guidance department also is developing a guidance curriculum K–12 to be coordinated by counselors. They have also completed an every-other-month inservice program with the area mental health agency. The most remarkable thing about these changes is that they occurred during a time of retrenchment in budgets and programs, as well as during a decline in the student population. (Hargens & Gysbers, 1984, pp. 120–121)

Develop Trust

Because of the tendency of people to resist change and because of the challenges and risks involved in making the transition to a comprehensive guidance program, guidance staff require time and privacy as they deal with the issues involved. Time and privacy are necessary to work through possible resistance to change that may not emerge otherwise and to develop trust and working relationships as a total staff. This is true particularly for school districts with guidance personnel at elementary, junior high or middle school, and high school levels. Current duties at these levels often do not emphasize full staff discussions about program directions and focus as much as does the comprehensive programmatic approach. Thus, provision for open dialogue, confrontation, and the processing of attitudes and feelings during the planning process is highly desirable.

Staff trust can be developed and nurtured through the full involvement of staff in the change process. In the section "Decide That You Want to Change" of this chapter, an example was given about how the guidance staff of one school district met several times as a full staff to assess the need for change. One result of these discussions was the decision to change; "to take charge of their own destiny" (Hargens & Gysbers, 1984, p. 121). Another result, and just as important, was the full involvement of the staff in the change process.

Having staff involved in the initial decision to make changes and then in the steps involved in the transition process can help bring about staff trust and commitment; we are all in this together. It also is important that staff members realize their advice and counsel will be put to legitimate use. Going through the frustrations and joys of making the transition to a comprehensive program can bond the individuals who are involved into a full-fledged guidance team.

Form Committees and Work Groups

Once consensus to change has been reached, the next step is to form committees and work groups to accomplish the tasks involved. Only two committees are recommended throughout the entire process: a steering committee and a school-community advisory committee. The majority of improvement tasks can be handled by forming work groups.

Steering Committee

The steering committee is responsible for managing the efforts needed to plan and implement an improved program. This committee is a decision-making body and is responsible for outlining the tasks involved and in making certain that the resources needed to carry out these tasks are available. It monitors the activities of the work groups and coordinates their tasks. The steering committee not only makes process-change decisions but also program-change decisions.

To carry out these responsibilities, one of the first tasks for the steering committee is to prepare a timetable of the steps it has chosen to take. Because it is the master timetable for program change, it requires careful thought and attention. Allow sufficient planning time for this phase of getting organized. Also, keep in mind that the timetable will probably be modified as the program improvement process unfolds.

There are a number of reasons for developing a master timetable. First, it provides those involved with an overview of the scope and sequence of the improvement process. It also shows the relationship of the steps and activities. In addition, potential problems can be identified and therefore anticipated and dealt with in advance. Finally, it provides those involved with an indication of the resources and materials required. Figure 2–1 presents an example of a timetable for the improvement process from Northside Independent School District, San Antonio, Texas.

The steering committee should be large enough to reflect a cross section of the ideas and interest of the staff but not so large as to be unwieldy and inefficient. Ordinarily, the steering committee is composed of guidance personnel or representatives from each grade level or building involved. Building administrators and the superintendent or a member of the cabinet are essential members, as are such individuals as the directors of vocational education and special education. Sometimes teachers, parents, school board members, or students also may serve. The chairperson of the steering committee is the guidance program leader. If no such title exists, then the person who is administratively responsible for the guidance program should be chairperson.

In addition to considering the steps, resources, and strategies needed to make the transition to a comprehensive program, the steering committee is responsible for developing a plan for public relations. This may be done later in the program improvement process, but whenever it is done, careful planning is required. Effective public relations don't just happen, nor can they be separated from the basic comprehensive program. In fact, the best public relations begin with a sound, comprehensive program. The best public relations in the world cannot cover up an ineffective guidance program that does not meet the needs of its consumers.

School-Community Advisory Committee

The school-community advisory committee is composed of representatives from the school and community. The membership on this committee will vary according to the size of the school district and the community, but could include such individuals as an administrator (assistant superintendent, principal); the guidance program leader; the director of vocational education; a representative of the teaching staff; a representative of the student body; representatives from business, industry, and labor; a representative from the mental health community;

Figure 2–1
Sample Timetable

Guidance Program Development Plan
1982–1986

'82–'83: *Planning Phase*
    Needs Assessment
    Goals/Outcomes Clarification
    Program Definition
    Current Program Design
    Building Support

    Results: Policy Established: Rationale, Assumptions, Program
    Definition

'83–'84: *Designing Phase*
    Establish Program Model
    Specify Client and Client Goal Priorities
    Specify Program Delivery Priorities
    Establish Model District Design ("Basic Structure")
    Define Guidance Staff Roles/Responsibilities
    Compare Current Local Designs with District Model
    Design Realistic Local Model Programs
    Local: Plan Specific Changes to be Made in '84–'85
    District: Identify Staff Development Needs and Plan for Meeting
    Them

    Results: District Design, Local Designs, Job Descriptions, Local
    Plans of Action for Changing, Districtwide Staff Development
    Plan

'84–'85: *Implementing Phase*
    Identify Needed Resources
    Local: Implement Changes
    District: Plan Overall Program Evaluation
        Implement Staff Development Program
        Plan Staff Evaluation Process

    Results: Changing Programs, Program and Staff Evaluation Plans,
    Developing Staff, Resource Development Plan

'85–'86: *Evaluation/Redesign Phase*
    Evaluate Program/Redesign Program as Necessary
    Continue Changes
    Continue Staff Development
    Implement Staff Evaluation Process
    Plan Future Actions

a representative from the Parent Teachers' Association; and a newspaper editor or other media representative. If any of these individuals are serving on the steering committee (with the exception of the guidance program leader), they probably should not serve here.

The school-community advisory committee acts as a liaison between the school and community and provides recommendations concerning the needs of students and the community. A primary duty of the committee is to advise those involved in the guidance program improvement effort. The committee is not a policy or decision-making body; rather it is a source of advice, counsel, and support. It is a communication link between those involved in the guidance program improvement effort and the school and community. The committee meets throughout the transition period and continues as a permanent part of the improved guidance program. A community person should be chairperson.

The use and involvement of an advisory committee will vary according to the program and the community. It is important, however, that membership be more than in name only, not one that is named at the beginning and then forgotten. Members will be particularly helpful in developing and implementing the public relations plan for the community.

Community involvement and interaction are important; there is no doubt about that. However, it is more difficult to accomplish than it may seem. This conclusion was reached in a study of the impact of the plan of the Rural American Series to develop and implement career guidance programs.

> The third major conclusion is that involving the community and developing good inter-institutional cooperation is more difficult than it would seem on the surface. In many instances in this field test, limited community involvement and institutional cooperation occurred. Some sites were better at developing linkages between groups and individuals due to the coordinator's skill and possibly due to the existence of prior such linkages. Distance was certainly a factor in inter-institutional roles in regard to the planning of career guidance programs. In many cases, increased positive cooperation which was desirable just did not take place. (Altschuld, Kimmel, Axelrod, Stein, & Drier, 1978, p. 22)

This statement was not included to discourage the use of advisory and community involvement committees. Rather it was included to point out that the process is more complex than many people imagine. Careful planning and continuous effort are required by all involved. It is difficult to do, but the time and effort spent will be well worth it.

Work Groups

To accomplish some of the work involved in making the transition to a comprehensive program, we recommend the use of work groups. Work groups are small groups of staff members, usually counselors, but sometimes others including administrators, teachers, parents, and students who are assigned specific tasks that need to be completed as part of the transition process. Assignments to work groups will vary depending upon the tasks involved. Work groups form and disband as needed.

Here are some suggestions concerning work groups.

1. Use as many work groups as possible because it reduces the overall work-load and provides opportunities for as many people as possible to become involved and learn about remodeling and revitalizing the guidance program.
2. Some work groups should include counselors only; some should include administrators or others. Specific suggestions are provided in subsequent chapters.
3. Work groups are responsible to the steering committee. Work group leadership is drawn from the steering committee. In fact, in the first phases of the improvement process, the steering committees' agendas will consist of work group reports.
4. Charges to work groups need to be specific and feasible. Each group exists for one purpose; when that purpose is accomplished, the work group disbands.
5. Work group membership should include cross-grade level representation when appropriate. This enhances trust and builds knowledge among the members that will provide a foundation for the comprehensive guidance program.

Guidance Program Leader's Roles and Responsibilities

The school district's guidance program leader will have the primary responsibility for organizing and managing the program improvement process. Some suggestions for program leaders regarding the organizational phase follow.

Without your taking the primary leadership role for these efforts, they will not get done. You must cause, lead, implement, and maintain the work accomplished during this important time in your school system. We see you as the manager of the improvement project as well as the program, and as the leader and supervisor of the staff.

As the manager of the improvement process, you must develop and monitor the plan for change. Specifically, you must develop the proposal to change and the timeframe you anticipate that it will take. You must form the steering committee, chair it, and plan its agendas and meeting schedule. You also form, or cause to form, the advisory committee and the various work groups. You need to attend as many meetings of the work groups as feasible to keep them on task, and you must attend all steering and advisory committee meetings. They are, after all, steering and advising the program for which you are accountable.

As the guidance program leader you not only continue your usual duties, but you also add the responsibilities of being the primary missionary for the improved program. You must be very clear about the model you and your district want to adopt or adapt. The success of this project is directly linked to your conceptualization of the model program. For a while you will be the only person who may grasp the new design, student competencies, the comprehensive nature of the program, and the means for redirecting the activities of the staff.

As the leader and supervisor of the staff, you develop the mechanisms for educating and involving counselors and administrators. You provide staff leadership to the steering committee members; ultimately, they provide peer leadership to their colleagues, under your direction.

You need to keep the purposes for changing the program in front of everyone for the duration of the project. Remember you are doing all this to better help student growth and development by the more appropriate use of counselors' unique talents and skills. We advise you to develop a support system for yourself. This might include committed counselors in the district, your own supervisor(s) who are eager for the changes to come, and guidance program leaders from other districts who have embarked on similar projects. Involvement in the state and national Associations for Counselor Education and Supervision (ACES) provides useful assistance and affiliation as well.

Conducting Meetings

From the above discussion of leaders' roles and responsibilities, it is obvious that meetings of various kinds will occupy a considerable amount of your time. Because of this, let's review types of meetings and some procedures and practices for conducting them. As the improvement process unfolds, you will probably be involved in three types of meetings: namely, specific task meetings, open agenda meetings, and information sharing meetings.

The primary purpose of each meeting you conduct should be clearly stated. In addition, leadership (sometimes a role rather than a person) should be defined, and the methods of achieving the purpose of the meeting should be presented at the beginning of the meeting. Assuming the above have been taken care of, here are some ideas that can make meetings effective and can allow the personal and professional dignity of everyone involved to be preserved and enhanced.

- *Set a Time Limit*—contract when possible—get agreement, start and finish on time.
  (Time and energy are two of the only real possessions we have).
- *What Kind of Meeting Is This?*—purpose, leader, methods . . .
- *No Voting*—if possible, try to work toward concensus, especially in small groups that will continue to work together.

- *Have Mutually Agreed Upon "Facilitation Tools"*—stop action—"we're stuck", "we're off task"; process tools—during and especially at the end; *use* the open agenda—as a tool.
- *Have Some Agreed-Upon Form of Conflict Resolution*
  When we conflict, how will we handle it?
  Helps establish meetings as a "safe place" for humans where risks can be taken.
- *Check on Physical Environment*—heat, cold, seating arrangement, noise level, lighting.
- *Brainstorming*—use it whenever possible—and go by the rules.
- *Rotate Leadership*—if practical and efficient.
- *Jobs*—good meetings end with people taking on tasks, even if it's only the awareness of what to be thinking about before the next meeting.
- *"Tough Love"*—agree to practice personal, caring, gentle confrontation *when needed.*
- *Encourage a "Positive Attention" Environment*—both verbal and nonverbal.
- *Have a "No Discount" Agreement*—watch for put-downs, especially of self, no suicide statements (this isn't important but---) watch what you laugh at.
- *No Arm Wrestling*—subtle plays for leadership, asking permission when not necessary.
- *Personal Ownership*—(I statement)—who is "we" or "they" or "You-all"?
- *Concerning Silence*
  Silence, at times, can be ok—the birthing of new ideas or awareness.
  When decisions are being made—silence is consent (especially for groups that operate together regularly).
- *Watch Out For "Shotgun Statements"*—"People are not handing in reports", "Teachers in this school are really punishing students."
- *Plops*—don't let people's ideas or comments be ignored.
- *Play*—don't disrupt—timing is the key.
- *Gestalt*—periodically check out group and self, trust "gut level" (intuition), make sure you check yourself (I'm tired, angry with spouse, have another meeting in 4 minutes).
- *Closure*—what's next for me and the group? Whom do I need to talk to later?

Concluding Thoughts

Early on in this chapter it was pointed out that the task of making the transition from an undefined program to a defined program is complex and difficult. It requires time and perseverance. Although the time required may seem long, it does provide the opportunity for counselors (and everyone else) to learn how to master it. Thus, the getting organized phase of improving and revitalizing guidance programs should be designed to assist those involved to develop a vision of what the comprehensive program will look like and to become committed to working to make it happen. Our premise is that staff development enables people to have vision and involvement and raises their level of commitment. Staff development begins during the getting organized phase and must be carried out throughout the program improvement and revitalization process.

References

Altschuld, J. W., Kimmel, K. S., Axelrod, V., Stein, W. M., & Drier, H. N. (1978). *From idea to action: Career guidance plans of rural and small schools.* Columbus, OH: National Center for Research in Vocational Education.

Aubrey, R. F. (1973). Organizational victimization of school counselors. *School Counselor, 20,* 346–354.

Ballast, D. L., & Shoemaker, R. L. (1978). *Guidance program development.* Springfield, IL: Charles C Thomas.

Campbell, R. E. (1980). *The career planning support system.* Columbus, OH: National Center for Research in Vocational Education.

California State Department of Education. School Climate and Student Support Services Unit. (1987). *Program quality review for guidance and counseling: Procedures manual.* Sacramento, CA: State Department of Education.

Commission on Precollege Guidance and Counseling. (1986). *Keeping the options open: Recommendations.* New York: College Entrance Examination Board.

Drier, H. N. (1979). *Cooperative rural guidance system.* Columbus, OH: National Center for Research in Vocational Education.

Engel, E., Castille R., & Neely, J. (1978, March). *Why have a traumatic time creating an accountable developmental guidance program when somebody else already had that particular nervous breakdown?* Paper presented at the convention of the American Personnnel and Guidance Association, Washington, DC.

Ewens, W. P., Dobson, J. S., & Seals, J. M. (1977). *Career guidance—A systems approach.* Dubuque, IA: Kendall/Hunt.

Hargens, M., & Gysbers, N. C. (1984). How to remodel a guidance program while living in it: A case study. *School Counselor, 32,* 119–125.

Jones, G. G., Dayton, C. A., & Gelatt, H. B. (1977). *New methods for delivering human services.* New York: Human Sciences Press.

Mitchell, A. M., & Gysbers, N. C. (1978). Comprehensive school guidance and counseling programs. In *The status of guidance and counseling in the nation's schools* (pp. 23–39). Washington, DC: American Personnel and Guidance Association.

Ryan, T. A. (1978). *Guidance services.* Danville, IL: Interstate Printers and Publishers.

Wilson, P. J. (1986). *School counseling programs: A resource and planning guide.* Madison, WI: Department of Public Instruction.

CHAPTER 3

A COMPREHENSIVE GUIDANCE PROGRAM: PERSPECTIVE, STRUCTURE, AND CONTENT

Once the getting organized phase of the transition to a comprehensive guidance program is under way, the next phase of the improvement process begins. This phase involves consideration of the foundation, structure, and content of a comprehensive program. Consideration needs to be given to a perspective of human growth and development on which to build the program as well as to how the program relates to other educational programs. Also considered must be the competencies the program will assist students to acquire and the structure and content of the program. What student competencies should the guidance program be responsible for? How should a comprehensive program be structured? What are its components? What is the content of these components?

To assist you in considering these issues, chapter 3 opens with a presentation of a perspective of human growth and development that can be used as a foundation for a comprehensive guidance program and for identifying the knowledge, skills, and attitudes (competencies) that students need to facilitate their development. This perspective is called _life career development_ (Gysbers & Moore, 1975, 1981). Next, the two major delivery systems in the schools for life career development—the instruction program and the guidance program—are identified. Then, chapter 3 focuses on the selection of student competencies and domains for the guidance program. Finally, specific and detailed attention is given to the structure and content of the guidance program.

The Life Career Development Perspective

Life career development is defined as self-development over the life span through the integration of the roles, settings, and events in a person's life. The word _life_ in the definition indicates that the focus of this conception of human growth and development is on the total person—the human career. The word *career* identifies and relates the many and often varied roles in which individuals are involved (student, worker, consumer, citizen, parent); the settings in which individuals find themselves (home, school, community); and the events that occur over their lifetimes (entry job, marriage, divorce, retirement). The word *development* is used to indicate that individuals are always in the process of becoming. When used in sequence, the words *life career development* bring these separate meanings together, but at the same time a greater meaning evolves. Life career development describes total individuals: unique individuals, with their own life styles (Gysbers & Moore, 1975, 1981).

In the definition of life career development, the word career has a substantially different meaning from that in some other definitions. Here it focuses on all aspects of life, not as separate entities but as interrelated parts of the whole person. The term career, when viewed from this broad perspective, is not a new word for occupation. People have careers; the work world or marketplace has occupations. Unfortunately, too many people use the word career when they should use the word occupation. Also, the term career is not restricted to some people. All people have a career; their life is their career. Finally, the words life career development do not delineate and describe only one part of human growth and development. Although it is useful to focus at times on different aspects of development—physical, emotional, and intellectual—there also is a need to integrate these aspects of development. Life career development is advocated as an organizing and integrating concept for understanding and facilitating human growth and development.

Wolfe and Kolb (1980) summed up the life view of career development as follows:

> Career development involves one's whole life, not just occupation. As such, it concerns the whole person, needs and wants, capacities and potentials, excitements and anxieties, insights and blindspots, warts and all. More than that, it concerns him/her in the ever-changing contexts of his/her life. The environmental pressures and constraints, the bonds that tie him/her to significant others, responsibilities to children and aging parents, the total structure of one's circumstances are also factors that must be understood and reckoned with. In these terms, career development and personal development converge. Self and circumstances—evolving, changing, unfolding in mutual interaction—constitute the focus and the drama of career development. (pp. 1–2)

One goal of a comprehensive school guidance program, founded on the concept of life career development, is to assist students to acquire competencies to handle current "here-and-now" issues that affect their growth and development. These issues may include changes in the family structure, expanded social relationships, substance abuse, sexual experimentation, changes in physical and emotional maturation, and peer pressure. In addition, another goal is to create career consciousness in students to assist them to project themselves into possible future life roles, settings, and events; analyze them; relate their findings to their present identity and situations; and make informed personal and career choices based on their findings.

Life Career Development Domains

Four domains of human growth and development are emphasized in life career development: Self-knowledge and Interpersonal Skills; Life Roles, Settings, and Events; Life Career Planning; and Basic Studies and Occupational Preparation (Gysbers & Moore, 1981).

Self-knowledge and Interpersonal Skills

In the Self-knowledge and Interpersonal Skills domain the focus is on helping students understand themselves and others. The main concepts of this domain involve students' awareness and acceptance of themselves, their awareness and acceptance of others, and their development of interpersonal skills. Within this domain, students begin to develop an awareness of their personal characteristics—interests, aspirations, and abilities. Students learn techniques for self-appraisal and the analysis of their personal characteristics in terms of a real-ideal self-continuum. They begin to formulate plans for self-improvement in such areas as physical and mental health. Individuals become knowledgeable about the interactive relationship of self and enviornment in such a way that they develop personal standards and a sense of purpose in life. Students learn how to create and maintain relationships and develop skills that allow for beneficial interaction within those relationships. They can use self-knowledge in life career planning. They have positive interpersonal relations and are self-directed in that they accept responsibility for their own behavior.

Life Roles, Settings, and Events

The emphasis in this domain is on the interrelatedness of various life roles (such as learner, citizen, consumer), settings (such as home, school, work, and community), and events (such as job entry, marriage, retirement) in which students participate over the life span. Emphasis is given to the knowledge and understanding of the sociological, psychological, and economic dimensions and structure of their world. As students explore the different aspects of their roles, they learn how stereotypes affect their own and others' lives. The implication of futuristic concerns is examined and related to their lives. Students learn of the potential impact of change in modern society and of the necessity of being able to project themselves into the future. In this way they begin to predict the future, foresee alternatives they may choose, and plan to meet the requirements of life career alternatives. As a result of learning about the multiple dimensions of their world, students understand the reciprocal influences of life roles, settings, and events and can consider various life-style patterns.

Life Career Planning

The Life Career Planning domain is designed to help students understand that decision making and planning are important tasks in everyday life and to recognize the need for life career planning. Students learn of the many occupations and industries in the work world and of their grouping according to occupational requirements and characteristics as well as personal skills, interests, values, and aspirations. Emphasis is placed on students' learning of various rights and responsibilities associated with their involvement in a life career.

The central focus of this domain is on the mastery of decision-making skills as a part of life career planning. Students develop skills in this area by identifying the elements of the decision-making process. They develop skills in gathering information from relevant sources, both external and internal, and learn to use the collected information in making informed and reasoned decisions. A major aspect of this process involves the appraisal of personal values as they may relate to prospective plans and decisions. Students engage in planning activities and begin to understand that they can influence their future by applying such skill. They begin to accept responsibility for making their own choices, for managing their own resources, and for directing the future course of their own lives.

Basic Studies and Occupational Preparation

The fourth domain, Basic Studies and Occupational Preparation, is the largest component in terms of amount of content and number of activities. This domain contains the knowledge, skills, and understandings found in such disciplines as English, social studies, mathematics, fine arts, industrial arts, home economics, physical and health education, foreign language, and vocational-technical education.

These areas of education are basic to students' total development, but because of new and emerging challenges to education, now need to be viewed in interdisciplinary ways. The roles, settings, and events of a student's life career and the interrelated worlds of education, work, and leisure can serve as a primary content focus for knowledge acquisition and skill development in basic studies and occupational preparation. Also, because the education, work, and leisure worlds are undergoing constant change, students need to update their knowledge and skill in basic studies and occupational preparation. Thus, a necessary emphasis within this domain involves the continuous acquisition and refinement of basic and occupational knowledge and skills throughout life.

Two Major Delivery Systems

Elementary and secondary education as envisioned from a life career development perspective include two major, interrelated delivery systems: the instruction program and the guidance program. Each delivery system emphasizes specific student competencies, but at the same time there are areas of collaboration. Competencies that students are to gain through the instruction program usually are grouped under such titles as fine arts, vocational-technical education, science, physical education, mathematics, social studies, foreign language, and English. Competencies that students are to gain through the guidance program can be derived from such domains as Self-knowledge and Interpersonal Skills; Life Roles, Settings, and Events; and Life Career Planning.

In a school setting, even though the instruction program is by far the largest in terms of numbers of student competencies, it is not more important than the guidance program. That is why the circles in Figure 3–1, which depict the delivery systems, are equal in size. Figure 3–1 also illustrates the fact that

Figure 3–1

Two Major Education Delivery Systems From a Life Career Development Perspective

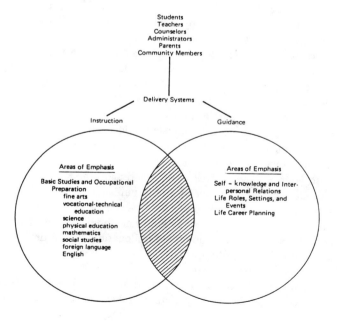

separate learnings in each system (nonshaded area) require specific attention. At the same time these learnings overlap (shaded area), requiring that the basic studies and occupational preparation program support the guidance program at times, and at other times that the guidance program support the basic studies and occupational preparation program. It is not a case of either/or but both/and.

Richardson and Baron (1975) outlined a similar schema but labeled their systems as two major purposes of education: social learnings and personal learnings. They pointed out that teachers were primarily responsible for the instructional function—that of "guiding and learning of developmental tasks in the area of 'social learnings' " (p.21)—whereas counselors were primarily responsible for the counseling function—that of "guiding the learning of developmental tasks in the area of 'personal learnings' " (p.21). They also pointed out that the counseling program contains developmental and crisis emphases, whereas the instructional program focuses on developmental and remedial elements.

Selecting Student Competencies and Domains for the Guidance Program

One task in developing a guidance program is the selection of student competencies. What knowledge will students gain, what skills will students develop, and what attitudes will students form as a result of participating in the guidance program? Another task is selecting the domains that will group the competencies into meaningful categories.

To complete these tasks, begin by reviewing the educational goals of your school district and your state. The chances are good that goals from these two sources will focus in part on such guidance-related goals as educational achievement and career development. At the same time examine the professional literature and relevant professional association position statements. From these two sources will come ideas about possible competencies and domains others have identified. Also, review previous needs assessment and achievement data of students in your school. Such a review will add actual data about students to more general statements derived from broad goal statements and the professional literature about competencies to be acquired.

Based upon your review of these sources and data, the task is to establish the domains and select the competencies for your guidance program. What are some broad headings (domains) that capture the essence of the goals and data from the above sources? Consider using no less than three or more than six broad headings or domains. Then think about the student outcomes (competencies) that fit under each domain or heading.

Because this is a somewhat abstract, complex process, three examples of domains and competencies follow. The first example uses life career development as a base and shows sample goals by domain and sample competencies by grade level. The second example presents the domains and competencies used by the state of Missouri (Vocational Special Needs/Guidance Services, 1988). The third example presents the domains and competencies used by Northside Independent School District, San Antonio, Texas (1985).

Example 1: Life Career Development Model

The Life Career Development Model uses three domains as follows:

- Self-knowledge and Interpersonal Skills
- Life Roles, Settings, and Events
- Life Career Planning

Grouped under each domain are five broad goals as follows:

Self-knowledge and Interpersonal Skills

Students will develop and incorporate an understanding of unique personal characteristics and abilities of themselves and others.

Students will develop and incorporate personal skills that will lead to satisfactory physical and mental health.

Students will develop and incorporate an ability to assume responsibility for themselves and to manage their environment.

Students will develop and incorporate the ability to maintain effective relationships with peers and adults.

Students will develop and incorporate listening and expression skills that allow for involvement with others in problem-solving and helping relationships.

Life Roles, Settings, and Events

Students will develop and incorporate those skills that lead to an effective role as a learner.

Students will develop and incorporate an understanding of the legal and economic principles and practices that lead to responsible daily living.

Students will develop and incorporate understanding of the interactive effects of life styles, life roles, settings, and events.

Students will develop and incorporate an understanding of stereotypes and how sterotypes affect career identity.

Students will develop and incorporate an ability to express futuristic concerns and the ability to imagine themselves in these situations.

Life Career Planning

Students will develop and incorporate an understanding of producer rights and responsibilities.

Students will develop and incorporate an understanding of how attitudes and values affect decisions, actions, and life styles.

Students will develop and incorporate an understanding of the decision-making process and how the decisions they make are influenced by previous decisions made by themselves and others.

Students will develop and incorporate the ability to generate decision-making alternatives, gather necessary information, and assess the risks and consequences of alternatives.

Students will develop and incorporate skill in clarifying values, expanding interests and capabilities, and evaluating progress toward goals.

Then, for each of the goals, competencies are listed by grade level K–12. For example, under the first goal of the Self-knowledge and Interpersonal Skills domain, the following sample competencies are listed.

Domain Self-knowledge and Interpersonal Skills
Goal   Students will develop and incorporate an understanding of the unique personal characteristics and abilities of themselves and others.

K. I can tell what I look like and some things I like to do.
1. I can tell something special about myself.
2. I can tell something special about other people I know.
3. I can describe myself to someone who doesn't know me.
4. I can tell how people are different and that they have different skills and abilities.
5. I can tell how my special characteristics and abilities are important to me.
6. I can tell how my characteristics and abilities change and how they can be expanded.
7. I can compare the characteristics and abilities of others I know with my own and accept the differences.
8. I can list the skills I already possess and those I hope to develop in the future.

9. I can discuss the value of understanding my unique characteristics and abilities.
10. I can describe and analyze how an individual's characteristics and abilities develop.
11. I can explain which characteristics and abilities I appreciate most in myself and others.
12. I can compare my characteristics and abilities with those of others and appreciate and encourage my uniqueness.

Example 2: State of Missouri

The state of Missouri uses three domains as follows:

- Career Planning and Exploration
- Knowledge of Self and Others
- Educational/Vocational Development

Grouped below under each domain are a number of subdomains, or categories. (Vocational Special Needs/Guidance Services, 1988).

Career Planning and Exploration

Planning and developing career
Understanding how being male or female relates to job and careers
Making decisions about college
Planning high school classes
Learning how to use leisure time now and in the future

Knowledge of Self and Others

Understanding and accepting self
Understanding and getting along with others
Knowing how drugs and alcohol affect me and my friends
Learning about marriage and family responsibilities

Educational/Vocational Development

Making decisions
Finding jobs
Improving basic skills and study/learning skills
Learning from friends and others who have graduated
Vocational selection and training

Example 3: Northside Independent School District

Northside Independent School District (1985) uses six broad domains under which subgroupings and specific competencies are listed.

  I. Students will understand and respect themselves and others.
    A. Self-knowledge
      1. Become aware of themselves physically and emotionally

      2. Understand that they are unique, with different characteristics and abilities
      3. Respect themselves and their individuality
   B. Interpersonal Skills
      1. Be aware of the unique personal characteristics and abilities of others
      2. Understand the importance of the uniqueness of others
      3. Develop and maintain skills to relate effectively with others

II. Students will behave responsibly in the school, the family, and the community.
   A. School
      1. Be aware of need to behave responsibly
      2. Develop an attitude that maximizes educational achievement
      3. Understand the need to behave responsibly
      4. Assume responsibility for themselves and manage their environment.
   B. Family
      1. Awareness of the family entity
      2. Understanding of the family entity
      3. Respecting the family entity
   C. Community
      1. Awareness of their responsibility to the community
      2. Understanding and respect of their role in the community
      3. Exhibiting responsible behaviors within the community

III. Students will develop decision-making skills
   A. Making wise choices
      1. Awareness of how decisions are made
      2. Exploration of use of the process
      3. Implementation of the decision-making process
   B. Manage change successfully
      1. Be aware of inevitability of change
      2. Understand effects of change
         a. individual
         b. group
      3. Manage change
         a. individual
         b. group
   C. Solve problems
      1. Know how to identify problem
      2. Understand steps involved in solving problems
      3. Solve problems

IV. Students will use their educational opportunities well
   A. Classroom
      1. Awareness of educational opportunities
      2. Exploring of opportunities
      3. Utilizing of opportunities
   B. School setting
      1. Awareness of alternatives/opportunities

    2. Exploring alternatives/opportunities
    3. Selecting appropriate alternatives/opportunities
  C. Future educational opportunities
    1. Awareness of alternatives/opportunities
    2. Exploring of alternatives/opportunities
    3. Utilizing of appropriate alternatives/opportunities

V. Students will communicate effectively
  A. Awareness of need to communicate
  B. Understanding necessary skills for communicating
  C. Application of effective communication skills

VI. Students will plan and prepare for personally satisfying and socially useful lives
  A. Personal
    1. Awareness of necessity for personal goal setting
    2. Using past and present experiences to set goals
    3. Setting appropriate goals
  B. Social
    1. Awareness of responsibility for socially useful lives
    2. Exploring opportunities available for socially useful lives
    3. Choosing appropriate activities

To put these domains and competencies into operation, Northside identifies "strands." Based on the above, 15 strands are identified as follows: Students

1. Understand and respect themselves;
2. Understand and respect others;
3. Behave responsibly in school;
4. Behave responsibly in the family;
5. Behave responsibly in the community;
6. Make wise choices;
7. Manage change successfully;
8. Solve problems;
9. Use their educational opportunities in classroom well;
10. Use their educational opportunities in school well;
11. Use their educational opportunities in community well;
12. Plan to use their future educational opportunities well;
13. Communicate effectively;
14. Plan and prepare for personally satisfying lives; and
15. Plan and prepare for socially useful lives.

A Program Structure

Selecting a comprehensive guidance program structure is another major task in the improvement process. The structure serves as an ideal against which you can compare your current program; it serves as a template to lay over the top of the current program so that similarities and differences can be seen. Having made this comparison, you can then *adopt* those components of the structure that fit your situation, *adapt* other components of the structure as needed, or *create* new components in response to unique local needs.

The structure we recommend for a comprehensive guidance program contains seven components organized around two major categories (Gysbers & Moore, 1981, p. 62).

Structural Components
 1. Definition
 2. Rationale
 3. Assumptions

Program Components
 4. Guidance Curriculum
 5. Individual Planning
 6. Responsive Services
 7. System Support

The first three components identify broad areas of competencies students will possess as a result of the program and where the program fits in relation to other educational programs (definition), offer reasons why the program is important and needed (rationale), and provide the premises upon which the program rests (assumptions). We have labeled these components structural components. The next four components delineate the major activities, and the roles and responsibilities of personnel involved in the guidance program. These are labeled program components and include the guidance curriculum, individual planning, responsive services, and system support.

Structural Components

Definition

A definition of the guidance program identifies the centrality of guidance within the educational process and delineates, in broad outcome terms, the competencies students will possess as a result of their involvement in the program. Two examples of a definition of guidance follow. The first is the definition of guidance used by the state of Missouri and the second is from Northside Independent School District, San Antonio, Texas.

State of Missouri

Guidance is an integral part of each school's total educational program. It is developmental by design and includes sequential activities organized and implemented by certified school counselors with the support of teachers, administrators, students, and parents. The guidance program includes

 1. guidance curricululm;
 2. individual planning;

3. responsive services; and
4. system support.

The program is designed to address the needs of all students by helping them to acquire competencies in career planning and exploration, knowledge of self and others, and educational and vocational development. (Vocational Special Needs/ Guidance Services, 1988, p.5)

Northside Independent School District

The guidance program in Northside Independent School District is a comprehensive program based on individual, school, and community needs and is organized around skill development goals. The program is delivered through the direct service program components of guidance curriculum, individual planning, system support, and responsive services. Additionally the guidance program provides indirect services supporting the total educational program.

The guidance program is a developmental educational program responsible for assisting students develop and maintain the skills needed to

- understand and respect themselves and others;
- behave responsibly in the school, the family, and the community;
- make wise choices, manage change successfully, and solve problems;
- use their educational opportunities well;
- communicate effectively; and
- plan and prepare for personally satisfying and socially useful lives.

Northside's guidance program is designed to assist systematically all students in our schools. The developmental perspective recognizes that every student must have sound emotional and social skills in order to achieve optimum benefit from the educational program. The guidance program also provides mechanisms for assisting individuals resolve problems which prevent their healthy development or which require remedial attention. (Northside Independent School District, 1985, p. 3)

Rationale

A rationale discusses the importance of the guidance program as an equal partner with other programs in education. It focuses on reasons why students need to acquire guidance competencies and have access to the assistance that a comprehensive guidance program provides. It should be based on the goals of your school, community, and state. Some examples of the points you may wish to consider in writing the rationale for your comprehensive guidance program are as follows:

Student Development

1. Students today face depersonalization in many facets of their lives as bureaucracies and impersonal relations are commonplace. They often feel pow-

erless in the face of masses of people, mass communication, and mass everything else, and need help in dealing with these feelings, not at the expense of society but in the context of society. Their feelings of control over their environment and their own destiny, and their relations with others and institutions are of primary importance in guidance programs. Students must be viewed as totalities, as individuals. Their development can be best facilitated by guidance programs that begin in kindergarten and continue to be available through grade 12.

Self-Knowledge

2. Formerly, students were brought up in a fairly stable society in which their roles were defined and relationships with others were fairly constant. Now they face an increasingly mobile society, in which relationships with both people and things are becoming less and less enduring. Society is characterized by transience and impermanence. Traditional beliefs and ways of doing things no longer seem sufficient for coping with the environmental demands. As a result, many students have problems defining their roles; thus, the quests for answers to: Who am I? and Where do I fit in? Guidance programs can help individuals respond to such questions through the development of self-appraisal and self-improvement competencies. Through these learnings, students can become more aware of personal characteristics such as aptitudes, interests, goals, abilities, values, and physical traits and the influence these characteristics may have on the persons they are and can become. Being able to use self-knowledge in life career planning and interpersonal relationships and to assume responsibility for one's own behavior are examples of needed competencies that students can acquire through participation in a comprehensive guidance program.

Decision Making

3. Students need help in decision-making because planning for and making decisions are vital tasks in the lives of all individuals. Everyday decisions are made that influence one's life career. Mastery of decision-making skills and the application of these skills to life career planning are central learnings in a guidance program. A preliminary task to effective decision making is the clarification of personal values. The degree of congruence between what individuals value and the outcomes of decisions individuals make contributes to personal satisfaction. Included in decision making are the skills for gathering and using relevant information. Understanding the influence of planning on one's future and the responsibility one must take for planning are components of the life career planning process. Life career planning is ongoing. Change and time affect one's planning and decisions. A decision outcome that is satisfactory and appropriate for the present may, with time or change, become unsatisfactory or inappropriate. Thus, the ability to evaluate decisions in view of new information or circum-

stances is vital. Being able to clarify personal values, identify steps needed to make personal decisions, gather relevant information, and apply decision-making skills to life career plans are examples of desired and needed outcomes for a guidance program.

Changing Environments

4. Increasing societal complexity affects not only interpersonal relationships and feelings of individuality but also other life roles, settings, and events, specifically including those associated with the worlds of education, work, and leisure. Changes resulting from advances in technology are perhaps more apparent as they affect the world of work. No longer are students well acquainted with the occupations of family and community members or their contributive roles to the common good of society. Parents' occupations are removed from the home and often from the immediate neighborhood. In addition, because students over their lifetimes will be assuming a number of roles, functioning in a variety of settings, and experiencing many events, learnings in this area emphasize their understanding of the various roles, settings, and events that interrelate to form their life careers. The roles of family member, citizen, worker, and leisure participant; settings such as home, school, community, and work; and events such as birthdays, educational milestones, job entry, and job change are identified and examined in terms of their influence on life styles. Guidance programs can help students develop an understanding of the structure of the family and education, work, and leisure requirements and characteristics. The effect of change—natural as well as unexpected, social as well as technological, in self as well as in others—is a needed major learning for students that a comprehensive guidance program can provide.

Placement Assistance

5. As students are and will be moving from one setting to another, they need specific knowledge and skills in order to make such moves as effectively as possible. They need help in placement. Although placement is defined broadly, specific attention should be given to intra- and intereducational and occupational transitions and to the personal competencies needed to make such transitions. Personal competencies needed include knowledge of the spectrum of educational courses and programs, an understanding of the relationships they may have to personal and societal needs and goals, and skills in using a wide variety of information and resources. They also include an understanding of the pathways and linkages between those courses and programs and potential personal goals. Stress is placed on the need for employability skill development including resume writing, job searching, and job interviewing.

Relevant Education

6. Some of the dissatisfaction of youth with education stems from the feeling that what they are doing in school is not relevant to their lives. A comprehensive guidance program is needed to seek to create relevance in the schools and to show individuals how the knowledge, understandings, and skills they are obtaining and the courses they are taking will help them as they progress through their life careers.

Assumptions

Assumptions identify and briefly describe the premises upon which a guidance program rests. Assumptions give the program its shape and direction, its nature and structure. Examples of assumptions are as follows:

1. *The guidance program helps develop and protect students' individuality.* The guidance program and personnel provide assistance to all students to ensure that they become aware of their needs, interests, and abilities; develop and pursue immediate and long-range personal goals; and respect the individuality of others.
2. *The guidance program helps students function effectively within groups.* The guidance program and personnel help all students learn to participate productively with others in the school, home, and community.
3. *The guidance program serves all students at all education levels.* The guidance program is designed to address the needs of all students at all levels—children, youth, and adults.
4. *The guidance program assists students in their personal, social, career, and educational development.* A comprehensive guidance program is not limited to only one or two of the significant areas of student development but recognizes the school's responsibility to nurture the whole child. Program goals and activities address all four major developmental areas.
5. *The guidance program provides consultation and coordination services to the teachers, parents, administration, and community representatives who work with students.* Counselors, by virtue of their training and their role, serve as resource persons and liaison between students and those individuals and agencies who play a significant role in their lives.
6. *The guidance program provides developmental as well as preventive and remedial services.* The guidance program and personnel have a developmental focus which maximizes the prevention of problems, a preventive focus which provides for early intervention for the onset of problems, and a remedial emphasis to assist with the solutions of problems that have arisen.
7. *The guidance program is both an integral part of and an independent component of the total education program.* The guidance program is a necessary part of the total school program. Many outcomes of the guidance program are supportive of the goals of the total program; guidance services and activities facilitate the efforts of other school personnel in those areas in which others have primary responsibility. The guidance program also has identifiable outcomes of its own,

for which guidance personnel have primary responsibility, but in which all personnel share.

8. *The guidance program is continuously refined through systematic planning, designing, implementing, and evaluating.* In order to ensure that the guidance program is responsive to the individual students' and the community's needs, careful program development, monitoring, evaluation, and redirection must occur on an ongoing basis. The program design includes three direct service components: curriculum, individual planning system, and responsive service. (Northside Independent School District, 1985, p. 2)

Program Components

An examination of the needs of students, the variety of guidance methods, techniques, and resources available, and the increased expectations of policy-makers, funders, and consumers indicates that a new structure for guidance programs in the schools is needed. The traditional formulations of guidance— the six services (orientation, information, assessment, counseling, placement, and follow-up)—and the three aspects of guidance (educational, personal-social, and vocational), though perhaps once sufficient, are no longer adequate ways to organize guidance programs in today's schools.

When described as services, guidance is often cast as ancillary and is seen as only supportive to instruction, not as equal and complementary. The three-aspects view of guidance frequently has resulted in fragmented and event-oriented activities and, in some instances, in the development of separate kinds of programs and counselors. Educational guidance is stressed by academic-college personnel, personal-social guidance becomes the territory of mental health workers, and vocational guidance becomes the focus of vocational education and manpower-labor economists.

If the proposition that these traditional structures are no longer adequate is acceptable, then the question is: What is an appropriate one? One way to answer this question is to ask what should be expected of a comprehensive guidance program.

1. Are there knowledges, skills, and attitudes needed by all individuals that should be the instructional responsibility of guidance programs?
2. Do individuals have the right to have someone in the school system sensitive to their unique life career development needs, including needs for placement and follow-through?
3. Should guidance staff be available and responsive to special or unexpected needs of students, staff, parents, and the community?
4. Does the school program and staff require support that can be best supplied by guidance personnel?

An affirmative response to these four questions implies a structure that is different from the traditional services or aspects model. In addition, a review of the variety of guidance methods, techniques, and resources available today and an understanding of expectations of policymakers and consumers of guidance also suggest a model different from the traditional services or aspects model. The structure suggested by an affirmative answer to the four questions and by a review of the literature is a program model of guidance techniques, methods, and resources containing four interactive components: *guidance curriculum, individual planning, responsive services*, and *system support* (Gysbers & Moore, 1981).

The curriculum component was chosen because a curriculum provides a vehicle to impart to all students guidance content in a systematic way. The next component, individual planning, was included as a part of the model because of the increasing need for all students to continuously and systematically plan, monitor, and understand their growth and development; to consider and take action on their next steps personally, educationally, and occupationally. The responsive services component was included because of the need in comprehensive guidance programs to respond to the direct, immediate concerns of students whether these concerns involve crisis counseling, referral, or consultation with parents, teachers, or other specialists. Finally, the system support component was included because it was recognized that, for the other guidance processes to be effective, a variety of support activities such as staff development, testing and research, and curriculum development are required. System support also was included because of the need for the guidance program to provide *appropriate* support to other programs in the school.

These components, then, serve as organizers for the many guidance methods, techniques, and resources required in a comprehensive guidance program. In addition, however, they also can serve as a check on the comprehensiveness of the program. In our opinion a program is not comprehensive unless it has activities in each of the components.

Guidance Curriculum

One of the assumptions upon which our conception of guidance is based is that there is guidance content that all students should learn in a systematic, sequential way. This means counselor involvement in the curriculum; it means a guidance curriculum. This is not a new idea; the notion of a guidance curriculum has deep, historical roots. What is new, however, is the array of guidance and counseling techniques, methods, and resources currently available that work best as a part of a curriculum. What is new, too, is the concept that a comprehensive guidance program has an organized and sequential curriculum. (ASCA, 1984; Commission on Precollege Guidance and Counseling, 1986; ERIC/CAPS, 1983).

Description. The guidance curriculum typically consists of student competencies (organized by domains) and structured activities presented systematically through such strategies as:

- *Classroom Activities*—Counselors teach, team teach, or support the teaching of guidance curriculum learning activities or units in classrooms. Teachers also may teach such units. The guidance curriculum is not limited to being taught in one or two subjects but should include as many subjects as possible in the total school curriculum. These activities may be conducted in the classroom, guidance center, or other school facilities.
- *Group Activities*—Counselors organize and conduct large group sessions such as career days and educational/college/vocational days. Other members of guidance, including teachers and administrators, also may be involved in organizing and conducting such sessions.

Although the counselor's responsibilities include organizing and implementing the guidance curriculum, the cooperation and support of the entire faculty and staff are necessary for its successful implementation.

Domain and Competency Sequencing and Layout. As you select the domains you will use in the guidance curriculum and identify the competencies to be included in each domain, keep in mind the following assumptions about human growth and development:

1. Individual development is a process of continuous and sequential, but not necessarily uninterrupted or uniform, progress toward increased effectiveness in the management and mastery of the environment for the satisfaction of psychological and social needs.
2. The stage, or level, of individuals' development at any given point is related to the nature and accuracy of their perceptions, the level of complexity of their conceptualizations, and the subsequent development rate and direction. No individual in an educational setting is at a zero point in development; hence change must be measured from some relative point rather than from an absolute.
3. Positive developmental changes are potential steps toward the achievement of higher-level purposive goals. This interlocking relationship dictates that achievement at a particular growth stage be viewed as a means to further development rather than as an end result.
4. Environmental or situational variables provide the external dimension of individual development. Knowledge, understanding, skills, attitudes, values, and aspirations are the product of the interaction of these external variables with the internal variables that characterize the individual.
5. The developmental learning process moves from a beginning level of awareness and differentiation (*perceptualization*), to the next level of conceptualizing relationships and meanings (*conceptualization*), to the highest level of behavioral consistency and effectiveness by both internal and external evaluation (*generalization*). (Wellman & Moore, 1975, pp. 55–56)

A major task in the development of the guidance curriculum is to organize and lay out student competencies so that they follow a theoretically sound scope and sequence. Note the concepts perceptualization, conceptualization, and generalization discussed in assumption 5. These concepts can serve as guidelines for this very important task. What follows is a detailed discussion of these concepts and how they function in making decisions about the scope and sequence of student competencies K–12 (Wellman & Moore, 1975).

Perceptualization Level

a. Student competencies concerned with environmental orientation
b. Student competencies concerned with self-orientation

Competencies at this level emphasize the acquisition of knowledge and skills, and focus attention on selected aspects of the environment and self. The knowlege and skills most relevant are those individuals need in making appropriate life role decisions and in responding to the demands of the school and social environment. Attention is the first step toward the development and maturation of interests, attitudes, and values. Competencies at the perceptualization level reflect accuracy of perceptions, ability to differentiate, and elemental skills in performing functions appropriate to the individual's level of development. Competencies at this level are classified under two major categories, *environmental orientation* and *self-orientation*.

Competencies classified under environmental orientation emphasize the individual's awareness and acquisition of knowledge and skills needed to make life role decisions and to master the demands of life career settings and events. The competencies at this level are essentially cognitive in nature and have not necessarily been internalized to the extent that the individual attaches personal meaning to the acquired knowledge and skills. For example, individuals may acquire appropriate study skills and knowledge, but it does not necessarily follow that they will use these skills and knowledge in their study behavior. However, such knowledge and skills are considered to be prerequisites to behavior requiring them. Thus, the acquisition of knowledge and skills required to make growth-oriented decisions and to cope with environmental expectations is viewed as the first step in individuals' development, regardless of whether subsequent implementation emerges. A primary and universally applicable goal of guidance is the development of knowledge and skills to enable individuals to understand and meet the expectations of their school and social environment and to recognize the values underlying social limits.

Competencies classified under self-orientation focus on the development of accurate self-perceptions. One aspect of an accurate awareness of self is the knowledge of one's abilities, aptitudes, interests, and values. An integral part of identity is individuals' ability to understand and accept the ways that they are alike and different from other individuals. Attention to life career decisions and demands relevant to immediate adjustment and future development are considered a prerequisite to an understanding of the relationships between self and environment. An awareness, and perhaps an understanding, of feelings and motivations is closely associated with self-evaluation of behavior, with the formation of attitudes and values, and with voluntary, rationally based modification of behavior. The goal of guidance at this level is to help individuals make accurate assessments of self so that they can relate realistically to their environment in their decisions and actions. The goal of guidance is individuals' development of self-awareness and differentiation that will enable appropriate decision making and mastery of behavior in the roles, settings, and events of their lives.

Conceptualization Level

a. Student competencies concerned with directional tendencies
b. Student competencies concerned with adaptive and adjustive behaviors

Individual competencies at the conceptualization level emphasize action based on the relationships between perceptions of self and perceptions of environment. The types of action sought are categorized into personally meaningful growth decisions and adaptive and adjustive behavior. The general goal at this level of development is that individuals will (a) make appropriate choices, decisions, and plans that will move them toward personally satisfying and socially acceptable development; (b) take action necessary to progress within developmental plans; and (c) develop behavior to master their school and social environment as judged by peers, teachers, and parents. The two major classifications of conceptualization objectives are *directional tendencies* and *adaptive and adjustive behavior*.

The directional tendencies relate to individuals' movement toward socially desirable goals consistent with their potential for development. These competencies are indicators of directional tendencies as reflected in the choices, decisions, and plans that individuals are expected to make in ordering the course of their educational, occupational, and social growth. The acquisition of knowledge and skills covered by competencies at the perceptual level is a prerequisite to the pursuit of competencies in this category, although the need to make choices and decisions may provide the initial stimulus for considering perceptual competencies. For example, a ninth grader may be required to make curricular choices that have a bearing upon post-high school education and occupational aspirations. The need to make an immediate choice at this point may stimulate an examination of both environmental perceptions and self-perceptions as well as a careful analysis of the relationships between the two. To this extent, then, the interrelationship and interdependence of perceptual and conceptual competencies preclude the establishment of mutually exclusive categories. Furthermore, the concept of a developmental sequence suggests this type of interrelationship. Any choice that may determine the direction of future development is considered to represent a directional tendency on the part of individuals, and competencies related to such choices are so classified.

The expected emergence of increasingly stable interests and the strengthening and clarification of value patterns constitute additional indicators of directional tendencies. Persistent attention to particular persons, activities, or objects in the environment to the exclusion of others (selective attention) is an indication of the development of interests through an evaluation of the relationships of self to differentiated aspects of the environment. Objectives that relate to value conceptualization, or the internalization of social values, complement interest development. Here individuals are expected to show increased consistency in giving priority to particular behavior that is valued personally and socially. In a sense, the maturation of interests represents the development of educational and occupational individuality, whereas the formation of value patterns represents the recognition of social values and the normative tolerances of behavior.

Competencies in these subcategories include consistency in the expression of interests and values and the manifestation of behavior compatible with the emerging interests and value patterns. For example, high school students may be expected to manifest increasing and persistent interest (measured or expressed) in particular persons, activities, and objects. They may be expected to develop a concept of self that is consistent with these interests and to place increasing importance, or value, on behaviors, such as educational achievement, that will lead to the development of related knowledge and skills and to the ultimate achievement of occupational aspirations. The directional tendency emphasis is upon achieving increased consistency and strength of interests and values over a period of time. The incidental or occasional expression of an immediate interest or value with little or no long-range impact upon the behavior of individuals should not be interpreted as an indication of a directional tendency.

The second major category of objectives at the conceptualization level includes objectives related to the application of self–environment concepts in coping with environmental presses and in the solution of problems arising from the interaction of individuals and their environment. Competencies in this area of functioning are designated as adaptive and adjustive behavior.

Adaptive behavior refers to individuals' ability and skill to manage their school and social environment (with normative tolerances) to satisfy self-needs, to meet environmental demands, and to solve problems. There are two types. First, individuals may, within certain prescribed limits, control their environmental transactions by selection. For example, if they lack the appropriate social skills, they may avoid social transactions that demand dancing and choose those where existing abilities will gain the acceptance of the social group. Second, individuals may be able to modify their environment to meet their needs and certain external demands. For example, students who find sharing a room with a younger brother or sister disruptive to studying may be able to modify this situation by arranging to study elsewhere.

Adjustive behavior refers to the ability and flexibility of individuals to modify their behavior to meet environmental demands and to solve problems. Such behavior modification may include the development of new abilities or skills, a change of attitudes, or a change in method of operation or approach to the demand situation. In the examples of adaptive behavior just mentioned, individuals might use adjustive behavior by learning to dance rather than avoiding dancing, and they might develop new study skills so they are able to study while sharing a room.

The basic competencies in this area involve an individual's ability to demonstrate adaptive and adjustive behavior in dealing with school and social demands and in solving problems that restrict the ability to meet such demands. The competencies may be achieved by applying existing abilities or by learning new ways of meeting demands.

Generalization level

    a. Student competencies concerned with accommodation
    b. Student competencies concerned with satisfaction
    c. Student competencies concerned with mastery

Competencies at the generalization level imply a high level of functioning that enables individuals to (a) accommodate environmental and cultural demands; (b) achieve personal satisfaction from environmental transactions; and (c) demonstrate competence through mastery of specific tasks and through the generalization of learned behavior, attitudes, and values to new situations. Behavior that characterizes the achievement of generalization-level competencies may be described as purposeful and effective by one's own or intrinsic standards and by societal or extrinsic criteria. Individuals should be able to demonstrate behavioral consistency, commitment to purpose, and autonomy in meeting educational, occupational, and social demands. Persons exhibiting such behavior therefore are relatively independent and predictable.

Guidance competencies at this level are classified as *accommodation, satisfaction*, and *mastery*. The concept of sequential and positive progress implies a continuous process of internalization, including applicational transfer of behavior and a dynamic, rather than a static, condition in the achievement of goals. The achievement of generalization competencies may be interpreted as positive movement (at each level of development) toward the ideal model of an effective person (self and socially derived) without assuming that individuals will ever fully achieve the ideal.

Accommodation competencies relate to the consistent and enduring ability to solve problems and to cope with environmental demands with minimum conflict. Accommodation of cultural and environmental demands requires that individuals make decisons and take action within established behavioral tolerances. The applicational transfer of adaptive and adjustive behavior, learned in other situations and under other circumstances, to new demand situations is inferred by the nature of the competencies classified in this category. The achievement of accommodation competencies can probably best be evaluated by the absence of, or the reduction of, unsatisfactory coping behavior. The wide range of acceptable behavior in many situations suggests that individuals who perform within that range have achieved the accommodation competencies for a particular demand situation, whereas if they are outside that range, they have not achieved these competencies. For example, a student is expected to attend class, to turn in class assignments, and to respect the property rights of others. If there is no record of excessive absences, failure to meet teacher assignment schedules, or violation of property rights, it may be assumed that the student is accommodating these demands with normative tolerances. In a sense, the objectives in this category represent the goal that individual behavior conform to certain limits of societal expectancy, whereas the other categories of generalization competencies tend to be more self-oriented. The achievement of accommodation competencies may infer congruence of individual values with the values of one's culture. Caution should be exercised in drawing such inferences, however, because the individual may demonstrate relative harmony externally but have serious value conflicts that do not emerge in observable behavior.

Satisfaction competencies reflect the internal interpretation that individuals give to their environmental transactions. Individual interests and values serve as criteria for evaluating the decisions made and the actions taken within the guidance domains. Although the evaluations of parents, peers, and authority figures may influence individuals' interpretations (satisfactions), these competencies become genuine only as they are achieved in congruence with the motivations and feelings of individuals. The description of satisfaction competencies consistent with guidance programming should include individuals' evaluation of affiliations, transactions, and adjustments in terms of personal adequacy, expectations, and congruency with a perceived ideal life style. Expressed satisfaction, as well as behavioral manifestations from which satisfaction may be inferred, such as persistence, would seem to be appropriate criterion measures. Also, congruency between measured interests and voluntarily chosen career activities should be considered.

Mastery competencies include the more global aspects of achievement and generalization of attitudinal and behavioral modes. Long-range goals, encompassing large areas of achievement, are emphasized here rather than the numerous short-range achievements that may be required to reach a larger goal. For example, a young child becomes aware of task demands and different ways to meet them (perceptualization). At the conceptualization level, task-oriented behaviors are developed and made meaningful. Generalization (mastery) competencies reflect the internalization of these behaviors so that tasks are approached and achieved to the satisfaction of self and social expectations. In the social area, competencies relate to social responsibility, and individuals' contributions with respect to social affiliations and interactions appropriate to their developmental level. All of the competencies in this category are framed in the context of self and social estimates of potential for achievement. Therefore, criteria for the estimation of achievement of mastery competencies should be in terms of congruency between independent behavioral action and expectations for action as derived from self and social sources. For example, a mastery competency in the educational area might be achieved by high school graduation by one individual, whereas graduate work at the university level might be the expected achievement level for another individual.

Individual Planning

Concern for student development in a complex society has been a cornerstone of the guidance movement since the days of Frank Parsons. In recent years the concern for student development has intensified as society has become even more complex. This concern is manifested in many ways, but perhaps it is expressed most succinctly in a frequently used goal for guidance: helping students become the persons they are capable of becoming.

Casting guidance and counseling in a personal development, personal advocacy role is not new. Lortie (1965) suggested that one grouping of tasks counselors might accept as part of their role would be that of advocate. Building on this same theme, Cook (1971) urged that school counseling and guidance claim the role of student advocate, with the end result being the enhancement of students' development. Similarly, Howard Miller, president of the Los Angeles Board of Education, supported the need for guidance and counseling programs to attend to the individual development of students. Writing in the *Los Angeles Times*, Sunday, July 17, 1977, about needed next steps for the Los Angeles schools, he described the kind of school programs that were needed. Among the critically important programs he described were "extensive counseling resources insuring personal direction and monitoring for each student" (Miller, 1977).

To accomplish the purposes of this component of the model, activities and procedures are needed to assist students to periodically monitor and understand their growth and development in terms of their goals, values, abilities, aptitudes, and interests (competencies) so that they can take action on their next steps educationally and occupationally. This means that counselors and others with guidance responsibilities serve in the capacity of personal-development-and-placement specialists. Personalized contact and involvement with individuals are required.

Description.   Individual planning consists of activities that help students to plan, monitor, and manage their own learning and their personal and career development. The focus is on assisting students to develop, analyze, and evaluate their educational, occupational, and personal goals and plans.

Individual planning is implemented through such strategies as:

- *Individual Appraisal*—Counselors assist students to assess and interpret their abilities, interests, skills, and achievement. The utilization of all test information and data becomes an important aspect of developing immediate and long-range plans for students.
- *Individual Advisement*—Counselors assist students to use self-appraisal information along with personal-social, educational, career, and labor market information to help them plan for and realize their personal, educational, and occupational goals. The involvement of students, parents, and school in planning a 4-year program of studies that meets the individual needs of students is a critical part of individual advisement.
- *Placement*—Counselors and other education personnel assist students to make the transition from school to work or to additional education and training.

The Individual Advisory System.*   One way we recommend that school staff be organized to respond to the individual planning needs of students is to use the Individual Advisory System (IAS). This system is based on the belief that satisfaction on the part of the faculty, students, and parents will result more easily if every student in school is able to relate personally, in a comfortable way, with at least one adult. In order for this one-to-one relationship to exist it is necessary to involve faculty members in a program that includes all students and their parents. Each teacher, counselor, administrator, and specialist acts as an advisor to a group of 15 to 20 students. Thus, within these groups students relate to one another as human beings sharing more than subject-matter concepts. The faculty members relate to one another as advisors sharing ideas about successfully dealing with their advisees. Parents relate to an individual in school who knows more about their child than grades earned in a particular class.

Program planning, parent contact, and personal development are the three main areas of the advisor's role. But advisors have other responsibilities to their

*This section on the Individual Advisory System, which encompasses material up to the heading "Responsive Services," was written by Suzanne Fitzgerald Dunlap and Edna Erickson Bernhardt when they were research associates, University of Missouri-Columbia. It was based on material developed as a result of an ESEA, Title II Project, Ferguson-Florissant School District, 1975. Reproduced by permission of the authors and the Ferguson-Florissant School District.

advisees and to their school. The following list contains eight categories of advisor responsibility with the definition of each. Obviously, advisors will not cover every area with every advisee completely. Also inservice workshops are needed to assist advisors in developing skills in each of the eight areas.

> *Program Planning*: Any activity dealing with the act of choosing school courses, such as course selection, evaluation of course schedule, or tentative long-range educational planning.
>
> *Self-assessment*: The analysis advisees make of their behavior, performance, or actions in an effort to strive for continuous self-improvement and understanding. All goal setting activities are included in this category.
>
> *School Awareness:* Any activity that contributes to an awarenss of the school and its programs, philosophies, and actions.
>
> *Parent Relations/Conferences*: Those special activities designed to increase parent participation in the schooling process of their children and to ensure frequent positive contact among the advisor, student, and parent.
>
> *Feedback/Evaluation*: Information that a school needs to hear, formally or informally, so that it can change itself to better suit the needs and desires of the people it serves. This cateogry does *not* mean feedback to the student. It means feedback a student gives *to the school*.
>
> *Decision-making Skills*: The conscious application of a process to make decisions. Although decision making is woven into activities in many categories, it also is a distinct category to aid advisors in teaching the process.
>
> *Career Planning/Preparation*: Activities to help students select and prepare for careers.
>
> *School/Community Issues*: Activities concerned with the human aspects of individuals working together. Included are human development activities and group building. This area also includes any discussions needed about current schoolwide issues that might arise during a school year, such as vandalism, a special decision the school needs to make, or any shared concern. (Hawkins & Cowles, 1975, pp. 7–9)

Being an advisor makes it possible to give all assigned students personal care and attention. An advisor has 15 to 20 advisees for all of their high school years, if this is mutually satisfactory. A student chooses an advisor in one of several ways. The choice may be based on curriculum or out-of-school interests of the advisor. A student may choose an advisor he or she already knows. A group of students may choose the same advisor so they can be together.

Advisors are given folders for the records of their advisees. This allows for easy access to student files during advisor-advisee meetings. In some schools folders are kept in an advisement center, where advisor-advisee meetings may also be held. Meetings are held at a regularly scheduled time. The scheduled advisement period usually takes priority over any other commitment students might have.

The Individual Advisory System acknowledges the need of students to have long-term, personal relationships with advisors. The IAS provides the time and structure necessary for this involvement to occur. It is accurate to say, then, that the work of school staff is supported and enhanced by the IAS.

The counselor's role in the high school has traditionally included at least a number, if not all, of the following functions:

1. Crisis-oriented counseling;
2. Administering and interpreting tests;
3. Educational or vocational guidance for seniors;
4. Scheduling and student registration; and
5. Student record upkeep.

The counselor's role in the high school that uses the IAS includes:

1. Providing advisors with backup support by dealing with crisis-oriented referrals;
2. Administering and interpreting tests along with the other advisors;
3. Helping advisors develop skills in providing students with educational or vocational information;
4. Scheduling and student registration of 15 to 20 advisees;
5. Student record upkeep of 15 to 20 advisees;
6. Developing out-of-school learning programs; and
7. Helping advisors develop skills in active listening, group dynamics, parent conferencing, and conflict resolution.

When we compare the two role descriptions, it becomes evident that the number of responsibilities does not vary greatly. What is strikingly different is the manner in which each method meets students' needs and uses the counselors' talents.

Traditionally, one counselor has been responsible for as many as four to five hundred students or more in a school. As a result, interaction between these students and the counselor has often been limited to brief encounters during registration times or other encounters during problematic times. Interaction between teacher and counselor has been limited, too, to faculty meetings, workshops, and brief consultations regarding problem students. The school program has simply not included the means for significant and consistent dialogue between counselors, faculty members, and students.

With the IAS at work in the high school, communication barriers between faculty members, and between faculty and students, are lessened. Personal caring becomes a priority in the school where there is equal involvement on the part of every faculty member and every student. Counselors become members of a team whose overall role includes meeting such student needs as receiving personal attention, learning self-assessment and goal setting, entering into meaningful dialogue with parents and teachers, getting to know an adult in the school, experiencing daily emotional growth, and developing decision-making skills.

At first glance it may seem to counselors that implementation of the IAS would serve only to minimize their function in a school. If suddenly every other faculty member is called upon to advise a small group of students (help them plan their school programs, facilitate their emotional growth, and maintain contact with their parents), how, then, do counselors' special talents come into play?

Counselors functioning in a program of advisement serve as prime resources for both advisors and students. Freed from an abundance of paperwork and now integrated into the mainstream of the high school, counselors are finally able to use their talents and training. Counselors will continue to fulfill many of the traditional roles, such as crisis counseling, but the IAS frees them to deliver a high level of professional services. Simply stated, an advisement program can enhance the work of counselors rather than jeopardize their position.

For some principals, student contact involves mainly disciplinary action with resulting negative feelings. The IAS does not guarantee principals freedom from that task, but personalized contact and program planning will increase student motivation and involvement in the school. This is not to say that principals will never have discipline problems, but IAS helps prevent such problems.

The IAS needs principals to function as advisors. This means that principals will also have the opportunity for full participation in helping relationships. In addition, principals can serve as models for other advisors. As model advisors, they need to sustain participation with enthusiasm. In fact, principals help provide long-term maintenance of the program.

As advisors, principals develop an increased sensitivity to the problems of advisement. Their full participation demonstrates the value and importance of advisement. Making changes is never easy. The rest of the staff need support as they learn the role of advisor and make necessary adjustments and improvements. Seeing principals share equally the responsibilities of advisor enhances the feeling of togetherness among the faculty. Everyone needs to feel trusted and cared for—counselors, teachers, administrators, and students. The environment should say to all within: You are trusted! Principals need to do all they can do to create this feeling, including placing confidence in IAS, the staff, the students, and themselves.

The skills needed to be an effective advisor are not so different from those required to be a good teacher, principal, or counselor. What is different is the one-to-one contact with a student outside of a curriculum-based situation. It is essential that advisors deal with their advisees in an honest and comfortable manner. In other words, advisors are most effective when they are themselves. Realizing this basic point will make the one-to-one contact easier to deal with. Once advisors reach this point, it is time to assess strengths and weaknesses and determine those areas where more skill development is needed.

Advisors must have skills useful in attending to the personal growth and well-being of advisees, helping each advisee outline a satisfactory learning program, and maintaining communication with the advisee's parents. Advisor skills include career planning and preparation, college information, conflict resolution, decision making, interpreting test scores, parent conferencing, program planning, record keeping, school awareness, and self-assessment. It is not realistic to expect every advisor to master each of the listed skills. Advisors need to share their knowledge and help one another develop the skills. As in the case of advisor responsibilities, it is helpful if advisors present inservice workshops for one another.

It is important to keep the basic purpose of an individual advisory system in focus when organizing the program. It is possible for an advisory-type system to be oriented toward school-system efficiency rather than personalized student learning. Although the system should be reasonably efficient, an overconcern for efficiency can distort its purpose. It is possible to have an IAS with no greater individualized student contact and involvement. A warmed-over homeroom approach, wherein students are seen only in a group and the goals are limited mainly to such administrative concerns as class scheduling, record keeping, and announcements will probably offer little personal development. Although class scheduling may be one responsibility of advisors and group meetings may be an appropriate method for discussion and efficient processing, the primary focus should always be on the facilitation of individual student development.

Benefits of an *Individual Advisory System* are as follows:

1. Better program planning;
2. Broader based decision making;
3. More personalized service for students;
4. More positive school climate; and
5. More positive staff relationships.

Responsive Services

Problems relating to academic learning, personal identity issues, drugs, and peer and family relationsips continue to be a part of the educational scene. As a result there is a continuing need for crisis counseling, diagnostic and remediation activities, and consultation and referral to be an ongoing part of a comprehensive guidance program. In addition, there is a continuing need for the guidance program to respond to the immediate information-seeking needs of students, parents, and teachers. The responsive services component organizes guidance techniques and methods to respond to these concerns and needs as they occur. In addition, the responsive services component is supportive of the guidance curriculum and individual planning components.

Description.   Responsive services consist of activities to meet the immediate needs and concerns of students whether these needs or concerns require counseling, consultation, referral, or information. Although counselors have special training and possess skills to respond to immediate needs and concerns, the cooperation and support of the entire faculty and staff are necessary for the component's successful implementation. Responsive services are implemented through such strategies as:

- *Consultation*—Counselors consult with students along with parents, teachers, other educators, and community agencies regarding strategies to help students deal with and resolve personal concerns.
- *Personal Counseling*—Counseling is provided on a small group and individual basis for students who have problems or difficulties dealing with relationships, personal concerns, or normal developmental tasks. It focuses on assisting students to identify problems and causes, alternatives, possible consequences, and to take action when appropriate.
- *Crisis Counseling*—Counseling and support are provided to students or their families facing emergency situations. Such counseling is normally short-term and temporary in nature. When necessary, appropriate referral sources may be used.
- *Referral*—Counselors use other professional resources of the school and community to refer students when appropriate. These referral sources may include:
  1. mental health agencies;
  2. employment and training programs;
  3. vocational rehabilitation;
  4. juvenile services;
  5. social services; and
  6. special school programs (special or compensatory education).

The responsive services component also provides for small group counseling. Small groups of students with similar concerns can be helped by intensive small group counseling. All students may not need such assistance, but it is available to all students.

Adjunct guidance staff—peers, paraprofessionals, volunteers—can aid counselors in carrying out responsive activities. Peers can be involved in tutorial programs, orientation activities, ombudsman functions, and—with special training—cross-age counseling and leadership in informal dialog. Paraprofessionals and volunteers can provide assistance in such areas as placement, follow-up, and community-school-home liaison activities.

System Support

The administration and management of a comprehensive guidance program require an ongoing support system. That is why system support is a major program component. Unfortunately, however, it is an aspect of a comprehensive program that is often overlooked or, if it is attended to, only minimally appreciated. And yet, the system support component is as important as the other three components. Why? Because without continuing support the other three components of the guidance program will be ineffective.

Activities included in this program category are by definition those that support and enhance activities in the other three program components. That is not to say that these activities do not stand alone. They can and often do. But for the most part, they undergird activities in the other three components.

Description.   The system support component consists of management activities that establish, maintain, and enhance the total guidance program. This component is implemented and carried out through activities in the following areas:

- *Research and Development*: Guidance program evaluation, follow-up studies, and the continued development and updating of guidance learning activities are some examples of the research and development work of counselors.
- *Staff/Community Public Relations*: This involves orienting staff and the community to the comprehensive guidance program through such means as the use of newsletters, local media, and school and community presentations.
- *Professional Development*: Counselors need to be involved regularly in updating their professional knowledge and skills. This may involve participation in regular school inservice training, attending professional meetings, completing postgraduate coursework, and contributing to the professional literature.
- *Committee/Advisory Boards*: Serving on departmental curriculum committees and community committees or advisory boards is an example of activities in this area.
- *Community Outreach*: Included in this area are activities designed to help counselors become knowledgeable about community resources, employment opportunities, and the local labor market. This may involve counselors' visiting local businesses and industries and social services agencies on a periodic basis.
- *Program Management and Operations*: This area includes the planning and management tasks needed to support the activities of a comprehensive guidance program. It also includes reponsibilities that members of the school staff may need to fulfill.

Also included in the system support component are those activities in the school that support programs other than guidance. These activities could include being involved in the school testing program (helping interpret test results for use by teachers, parents, and administrators), serving on departmental curriculum committees (helping interpret student needs data for curriculum revision), and working with school administrators (helping interpret student needs and behaviors). Care must be taken, however, to watch the time given to these duties because the prime focus for counselors is the carrying out of the comprehensive guidance program. It is important to realize that if the guidance program is well run, it provides substantial support for other programs and personnel in the school and the community.

Concluding Thoughts

One goal of chapter 3 has been to present a theoretically sound *perspective* for comprehensive guidance programs, K–12. A second goal has been to present a theoretically sound *structure* around which a comprehensive guidance program could be organized and managed. A third goal has been to describe the *content* of this structure and to provide examples of lists of student competencies and the domains that organize them. If this structure and the content involved are to come together as a complete, comprehensive guidance program K–12, some imperatives must be followed. We must do the following:

1. Understand that a comprehensive guidance program is *student development oriented*, not school maintenance-administrative oriented;
2. Operate a comprehensive guidance program as a *one hundred percent program*; the four program components constitute the total program there are no add-ons;
3. Start the comprehensive guidance program the *first day of school and end it the last day of school*, not begin in the middle of October and end in April, so that administrative, nonguidance tasks can be completed; and
4. Understand that a comprehensive guidance program is *program-focused, not position-focused*.

References

American School Counselor Association. (1984.) *The school counselor and developmental guidance: Position statement*. Alexandria, VA: Author.

Commission on Precollege Guidance and Counseling. (1986). *Keeping the options open: Final report*. New York: The College Board.

Cook, D. R. (Ed.). (1971). *Guidance for education in revolution*. Boston: Allyn & Bacon.

ERIC/CAPS Fact Sheet (1983). *Comprehensive guidance program design*. Ann Arbor: Counseling and Personnel Services Clearinghouse.

Gysbers, N. C., & Moore, E. J. (1975). Beyond career development—Life career development. *Personnel and Guidance Journal*, *53*, 647–652.

Gysbers, N. C., & Moore, E. J. (1981). *Improving guidance programs*. Englewood Cliffs, NJ: Prentice-Hall.

Hawkins, M. L., & Cowles, R. J. (1975). *Just a little care*. Florissant, MO: Ferguson-Florissant School District.

Lortie, D. C. (1965). Administrator, advocate or therapist? Alternatives for professionalization in school counseling. In R. L. Mosher, R. F. Carle, & C. C. Kehas (Eds.), *Guidance: An examination* (pp. 127–143). New York: Harcourt Brace Jovanovich.

Miller, H. (1977, July 17). Which way next for L.A. schools? *Los Angeles Times*, Part VIII, p. 5.

Northside Independent School District. (1985). *Comprehensive guidance program framework*. San Antonio, TX: Guidance Department.

Richardson, H. D., & Baron, M. (1975). *Development counseling in education*. Boston: Houghton Mifflin.

Vocational Special Needs/Guidance Services. (1988). *Missouri comprehensive guidance: A model for program development and implementation*. Jefferson City, MO: Department of Elementary and Secondary Education.

Wellman, F. E., & Moore, E. J. (1975). *Pupil personnel services: A handbook for program development and evaluation*. Washington, DC: U.S. Department of Health, Education, and Welfare.

Wolfe, D. M., & Kolb, D. A. (1980). Career development, personal growth, and experimental learning. In J. W. Springer (Ed.), *Issues in career and human resource development* (pp. 1–56). Madison, WI: American Society for Training and Development.

CHAPTER 4

ASSESSING YOUR CURRENT GUIDANCE PROGRAM

The next phase of the program improvement process involves assessing your current program. Current program assessment is a process for obtaining a concrete description of your school or school district's guidance program as it exists in the present. Quantitative and qualitative data are gathered, slicing the program from as many angles as is feasible. The current program assessment process is not a way of measuring students' needs, rather, it is a way of determining what the current guidance program is. Thus, the assessment is done using the components of the program model adopted by the district for implementation. The assessment process reveals what the current program is accomplishing and what its present form is. It provides the basis for identifying critical gaps in service delivery and for planning needed program changes.

Five steps involved in assessing your current program are discussed in this chapter:

Step 1: Identify current resource availability and use;
Step 2: Identify current guidance and counseling activities;
Step 3: Determine student outcomes;
Step 4: Identify who is served; and
Step 5: Gather perceptions.

As you will see, several steps can be carried out at the same time, depending on the personnel available and the program improvement plan established by the steering or school-community advisory committee as its organizational plan. Step 1 requires identifying the resources available and in use in the current guidance program. Resources include the counseling staff, their time, and their talent. Step 2 entails identifying and writing down by grade or school level—elementary, middle or junior high, or high school—all the guidance activities presently being conducted by the guidance, teaching, and administrative staff. In step 3 the intended outcomes for students are determined for each activity identified in step 2. What competencies do students acquire as a result of their involvement in an activity? In this step, a description of the students in your school or system is developed by gathering available information. Step 4 requires identifying the clients actually served by the current guidance program. This step is also an outgrowth of step 2. In step 5, perceptions of the program are gathered from students, teachers, administrators, counselors, parents, and community members.

Getting Ready

To accomplish the current program assessment, several work groups need to be formed. As mentioned, steps 2, 3, and 4 are interrelated, thus the groups gathering this information should either be the same or work closely together. Concurrently, other work groups can begin identifying current program resource use and collecting perceptions about the current program. One basic rule must apply to all work groups and to other data collection efforts: To make your data useful in future planning, it is important that you organize your current assessment according to the components of the program model your school or school district has adopted. If you have adopted the model using the guidance curriculum, individual planning, responsive services, and system support components described in chapter 3, you should organize your data collection and reporting according to these components. As you will see, the examples in this chapter use that model.

Because assessing your current program is a substantial undertaking, the guidance program leader has an important role to play. If you are the leader of the guidance program, you have the primary responsibility for data collection and for ensuring the full and appropriate summary, analysis, and dissemination of the results. We recommend, however, that all counselors in the building or district affected by the potential changes be involved in the current assessment. Accomplishing the assessment tasks helps the staff become familiar with the program model selected and feel comfortable that most of what they are currently doing fits into the components of the model—that the "new" program will not be completely different from the current program.

Involvement of administrators in work groups also is of value. Administrators so involved learn about the program model and are in a better position to support the changes called for in the future. Some administrators have been counselors in the past and have strong experience-based opinions on how the program can and should be changed. Of great value as well is the help that counselors provide to the students, staff, and climate of a building and, by their knowledge of the direction that the improved program is taking, they provide support for the implementation of changes in their schools or districts.

The work of some groups, however, is at times truly laborious. Staff who are not directly concerned with each minute detail may find it somewhat tedious, for example, to analyze the time study data for similarities and differences for each school or grade level. It is important to use administrators where they can make a solid contribution to the deliberations, and not let them get bogged down in data that are in fact the internal affairs of the guidance department.

If a steering committee is used, we recommend that steering committee members chair the various work groups. Then, steering committee meetings will provide the opportunity to monitor and coordinate the work of the various groups. In any case, some vehicle for coordinating the work groups' efforts will need to be established; a committee of committee chairs also would work.

In planning your current program assessment, current program description materials should be used. Many states have led schools and districts in the development of guidance program "handbooks" or "plans." Much useful information can and should be extracted from these existing documents to facilitate current assessment efforts. Usually, they provide a listing of current program activities. One caution, though: It has been our experience that often these "plans" have been just that—plans—and include activities that are not actually performed.

Finally, assessing the current program will take time, and you need to be realistic in establishing the timeframe. Some specific suggestions for accomplishing each of the steps are offered below that will help save you some time, but it still could take from 6 months to a year to complete an assessment. It is worthwhile to take the time needed to gather your data accurately because they are used to help the guidance staff understand the current design of their program and to educate others about the current status of the program. It also becomes the baseline from which your decisions for change are made and against which your changes will be evaluated.

Step 1: Identify Current Resource Availability and Use

The effectiveness of a program is measured in terms of the ratio of resources applied to the benefits accrued. Thus, gathering concrete information about the resources available and used in the guidance program is essential to any program decisions to be made. The more complete your knowledge of the resources currently available, the more room you have for creativity as you decide to redirect them for program improvements and the more specific you can be in your requests for additional resources. Having complete information about what is available is of benefit; in addition, most guidance program administrators will be encouraged by learning the actual quantity of resources available to them.

"Resources" is an ambiguous word, and further categorization is needed. For the purposes of our discussion, we have chosen human, financial, and political resources as useful categories. Human resources include staff members' time and talents. Financial resources are those applied through the budget to provide materials, equipment, and facilities for the guidance program. Political resources are represented by policy statements and supporters of the current program and staff. Because of the variety of resources used in a comprehensive guidance program, step 1 is a "giant step" that requires time and staff commitment to accomplish. Some ways that districts have assessed resource availability and use are described below.

Human Resources

Human resources that need to be assessed include counselors and guidance department paraprofessionals. Teachers and administrators often conduct guidance activities, so they may need to be included too. If your school or district uses community volunteers, such as business community representatives as career speakers or PTA volunteers as clerical support, you will need to list them as well. Assessing these human resources involves identifying their talents and the time they spend on the program.

Guidance Department Staff

The counseling staff is the basic resource of the guidance program. It is the counselors' *unique training and experiences* that allow us to seek accountability for helping students learn to make decisions, solve problems, and perform other tasks. Indeed, more often than not, when principals are asked to describe their guidance programs, they will say, "I have five counselors," or, "I have six counselors and a registrar."

There is, however, a widespread lack of information as to what counselors' unique talents are. As a result, in several projects we have been involved with, it has been useful to specify counselors' skills. There is a variety of ways to do this: to ensure that everyone concerned is aware of the certification requirements for school counselors; to publicize the training requirements for the master's degree in counseling; to publicize appropriately written job descriptions of school counselors; and to disseminate the American School Counselor Association (ASCA) role statement (1981).

A more extensive and potentially more useful way to make counselors' skills known is to ask them to identify their own modes of functioning within each of the components of the model program. Figure 4–1 displays an example of this from one district. The next step is to have counselors define their modes of functioning as they use them operationally in the schools. This approach also is useful in building a common terminology base among counselors of varied backgrounds and training. It has the additional benefit of helping counselors relate their skills to the model program design.

An essential piece of quantitative data is the current counselor-student *ratio*. During the discussions of the model program it is quite possible that everyone involved may be starry-eyed about the possibilities. The realities of case load

Figure 4–1
Counselor Functions by Program Component

1. *Guidance Curriculum*
   leading
   developing
   coordinating/facilitating
   evaluating

   planning
   consulting
   teaching/demonstrating
   communicating/describing

2. *Individual Planning*
   counseling/guiding
   developing/revising
   planning/evaluating the system
   conferencing
   communicating/coordinating/
   directing

   teaching (e.g.) decision skills
   referring
   informing/disseminating
   consulting

3. *Responsive Services*
   counseling
   referring/linking
   intervening
   informing/disseminating

   assessing/identifying/diagnosing
   monitoring/following up/following
   through
   case conferencing

4. *Support System*

   In order to carry out their responsibilities, counselors need the following
   support from the system:
   district guidance policy
   assessment programs
   appropriate financial allocations
   public relations program
   administrative leadership at district and campus levels
   coordinated articulation of activities
   time allocations
   testing programs
   district and community referral systems
   parent education and parent involvement programs
   community relations programs
   development of guidance curriculum
   guidance program development/review/evaluation/improvement

   In order to provide support for the total educational system, counselors will
   perform the following support functions:
   program development
   attendance
   supervision
   activities

   curriculum development
   discipline
   testing

must be ever-present; ultimately your program design will have to acknowledge what each counselor can be expected to do for 200, 500, or 1,000 students. Also, knowing whether the ratio is the same from school level to school level allows you to tailor your expectations accordingly. In some districts, the recognition of the disproportionately heavy loads at the elementary level when contrasted with the secondary level has led to immediate efforts to employ more elementary counselors.

In addition to ratios, typical patterns of *counselor-student assignment* need to be reviewed. Are counselors assigned to a grade level or to an alphabetical group? How are specialized counselors—vocational or special education—assigned their students? The rationale behind these assignments implies the philosophy of the guidance program; for example, case-load assignment by grade level may reflect a developmental philosophy, whereas assignment by alphabet may reflect an emphasis on responding to students with knowledge of their family context.

Clarification of counselors' unique talents provides qualitative data about the contribution they are able to make to students' growth and development. Assessing how counselors use their *time* provides quantitative data about the current guidance program. Because counselors are the basic program resource, the recording of their actual program-related behaviors is *the most critical data you will gather*. These data provide the most concrete information about the actual design of your current program, therefore it is essential that you gather this information.

In order for data to be meaningful and useful, you must plan your time usage study carefully. There are many decisions to be made and items to consider:

Why: What is the purpose of the time study? You need to write it out to ensure clarity. For example, "the purpose of the time study is to determine how the resource of counselor time is appropriated to the four components of the model program"; or, "the purpose of the time study is to determine how the resource of counselor time is appropriated to the functions identified as those used by counselors"; or, "the purpose of this study is to analyze the time that counselors spend doing various tasks." These three different purposes lead to different types of time studies: the first is a calendar study, and the second and third are log studies. You need to have a precise idea of why you are gathering the data. Also, you need to explain the purpose to the staff and to school administrators.

There may be concern that the data will be used for personnel evaluation rather than program description purposes. You need to decide if you are willing to provide for anonymity, or somehow you need to establish an appropriate trust level with the counselors.

Who: Whose time usage is to be assessed? Counselors' only? Paraprofessionals'? Other aides'? Teachers' or administrators' who may perform guidance functions? Besides being able to identify staff in broad categories, will it be important to sort the information collected by subsets of staff? It is usually useful to distinguish between the elementary, middle/junior high, and high school counselors, for example.

What: What do you really *need* to know? In the first of the three previous examples, the time allocated to each of the four program model components—guidance curriculum, individual planning, responsive services, and system support—was the information gathered. In the second example, specific information about each of the functions that counselors perform, such as individual counseling, small group counseling, and consultation is what was learned, both in terms of the overall time allocated and the relative balance of function use. In the third example, data relative to guidance program tasks were acquired. You may want a measure relative to student outcomes or one of the various clients served.

This is a golden opportunity to learn a great deal about what is actually happening in your program, but you need to resist the temptation to learn everything you always wanted to know but were afraid to ask. Because school counselors and other guidance staff are busy, consider carefully what you are asking them to record. Collect only data you know you will use. The simpler the time-recording system is, the more accurate your information will be.

When: Because this is a time usage study, there are several time questions you need to answer: When will you do the study: all year? a certain month? a scattering of days throughout the year? The study should cover enough time so that some activities that may occur only occasionally are not given undue attention. We recommend that you conduct the study all year. Begin by recording time on Monday of the first week; in the second week log your time on Tuesday; in the third week, Wednesday; and so on throughout the year.

DuBois (1975) recommended that the school year be divided into quarters and that 9 days be chosen randomly for each quarter. If information is needed quickly, then the best time for you should be chosen. Try for at least one week and remember to correct for the possible distortion that could occur in a short sample.

What increments of time will you be asking to have recorded: by minutes? by quarter hours? by half hours? by class periods? by the length of activities? When do you want the record keepers to log their time: as they go? at the end of the morning and afternoon? at the end of the day? Should they record time spent during the 8-hour work day? or count extra-hours work too? Your answers to these questions again depend on the way you plan to use the information and how precise you want the information to be.

In the first of our three examples begun above, the component data would be gathered for a full year by the blocks of time that the activities take. Counselors record the information on calendars. In the second example, the counselors record the number of minutes they spend doing each function as they do it during a 1-month period. In the third example, counselors record time they spend in activities in 15-minute segments. (See Appendix A for forms used to conduct this type of time study in the state of Missouri.)

Where: Is the staff to record time spent at school only? or should they and you acknowledge the work some of them do before and after school or in the evenings? Again, your answers depend on how you plan to use the information and if your plans for data aggregation allow you the variability that out-of-school data will bring. The counselors will ask you this question, so be prepared to answer it. We recommend that all time spent on the program be recorded, so that the time that is actually taken is reflected in the data.

How: The forms for data collection need to be as simple to use as possible, both for recording and for tallying. Ideally you will be able to use a computer for aggregating the data and generating the reports you need. Be sure to consider the dictates of the computer *before* developing your forms.

Directions for implementing the study must be precise and clear. Counselors need to be schooled in what the purpose of the study is and how to keep their records. The terminology used in the categories of the study needs to be thoroughly understood by everyone to ensure consistency of data. A system for fielding questions and for monitoring implementation of the study needs to be employed. If you are running this from a central office location, you must ensure that the campus guidance program leaders—the head or lead counselors—understand the study and its purposes and can monitor its implementation effectively.

As mentioned earlier, these data will be used again and again as your improvement efforts proceed. Once data are collected for the appropriate length of time, the next step is to aggregate them into a meaningful report. From data collected in our first example, Northside Independent School District learned that the current guidance program reflected a design similar to that displayed in Figure 4–2. From the data collected by the logging procedure, the picture displayed in Figure 4–3 was generated in Northside Independent School District. Both sets of data were totaled and figured into percentages, yielding a rather graphic picture of the shape of the current program in one case and the actual use the district was making of the counselors' unique skills in the other. The rank order of usage of functions was available as well. Finally, within the totals for individuals and for buildings, there were great ranges of time spent for the various functions. Each of these pieces of information was highly useful as the program improvement project unfolded.

Other Personnel

School staff members are important members of the guidance team, and as such their competencies and their contributions to the program need to be identified. In some schools, counselors share case loads with campus administrators. Paraprofessionals or secretaries fulfill essential roles; for example, career center technicians provide many guidance activities for students. Students also are important members of the guidance team. Working as peer counselors or aides in career centers, or making alumni presentations to younger students are just a few of the ways students may contribute. Such contributions need to be identified and listed in a similar way to staff participation. The same is true for business and community representatives and PTA volunteers.

Financial Resources

Budget

The place to begin the assessment of financial resources is the budget of the current guidance program. Even if there is no official budget—and this is often the case at the building level—funds are being spent for guidance activities, so begin there. Consider listing such items as salaries for counselors, secretaries, and aides; money spent for supplies such as paper, pencils, record folders; money spent for guidance program materials such as books, filmstrips, films and pamphlets, standardized tests, and scoring services. All expenses for guidance activities in the district should be included as well as any special funding from federal, state, or private foundations that is used. This information will give you a perspective about the share of the total educational budget that guidance has. In many cases, it is often much larger than the guidance staff thinks.

Materials

If you do not already have one, it is important to take an inventory of the materials you have available. You will want to categorize your inventory by the

Figure 4–2
1985–86 Calendar Data Aggregation
District Totals

Month	Curriculum	Individual Planning	Responsive Services	System Support
O C T	641.7 hrs. 11.3%	1477.3 hrs. 25.9%	1325.5 hrs. 23.2%	2257.3 hrs. 39.6%
N O V	672 hrs. 14.9%	1170.5 hrs. 26%	1278.5 hrs. 28.3%	1387.3 hrs. 30.8%
D E C	354.5 hrs. 10%	929 hrs. 26.1%	997.25 hrs. 28%	1276.75 hrs. 35.9%
J A N	256 hrs. 5.2%	1272.7 hrs. 26.6%	1115.25 hrs. 23.3%	2146 hrs. 44.9%
F E B	253 hrs. 5.6%	1266 hrs. 28%	910.5 hrs. 20.2%	2987 hrs. 46.2%
M A R	80.5 hrs. 2.3%	1683 hrs. 48.2%	606.75 hrs. 17.4%	1122.75 hrs. 32.1%
A M* P A R Y	582.5 hrs. 5.9%	2839 hrs. 28.8%	2675.25 hrs. 27.2%	3751.25 hrs. 38.1%
T O T A L S	2830.2 hrs. 7.8%	10637.5 hrs. 29.2%	8909 hrs. 24.5%	14028.35 hrs. 38.5%

*Two schools turned in April–May summaries.

Figure 4-3
Counselor Log Totals

	Elementary			Middle			High			District		
	Minutes	%	Rank	Minutes	%	Rank	Minutes	%	Rank	Minutes	%	Rank
Counseling—Indiv.	21,804	10.7	2	23,333	14.6	1	25,281	12.8	2	70,418	12.4	1
Counseling—Sm. Grp.	12,606	6.2	5	5,547	3.5	13	955	.4	21	19,108	3.4	13
Counseling—Parent	2,658	1.3	18	4,846	3.0	15	4,448	2.5	16	11,952	2.1	17
Guidance—Group	18,702	9.2	4	3,309	2.1	19	7,234	.6	12	29,245	5.1	9
Guidance—Indiv.	2,650	1.3	19	4,616	2.9	16	15,102	8.0	4	22,368	3.9	11
Conferencing—Staff	11,652	5.7	6	8,912	5.6	8	12,949	6.3	6	33,513	5.9	6
Conferencing—Parent	5,717	2.8	12	5,913	3.7	12	6,236	3.2	13	17,866	3.1	15
Conf. Staff/Parent	2,799	1.5	16	1,988	1.2	21	2,535	1.3	19	7,322	1.3	23
Consulting—Staff	5,321	2.6	13	8,311	5.2	9	7,926	3.9	11	21,558	3.8	12
Consulting—Parent	2,741	1.1	17	3,153	2.0	20	2,342	1.5	20	8,236	1.5	22
Cons. Other School Specialists	4,703	2.3	15	4,467	2.8	17	4,676	2.0	14	13,846	2.4	16
Coor. Other Agency	2,311	1.1	20	3,464	2.2	18	4,571	2.3	15	10,346	1.8	19
Testing—Indiv./Spec.	9,230	4.5	8	267	.2	23	320	.2	22	9,817	1.7	21
Testing—Dist. Prog.	38,919	19.1	1	835	.5	22	235	.1	23	39,989	7.0	3
Career Education	1,724	.8	21	6,518	4.1	11	2,794	1.4	18	11,036	1.9	18
Record Keeping	9,240	4.5	7	9,112	5.7	6	14,355	6.9	5	32,707	5.8	7
Guidance Activities	1,524	.7	22	5,259	3.4	14	3,055	1.7	17	9,838	1.7	20
Planning (Prog. & Case)	7,417	3.6	11	7,651	4.8	10	15,131	8.3	3	30,199	5.3	8
Enrollment & Registration	970	.5	23	9,203	5.8	4	8,787	4.2	9	18,960	3.3	14
Professional Resp.	8,821	4.3	9	8,918	5.6	7	34,280	19.4	1	52,019	9.2	2
Admin. Assignments	8,798	4.4	10	13,011	8.2	2	12,899	3.8	7	34,708	6.1	5
Misc. Paperwork	4,725	2.3	14	9,151	5.7	5	10,251	5.2	8	24,127	4.2	10
Special Education	19,166	9.4	3	11,371	7.1	3	8,163	3.9	10	38,700	6.8	4

Total Counselor Days 1322
Total Counselor Minutes 1,042,929

program model components and by student outcomes, as well as by grade level. The listing should include title, copyright date, a brief description of the content, and the use for which the resource was developed. Assuming that you will want to disseminate this list to the guidance staff, it also is helpful to include information about how to obtain the resource and about any restrictions on borrowing it.

Equipment

A study of your equipment inventory will reveal the quantity and kinds of equipment available as well as how it is distributed. How accessible is it to all staff? You may want to consider an equipment use study to determine if you are using the equipment to its maximum potential or to evaluate if your current distribution system is the best for you. Depending on the size of your program and the quantity of the equipment, you have a basic choice to consider: whether the equipment is best used if housed centrally and shared on a check-out basis, or permanently housed on each of the campuses.

Facilities

Baseline information as to the facilities available to the current guidance program is needed on a building-by-building basis. This, again, will show you the evenness of facility availability. As you begin to implement desired new program activities, it will provide realistic planning information about the space available currently. Any necessary remodeling takes time and planning. If additional space is needed, such as a classroom for developmental guidance or a guidance information or career center, that information must be ready for submission to the district as the superintendent makes the overall plans for the ensuing year.

Political Resources

Policy Statements

"Political" here means the support that is rooted in district or building policies, in state and federal laws, rules, or regulations, or in the standards adopted by accreditation or other professional associations to which your school or district subscribes. Knowing the philosophical tenets that undergird your program provides you the context within which to operate. The district may have an existing board policy about the guidance program. It surely has a statement about the educational mission of the district that has implications for the guidance program. In all likelihood there are procedural expectations for counselors expressed in administrative handbooks. You need to review these official pronouncements and extract and synthesize from them the basic political platform of the current guidance program.

If you have followed the suggestions we made in chapter 3, you have expressed a policy statement about the guidance program when adopting a program model; for example, if you are using the comprehensive program model described in chapter 3, the development of the three structural components—the definition, rationale, and assumptions—will provide you with the policy support that is most relevant to your efforts. Indeed, it is our opinion that unless you have these statements in hand, unless you know the model the district wants, your reorganization efforts may be ineffective.

Another useful survey is that of existing state and federal education laws, rules, and regulations that pertain to guidance. This is particularly true where the state holds close control over the educational system. Because guidance is still a relatively new part of the total educational program, there may not be much available in written rules and regulations; however, a visit with the state education department guidance staff often reveals much about state goals. This task is one that a work group can accomplish to learn much about the larger perspective. If you have not availed yourself of the statewide viewpoint, join the members of the work group on their visit to the capitol.

Finally, regional accreditation and professional associations have established standards relevant to guidance and counseling. Some of these standards include counselor-student ratios, and some hint at guidance program standards. Where they do, you may find them useful as you proceed through the program improvement process. Program standards have been established by the American School Counselor Association (Carroll, 1980; ASCA & NACAC, 1986) and the National Career Development Association, formerly the National Vocational Guidance Association (NVGA, 1979)—divisions of the American Association for Counseling and Development.

Staff Support/Nonsupport

"Political" also means the level of constituent support that is behind the momentum to change. Some counselors are eager for changes and will accept them; others resist change. If you are the guidance program leader, you need to consider the feelings of the staff and make preparations for working with both supportive and nonsupportive individuals.

Step 2: Identify Current Guidance and Counseling Activities

A major task in assessing the current program is to identify and record the activities in which the guidance staff—and other staff, if appropriate—are involved. The activities should be categorized by the components that organize the desired program structure as well as by grade or school level. This assessment phase provides qualitative data about the program; it provides the detail that fills in the outline of your current program structure.

There are several reasons for recording these activities in writing. First, the discipline of writing as opposed to speaking ensures preciseness. In addition, recording these activities renders them visible and thus more understandable to others. This is important because so much of what we do is invisible to others. Visibility helps counselors see the commonalities among their programs. In some districts it has provided a bridge between the elementary and secondary counselors; they have been able to focus on the similarities rather than on the differences of their programs. Finally, recording encourages counselors as they learn more about the new program model and how what they are currently doing fits into the model. In our experience, it has helped the counselors who are not in the mainstream of program remodeling and revitalization better understand the four program components described in chapter 3 by providing operational definitions for them.

We suggest that one or more work groups be used to accomplish this step 2 assessment. Groups can be organized by school level—elementary, middle/junior high, and high—or represent all school levels and be organized by the new program components. Every staff member should respond to the survey so that a complete picture is developed; however, if the staff is large, groupings of staff members may complete the surveys together. Buildings with multiple staff members are an obvious grouping. Clusters of elementary counselors, or other clusters of single staff members can be arranged.

The work groups need to devise the forms to be used. Each group should then distribute the forms to the staff for whom they are responsible, asking them to list the guidance and counseling activities by program components. The forms could contain a few examples by grade level in order to assist staff in knowing what to list. The work group members could generate their own examples. Some districts have found it useful to use the activities described in their original district handbooks. Make sure that the activities listed are actual activities, however, not those that the staff would like to do. The next step is to aggregate the data from individual staff members into a level-by-level, component-by-component composite.

Some districts have conducted specific activity or task assessments as well as the larger survey just described. In order to better understand the nature of its ''system support'' activities, one district conducted a study of the quasi-administrative and clerical tasks counselors perform. The process used was similar to that described above. A work group of counselors identified the tasks they performed that ''did not require a master's degree in guidance and counseling to do.'' Individual staff members then estimated the number of hours or days a year they spent on each of these tasks. These specifics were then totaled and their percentage of the total time was determined. Other districts have gathered this information in the original study, as in the Missouri time-task analysis (See Appendix A).

Another approach to this qualitative assessment of what actually occurs in the guidance program was used by a guidance program leader as she met with each building staff group. She interviewed them regarding a predetermined set of criteria that allowed her to gather the data to compare their programs to the program model adopted by the district. The same concept is being used in a self-study format whereby the leader provides the questions to a building staff. They complete the responses in writing and the comparison process ensues. Neither of these modes, however, provides the specific information about the range of activities that is so useful in understanding the texture of the current program; and neither mode is useful in accomplishing the next assessment step, determining the intended student outcomes of the current program activities.

Step 3: Determine Student Outcomes

Gathering Student Outcome Information

The next task is to identify the student outcomes for each activity. This entails taking one activity at a time and asking such questions as, Why do we do this? How are students different as a result of this activity? What do students know, what attitudes do they form, or what can students do that they could not do before? Note the following examples in the boxed material entitled "Activity Outcomes."

ACTIVITY OUTCOMES	
Activity	Outcome
Assist students in planning their schedules.	All students can select classes consistent with their abilities and interests.
Conduct Career Day.	Students who participate can identify an occupation consistent with their abilities and interests.

Although it is obvious that our major purpose as counselors is to serve students, not all of us have had experience in clearly stating the results of the work we do. For years as a profession we subscribed to the notion that what we did was not observable or measurable, or that what we did were processes and so the results were not visible.

If your district has been involved in the accountability movement, your task may be to merely synthesize available written statements. If, in adopting the guidance program model, you adopted an outline of student competencies, then your task is one of relating specific activities to student competencies. If neither of these options is available and your staff as a whole is not comfortable with the emphasis on outcomes, you are advised to use a work group—your steering committee counselors or a group of other counselor leaders—and guide them through the basic process of identifying student outcomes for the activities listed. It is by demonstrating our contribution to students' growth and development that our position in the educational setting is assured. Thus, this exercise allows you to test the validity of staff activities; if an activity has no visible outcome or if the identifiable outcome is of little significance, then continuing it may be inadvisable.

Having determined the intended outcomes of each activity, you can (a) generalize competencies, and (b) specify the clients you serve. The client data will be useful to you as you take step 4, described in the next section of this chapter; the competency information is useful now. By grouping activities under a component that is intended to deliver similar outcomes, you can make general statements about the intended outcomes of each program component. For example, the outcomes of the two activities cited above—schedule planning and Career Day— are related to students' development of educational and career plans. Aggregating the outcomes from all such activities would describe the outcomes of the individual planning component. With all the outcomes listed, you can draw larger generalizations about the intended outcomes of your total current program. This list then is ready for use in comparing the program you currently have and the program your district/school desires—the phase of the project described in chapter 6.

Gathering Student Status Information

An important part of assessing the current program is gathering information about the current status of students: What they know, learn, and need. If this has not already been accomplished in developing the rationale for your program, a work group should take on the task of identifying and collecting data about students. Possible sources of such data include standardized tests, criterion-referenced tests, attitude surveys, career development surveys, follow-up studies, and dropout studies. Demographic data, failure and absence rates, discipline reports, and mobility rates are reported by many schools and districts; the committee should amass as many of these reports as already exist in your system. When compiled, such information can provide insight into how well the current program is meeting student needs. It also tells you what the student needs are for your system. As with the activity information, the student data gathered in this step should be related as much as possible to the list of student outcomes you have just identified.

In addition to providing insight into how well the current program is meeting student needs, student data play another role in program development. They provide a baseline against which to compare students in future years. They provide opportunities to look at trends concerning student growth and development.

Step 4:   Identify Who Is Served

The fourth step in assessing your current guidance program is to identify who actually is served by your program—who the "clients" are—and the balance of services or the level of service that each subset of clients receives. The previous assessment has identified who your student clients are and, if the exercise was thoroughly done, caused you to acknowledge that there are many clients in addition to students. School counselors also serve teachers, administrators, students' parents, and the system itself.

After the staff have identified the activities they perform and the intended outcomes of each activity, the next question is: How do we know that all students for whom the activity was conducted reached the intended outcomes? Although the guidance staff may feel that the activities accomplished the desired results, there may be little evidence to prove it.

Thus, the next task is to identify the students who have attained the intended outcomes. Is it only the students who drop in to visit the guidance office? Is it all students? Is it all 10th-grade students? Indicate the number and percentage of students who have achieved a particular outcome and how it was determined that this outcome has been achieved. In this way the guidance staff defines the outcomes for specific subpopulations in the school. Follow this technique for each activity (or grouping of activities), and the result will be a listing of the outcomes that the activity is achieving and its impact on students (see Figure 4–4). It may be that only a small number of students attain many guidance outcomes, or there may be little proof that any outcomes are attained at all.

Another means for gathering data on clients served that has been used is a survey. It is not as precise as the method suggested above, but has yielded useful information. Counselors in one district were asked to "guesstimate" the percentage of their client-contact time that they spent with a listed set of clients. The original list was developed by a work group and distributed to all counselors. The group collected and tallied the results and were encouraged by the consistency of the "guesstimates." We believe that although this is an imprecise way to get information, if enough individuals submit input, any real aberrations are modified by the uniformity of the majority. The results of one survey of this type are presented in Figure 4–5.

The system-as-client is important to acknowledge also. In the districts with which we have worked, the most accurate data about this come from log keeping. By ensuring that the system-serving functions are distinct from the student-serving functions, the data may then be so analyzed. The results of one such log keeping for a group of high school counselors are presented in Figure 4–6.

Figure 4–4
Activity/Outcome/Impact

Activity	Outcome	Impact
Assist students in planning their schedules.	Students can select classes consistent with their abilities and interests.	1. Only 12% of the students change classes. 2. 1976 follow-up study of graduates: 68% reported curriculum satisfaction.
Conduct Career Day.	Students can identify an occupation consistent with their abilities and interests.	1. Participation-attendance records at the Career Day: low (only 30%). 2. Counselor contacts: high-quality response, but only 12% of the student body.

Figure 4–5
Guesstimates of Percentages of Time Spent With Clients
(75% of Total Time Spent in April, 1983)
Northside ISD, 1983

	Average* Elementary	Average* Middle	Average* High
Student Contacts			
Developmental Guidance			
Group	23	13	10
Individual	11	12	25
Basic Testing Program	7	3	10
Preventive (counseling)	12	18	11
Remedial (counseling, referral)	4	8	3
Adult Contacts			
District Administration	5	8	3
School Staff			
Principals	5	4	3
Teachers	9	9	7
Other Counselors	3	3	5
Special Education Staff	8	6	5
Other Specialists	3	3	3
Parents	7	10	8
Outside Agency Staff	2	2	1
Community Representatives	1	1	2

*Due to rounding, numbers do not add to 100%.

Figure 4–6
Personnel Support Versus System Support

% of Time	Personnel Support Function	Rank	VS.	% of Time	System Support Function	Rank
12.8	Individual Counseling	2		19.9	Professional Responsibilities	1
8.0	Individual Guidance	4				
6.3	Confer. Staff	6		8.3	Planning	3
4.2	Enrollment/Registration	8		6.9	Record Keeping	5
3.9	Consulting Staff	9		5.2	Misc. Paperwork	7
3.2	Confer. Parent	12		3.9	Special Education	9
2.5	Counseling Parent	13		3.8	Administrative Assignments	11
2.3	Coordinate Agencies	14				
2.0	Consulting Other School Specialists	15				
1.7	Guidance Activities	16				
1.5	Consulting Parents	17				
1.4	Career Ed.	18				
1.3	Confer. Student/Parent	19				
.6	Group Guidance	20				
.4	Small Group Counseling	21				
.2	Testing Individuals	22				
.1	Test District Prog.	23				
52.4				47.5		

Step 5: Gather Perceptions

The last step in the current program assessment process is to gather perceptions about the current program from students, teachers, counselors, administrators, parents, and community members. This phase of the assessment focuses on what individuals from such groups think about the activities of the current program. It does not necessarily focus on the realities of the current program nor on the perceived needs of individuals, the school, or society. Needs assessment comes later in the program improvement process.

The data gathered may help you identify supportive people and groups who may be used as resources, and inform you about what is right with the current program in your users' perceptions and about what might need to be changed. You can also use the baseline data in subsequent public relations efforts.

The most direct way to find out what people think about your current program is to ask them. We suggest that you ask the members of your advisory or steering committees to help you in this process. The parents on your advisory committee, for example, can help you word the questions to parents by suggesting proper terminology and effective ways to encourage parents to respond to your questions.

The same is true of the administrators on the committee. They are *representatives* from their groups to you.

One way to ask is to interview a representative sample of individuals from the various groups involved using a structured interview approach. Using separate work groups with the advisory and steering committee members as leaders can help accomplish this task. You may wish to consider having your advisory and steering committee members interview leaders of various subgroups because leaders are representatives of their groups; for example, the PTA representative to the advisory committee could interview the presidents of local unit PTAs. The danger here is that the leaders' opinions may not be representative of the mainstream of their groups.

There is a specific role for the guidance program leader to play in this process. Especially if there is widespread and generalized criticism of the current guidance program, there is merit to the leader asking key individuals such as superintendents, principals, and parent leaders direct questions such as: What do you like about the current guidance program? What do you dislike about it? What would you change about the program? What would you add to the program?

The advantages of using an interview approach are the direct contacts with members of the various groups and the in-depth responses that can be gathered. The disadvantages include the time-consuming nature of the task, the small number of people who can be contacted, and the difficulty in tabulating the results.

Another way to ask people for their perceptions is to use a questionnaire or a series of questionnaires. Questionnaires can be prepared and distributed to large numbers of people. Tabulating results is easy, particularly if you have access to a computer.

We would suggest the same cautions in the development of the questionnaires or questions as we did in the development of logs. Avoid the temptation to ask every question you ever wanted answered; keep the questions straightforward and simple. It is imperative that your questions be related to the components of your program model or to the outcomes desired for students and other clients rather than to counselors' functions. How you do your job is a professional decision. Needless to say, the questionnaires will have wording suitable to the population being polled; the questionnaire for elementary children will be different from the questionnaire for adults, but in order to be correlated, the substance must be the same. The questions and answers must correspond from one survey form to another if you want to aggregate the results and analyze them together. Comparisons of perceptions different groups hold are often useful.

A partial sample of a questionnaire used successfully to assess students' perceptions about the outcomes they achieved from participating in guidance activities is presented in Figure 4–7. The format of the questionnaire was used with all the groups surveyed by changing the statement "The guidance program helped

Figure 4–7
Guidance Program Questionnaire

Directions: Please read each statement carefully. There are no right or wrong answers. Just check the space that best decribes how you feel about each statement concerning the guidance activities in your school.

The guidance program helped me to:	Strongly Agree	Agree	No Opinion	Disagree	Strongly Disagree
1. *Plan my schedule*	___	___	___	___	___
2. *Interpret tests and other data*	___	___	___	___	___
3. *Recognize my abilities*	___	___	___	___	___
4. *Solve personal problems*	___	___	___	___	___
5. *Plan for education after high school*	___	___	___	___	___

Note: Courtesy of Guidance Department, Mesa Public Schools, Mesa, Arizona. Byron E. McKinnon.

me to . . .'' For example, if the questionnaire were to be used with parents, the statement could read, ''The guidance department helped my son or daughter to . . .'' In addition, the activities list can be changed to reflect the activities of your own program. It is recommended that a questionnaire of this type be prepared for the elementary, middle/junior, and senior high levels. The range of responses also can be modified to three—agree, no opinion, disagree—or two—simply yes or no.

As with any market research effort, selecting the population to be surveyed is very important. The sample must be representative of your program's consumers. Not all the perceptions held will be flattering and not all of them will be negative; there may not be much uniformity between consumer groups. The more accurate your sample, the truer the picture that you will have of your current program will be. Again, gathering the perceptions of all your constituents at once is a one-time activity and should be done with proper care. After you have made some program improvements, you may do some selective market research to gather opinions about the changes, with the current study results serving as baseline data.

If your system is small enough to do it by hand, or if you have access to a computer, it is best to survey random samples of students and parents. However, surveying total samples of counselors and administrators is advised. Whether you poll all your teachers or a random sample depends on the size of your school system. If it is small, poll them all. If it is large, identify a random sample. (If you are selecting the sample by hand, use a random sample table found in your basic statistics book.)

Leadership Roles and Responsibilities

If you are the guidance program leader, you are responsible for accomplishing the current program assessment. The scope of the undertaking will call upon all of your leadership, supervision, management, and administration skills. As you read through the descriptions of the various tasks to be undertaken in this phase of program improvement, you will no doubt come to that conclusion. This summary is provided to clarify your role. Essentially, you have specific responsibilities for the initiation, implementation, and closure of this phase of the program improvement project.

Initiation

As the program leader, you will need to keep the adopted program model in front of everyone involved in the project, including the decision makers and every member of the counseling staff. At this point you may be the only person who truly understands the concept. You will find yourself continually clarifying and explaining the model.

It is your responsibility to conceptualize the current program assessment process. As the guidance program leader, you need to identify the tasks to be performed and be able to explain them to the staff. We have suggested a multitude of tasks necessary for a complete assessment; you may not choose to do them all at this time or in the order we have set out. Ultimately, however, all the tasks are needed as the program improvement efforts continue.

Once school administrators have a vision of what an improved program will look like, they are eager for changes to occur. As the guidance program leader, you need to respond to their needs, but you also need to ensure that the program change decisions are the right decisions. This is why a factual assessment of the current program is so essential: to ensure making the right changes, not just responding to some individuals' pet concerns. You need to determine how much time you have to complete your assessment, and the steps that are most critical in order to progress at a reasonable rate. Thorough planning is essential, and so is effective use of your time.

If you are in a multi-school or building system, you need to share the leadership of the program with your staff leaders. These counselors can become the leaders of the subparts of the project and lead their colleagues by influence and delegated authority. You continue to lead by influence coupled with the authority of your position. You need to be sure that (a) the counselors selected are ready to be effective leaders, and (b) to work out mechanisms for being able to continue to provide leadership to them. The whole process becomes a matter of balance. In this case, you must strike a balance between knowing where you are going, what you need and want in results, and letting the staff of the work groups determine how they are going to provide results.

Implementation

You are the overall leader of the data collection efforts. You must staff your work groups to get the tasks done, and you must delegate effectively. Effective delegation means being explicit and precise in the charges you give work groups, and monitoring their progress as they proceed. We feel it is important, if possible, for you to meet with each work group and, indeed, to become a member of each group. Although you are the ultimate leader of these efforts, you do not have to have all the answers. We have found that thinking together with the work group members is a useful strategy. Every district with which we have worked has implemented its current program assessment somewhat differently. The data needs are the same, but the process routes may be different.

In your district you may need to engineer the development of the assessment instruments and procedures to be used for a variety of reasons. You need to ensure the adequacy of instrument development and then ensure that the instruments are relevant to the selected program model. Your perspective is broader than that of your staff and you are more aware of the resources available to you from other district or campus departments; you will know about reports generated by district departments, and you will know about district computer capabilities. Your involvement will allow you to coordinate the work of the various work groups. It is imperative that you not bombard the staff with a variety of similar surveys. It is also appropriate for you, as the guidance program administrator, to collect and present some of the data on your own. For example, you probably already have much of the budget and facilities information. Also, you are in a better position to survey other administrators.

There are a variety of ways in which you will be able to help the committees implement their processes. Your authority will facilitate data collection. You can ensure the involvement, understanding, and responsiveness of every staff member. You will need not only to educate the staff as to what they are doing and why, but also understand and manage the resistance of some staff members. If you are taking the steps in program improvement that we are suggesting, then you will be armed with the policy support you will need to answer the concerns. It also is helpful to remind staff that the current assessment needs to be accomplished only once; after the program redesigning efforts are completed, you will evaluate what you have done, but your basic program description will be finished. You may find that you need to mandate some of the work, particularly the time-usage study. The time-usage study will involve more work on the part of each staff member than will other aspects of the assessment, and the importance of its results is such that completeness and accuracy are imperative. Finally, there is a high correlation between your use of your supervisory skills of encouraging and praising and the success of this phase of the project. The more accessible you are to the staff, both to the work groups and to the staff as a whole, the more comfortable everyone will be with the new model and its implementation.

Closure

Your final set of responsibilities in accomplishing the current program assessment will be to help the work groups summarize and disseminate the data they have collected and to help the steering committee and the staff analyze the results. Organizing the presentation of the data is not easy. It is probable that you will want to present all of the data to the steering committee and to the counseling staff, but only an executive summary to other interested staff such as campus administrators and other guidance staff. It is useful to have leaders of the work groups present the information that their groups have gathered, but you must assume responsibility for ensuring that the information is understood. You will need to allow as much time to do this as is required. As much as an entire inservice education day has been used in some schools for this purpose. This allows the staff time to process the information and to begin drawing their own conclusions. It also provides them the opportunity to raise questions and to learn more about the implied program changes. The results that have been gathered are tangible and impressive, and by presenting them all together, perspective is maintained. It will be rewarding to staff to see the fullness of their program. As we mentioned above, this will probably be the first time that the entire program will seem visible, tangible, and concrete.

The data need to be analyzed by you, the steering committee, and, either together or separately, by the counselor leadership team—if they are not all a part of the steering committee. You must be clear about what the data say to you. You must draw conclusions about what the current program is and what it is accomplishing. Then you are in a position to state what the design of the current program is and what the current priorities are.

By "design" we mean the balance that has been struck between the program components or among the counselor functions. You can state that as of this time, for example, the largest component of the current guidance program is system support, the second is individual planning, third, responsive services, and fourth, guidance curriculum. You now know, for example, that the primary mode of operating for the counseling staff is individual counseling, the second is completing administrative assignments, the third is doing special education administrative work, and so on. An example of presenting that information from the Northside Independent School District's program improvement project is presented in Figure 4–8.

Figure 4–8
Northside Independent School District
Current Guidance Program Priorities
(Data Generated in Counselor Time Study, April, 1983)

Component	Priority/School Level		
	Elementary	Middle	High
Guidance Curriculum	4	4	4
Individual Planning	1	3	3
Responsive Services	3	2	2
System Support	2	1	1

As a result of aggregating the information gleaned in the study of how counselors applied their time, it was learned that the priorities of the program—in comprehensive guidance program terms—were as shown in the boxed material entitled "Program Priorities."

PROGRAM PRIORITIES

First Priority
  Elementary: Individual Planning
  Middle School: System Support
  High School: System Support

Fourth Priority
  Elementary: Guidance Curriculum
  Middle School: Guidance Curriculum
  High School: Guidance Curriculum

Next, you would state the priority order of the student outcomes addressed and that of the clients served by the current program. For example, you may have learned that at the elementary level 20% of your activities are aimed at helping students to be safe at home and in the neighborhood. Those activities thus have a high priority. At the high school level, you may have learned that 60% of your activities relate to scheduling and schedule changes. You also now know the rank order that applies to the clients you serve. You may have learned that your top priority clients are individual students who come to the counseling office, second are teachers, third are groups of students with remedial level needs whom you call in for group counseling, and so on.

If you have not already done so, these conclusions need to be written down. This will help you bring this phase of the project to closure and provide you baseline information with which to move on to subsequent steps without having to reanalyze the data every time you pick them up. The value of written statements, as mentioned earlier, forces you to be precise, provides a tangible focus for the steering committee and the counselors to endorse, and provides a vehicle for communicating with others about the results of the work that has been accomplished.

Concluding Thoughts

In summary, the assessment of your current program should have contributed to your program improvement project. The staff has been involved and has learned much about the program as it exists. The staff has a vision of the model to be adopted/adapted. A full, concrete description of the current program has been made.

You have broadened the involvement of staff in the program improvement process. Counselor leaders have been identified and are beginning to fulfill their role. All counselors and other relevant guidance program and administrative staff have been working in groups. The steering committee members have been used in operational roles to lead the work groups, in addition to their advisory capacity on the committee, and, thus, their investment in the overall project has increased.

In addition, a sense of the need for change has begun to emerge. By this time the counselors know that changes will come, but should feel reassured that the decisions to change are not being made hastily. This suggests that the leadership is seeking to make the right changes.

From a staff development perspective, the counselors have learned more about the adopted program model and the components through record keeping, data gathering, and discussion. They have begun to understand the relationship between their current program and the new program model. They have come to know their current program in concrete detail. They have begun to learn about and practice the important program development skills of planning and data gathering.

You, the steering committee, the guidance staff, and the administrators now know what resources you have available in the current program and how you use them. You know the activities that compose the current program, what your current program emphasizes, its variety, and the balance of your use of the components in the delivery system. You now know at least the probable student outcomes of your program and the scope of your impact on the students you serve. You know the clients your current program serves and the proportion of services it provides to the various subsets of these populations. You know the perceptions of your primary program users. In short, you, the steering committee, and the guidance and administrative staffs know the design and priorities of the current guidance program.

The scope of the current program assessment is such that, once done, there is a tendency to think that the program improvement project is completed. But, it is not. Although you can now relate your current program data to the program model, making judgments at this time is premature. Your next questions are: *What do we desire our guidance program to be?*—that is discussed in chapter 5; and *How does what we are doing now compare and contrast with what is desired from our program?*—that is discussed in chapter 6. The concreteness of your knowledge about what is and the vision you have about what could be will provide you the impetus to begin to navigate the difficult program improvement steps of planning the transition from where you are to where you want to be and, then, implementing changes.

References

American School Counselor Association. (1981). *ASCA role statements*. Alexandria, VA: Author.

American School Counselor Association, & National Association of College Admissions Counselors. (1986). *Professional development guidelines for secondary school counselors: A self-audit*. Alexandria, VA: AACD Press.

Carroll, M.R. (Ed.). (1980). Standards for guidance and counseling programs. *School Counselor, 28*, 81–86.

DuBois, P. (1975). *Module 4: Assessing current status*. Palo Alto, CA: American Institutes for Research.

National Vocational Guidance Association. Commission of Criteria for Career Guidance Programs. (1979). Guidelines for a quality career guidance program. *Vocational Guidance Quarterly, 28*, 99–110.

PART 2—Designing

CHAPTER 5

DESIGNING THE COMPREHENSIVE GUIDANCE PROGRAM

Once a comprehensive guidance program model has been selected and data have been gathered that describe the current guidance program, the next phase of the program improvement process is to design the specific program that is desired for your school district or school building. Conceptualizing the desired program in concrete terms is essential because, as you will find, the program improvement process is somewhat analogous to remodeling your home while you are living in it. A specifically drawn blueprint of the renovations for your home is needed so that the renovations may be made in an orderly sequence without totally disrupting your life style. The more precise the blueprint, the more efficient the renovation will be and the more certain the ultimate product will be to reflect what you want. The same is true for a comprehensive guidance program. Also, although at this point you may have a somewhat idealistic picture of the guidance program you want, you will need to begin to temper this vision with reality. You will need to be specific about the changes you want to make and feel confident that those changes are the *right* changes.

During the designing phase of the program improvement process you will continue to use the steering committee or the school-community advisory committee you established previously. By this time these committee members have become knowledgeable about the current program and have grasped the concept of the new program. As representatives of both the professionals who work in the program and the constituents who use the program, they can help in hammering out the hard decisions to be faced. Possible questions that need to be asked are:

- Which program component should have priority for the counselors?
- Of the competencies that students need to learn, which should be emphasized at each grade level or grade grouping?

- Who will be served and with what priority: all students in a developmental mode or some students in a remedial services mode? And, what are the relationships between services to students and services to the adults in the students' lives?
- What domains will describe the scope of the guidance program and what competencies and outcomes will have priority?
- What skills will be utilized by the school counselors: teaching, guiding, counseling, consulting, testing, record keeping, coordinating, or disseminating information, and with what priority?
- What school levels will benefit, and to what extent, from the resources appropriated to the program: elementary, middle/junior high, or high school?
- What is the relationship between the guidance program and staff and the other educational programs and staff: is the sole purpose of guidance to support the instructional program? Or does guidance have an identity and responsibilities of its own? Should it be a program or a set of services? (Henderson, 1987).

The answers to these questions are dictated by the priorities of the system in which the guidance program and school counselors find themselves, and by the quantity and quality of resources supplied to the program. The steering and advisory committees can help ensure that the changes you will be recommending will be responsive to the needs of the school district and the community, and they may help in generating the new resources you undoubtedly will need.

If you are the guidance program leader, you have primary responsibility for the decisions and their implementation, but we believe the broader your support base, the sounder your decisions will be. You will need to continue to clarify information and the impending decisions. You will need to move the decision process along. In all likelihood, you will have major responsibility for putting the vision of the model program in operation.

Establishing the design of your desired program entails describing in concrete terms the structure and contents of your improved guidance program. The comprehensive guidance program model you selected needs to be tailored to fit the realities of your school building and district. The basic question at this point is: *How do you want to use the resources available to the guidance program in your setting in order to have a comprehensive and well-balanced program?*

Chapter 5 describes seven steps to establish the design of the program for your district/building:

Step 1: Select basic program structure;
Step 2: List student competencies;
Step 3: Reaffirm policy support;
Step 4: Establish parameters for resource allocation;
Step 5: Specify student outcomes;

Step 6: Specify activities by components; and

Step 7: Write down and distribute the description of the desired program.

The first step entails selecting the structure that best will help you organize your program and defining the program components to fit your building or district situation. In the second step, the competencies that your program will help students learn and apply need to be listed. Suggestions are made to help you build the list that best fits your situation. Although, as we said earlier, you must have had policy support to begin the guidance program improvement process, in the third step it is important to reaffirm that support. With the newly conceptualized program defined to fit your building or district and with the basic competencies that your program will address identified, policy support should be elicited for these specific concepts. In the fourth step, the resources we discuss are the time and talents of the staff and the allocation of these resources to program component delivery and to student competency development. We suggest that the roles of staff members be defined and guidelines established for the use of counselors' time and talent. Also, the desired balance between program components needs to be established, and priorities for the competencies students are to acquire need to be set. In the fifth step, student outcomes/indicators are specified for different grade levels (e.g., K, 1, 2, etc.), grade groupings (e.g., K–3, 4–6, 7–9, 10–12), or school levels (e.g., elementary, middle/junior high, high school). The sixth step entails identifying the major activities that make up each of the comprehensive guidance program components. At this time, you develop the scope and sequence of the guidance curriculum, list the major activities that contribute to students' individual planning, and identify recurrent topics for which responsive services are sought. In the seventh and last step, we suggest forming an outline describing the comprehensive guidance program and distributing it. The description of the new program must be reviewed and understood by all concerned.

It is essential to establish the design that you want to have for your program so that the implementation that follows can be realistic. If you are from a school district that has more than one building, clarifying the desired design at the district level will ensure consistency of the program from one building to another. The district design should be general enough, however, to allow buildings to tailor their programs to meet local building and neighborhood needs.

Step 1: Select Basic Program Structure

With the assistance of your steering committee and school-community advisory committee and your district policymakers, decide what the guidance program structure will be for your district/building. Currently, the structure in use may follow the guidance services model (orientation, assessment, information, counseling, placement, and follow-up activities,) or it may be organized around the processes of counseling, consulting, and coordination, or the duties model. We recommend that, in place of these structures, a new structure be adopted that is more in keeping with a developmental guidance perspective. We recommend that the components described in chapter 3—guidance curriculum, individual planning, responsive services, and system support—be used as the organizers for your guidance program K–12. Local community, district, and state needs will dictate the specific content to be included in each program component as well as the overall balance among the components. The recommended components are again briefly described below, and an example of how one school district tailored this structure to its needs is included in Appendix B.

STRUCTURAL COMPONENTS

Definition: The program definition includes the mission statement of the guidance program and its centrality within the school district's total educational program. It delineates the competencies individuals will possess as a result of their involvement in the program. It summarizes the components and identifies the clients of the program.

Rationale: The rationale discusses the importance of guidance as an equal partner in the educational system and provides reasons why individuals in our society need to acquire the competencies that will accrue to them as a result of their involvement in a comprehensive guidance program. It includes the conclusions drawn from the student and community needs assessments or other clarifications of goals for the local educational system.

Assumptions: Assumptions are the principles that shape and guide the program. They may include statements regarding the essence of the contribution that school counselors and guidance programs make to students' development, the premises that undergird the comprehensiveness and the balanced nature of the program, and the relationship between the guidance program and the other educational programs. A statement that the program needs to be continuously planned, designed, implemented, and evaluated should be included as well.

PROGRAM COMPONENTS

Guidance Curriculum: The guidance curriculum is the center of the developmental part of the comprehensive guidance program. It contains statements as to the goals for guidance instruction and the competencies to be developed by students. The curriculum is organized by grade level; that is, a scope and sequence of learnings for Grades K–12 is established. It is designed to serve all students and is often called classroom or group guidance.

Individual Planning: The activities of the individual planning component are provided for all students and are intended to assist students in the development and implementation of their personal, educational, and career plans. They help students to understand and monitor their growth and development and to take action on their next steps educationally or vocationally. The activities in this component are delivered either on a group or individual basis with students and parents.

Responsive Services: The purpose of this component is to provide special help to students who are facing problems that interfere with their healthy personal, social, career, or educational development. It includes the provision of preventive responses to the students who are on the brink of choosing an unhealthy or inappropriate solution to their problems or of being unable to cope with a situation. Remedial interventions also are provided for students who have already made unwise choices or have not coped well with problem situations. This component includes such activities as individual and small group counseling, consulting with staff and parents, and referring students and families to other specialists or programs.

System Support: This component has two parts. It includes activities necessary to support the other three components and activities implemented by guidance staff that support other educational programs. Support that the guidance program needs includes such activities as staff development, community resource development, budget, facilities, and policy support. Support that the guidance staff provides to other programs includes the system related aspects of the individual planning activities (e.g., student course selection), linkage with the special education and vocational education programs, and guidance-related administrative assignments.

Step 2: List Student Competencies

Once you have selected your overall program structure, the next step is to decide on the competencies that the guidance program will take responsibility for helping students acquire. What knowledge will students gain, what skills will students develop, and what attitudes will students form as a result of their participation in the guidance program? For help in answering these questions, go to the results section of the current program assessment you have already completed. In that process you identified the intended student competencies resulting from guidance activities K–12 in the current guidance program. As we suggested earlier, compare these with lists generated from the goals of your school district, your state department of education, or your local community. Some school districts and some state departments of education have developed competency lists to be used as part of their graduation requirements. Use such lists in the comparison process. Also review the lists of competencies presented in chapter 3 and appendix C. Then decide on the list to be used in your program.

The above-mentioned sources will give you a plethora of ideas, but we recommend that you *build your own list*, one that fits your school district's and community's stated goals and priorities. One of your ultimate goals is to ensure the centrality of the guidance program within the school district's total educational program. The more direct the link between the school district's goals and your program, the more clearly related the guidance program will be to the basic mission of the school district. For example, if the district's educational philosophy includes such items as helping students to become good citizens, be responsible for their actions, and make wise choices, then these words should be incorporated in the student competencies addressed by the guidance program.

You need to proceed through the list-building process in as systematic a way as possible; that is, you first need to identify the broad areas of human growth and development that you established as the realm of the guidance program—in chapter 3 we called these categories domains. Next, competencies are specified for each domain and for each grade grouping, or end-point of a school level; for example, at the end of the 6th grade for the elementary guidance program, at the end of the 9th grade for the junior high school program, or at the end of the 12th grade for the high school program.

The preliminary work of assembling this list can be done by a work group. Reviewing lists of competencies generated by others may be confusing at first, but once the work group gets involved it is an exciting task. It allows professional counselors to focus on the contributions they can make to students' growth and development. At each stage of the development of the list—after establishing the domains stating the competencies—it should be reviewed and approved by the total guidance staff as well as by other key members of the school staff, administration, students, and the community. Use your school-community advisory committee to assist you in the process.

Finally, we stress the need to be parsimonious when it comes to the number of domains, goals, and competencies used as the basis for your improved program. The life career development model presented in chapter 3 used 3 domains and 5 goals per domain. This means that there were 15 goals for the overall program model. The Northside model presented in chapter 3 displayed 6 domains and 12 skill goals for the overall program model. We suggest that you not exceed these numbers because longer lists become difficult to manage effectively, especially given the resources typically available to the guidance program. This list of competencies is the heart of the comprehensive guidance program. Every activity conducted in each component of the program should aim toward mastery of one or more of these competencies.

Step 3: Reaffirm Policy Support

If you have followed the process of the program change outline so far and are using a steering committee or a school-community advisory committee, you already have a group of guidance-educated and supportive others, including administrators, parents, teachers, and business and industry personnel. At this point in the process, however, it is a good idea to reaffirm the support of the school system's policymakers and administrators for the program concept. Remember, they need to know what is envisioned for the guidance program and be willing to support the improvement efforts not only with the public but also with the guidance staff and other school staff members who may be anxious about the proposed changes.

To learn if you have the support of the administrators in your school or district, begin with your immediate supervisor. If you are at the district level, this means your assistant or associate superintendent; if you are at the building level, it means your principal. Remember, to ensure that the changes you envision are consistent with the district's vision, you need at least one of the administrators to help you keep in touch with the district's basic mission. You also will need the administrator to help you gain the support of the school district's board of education. In addition, you will need the administrator's assistance in enlisting the support of the other administrators, at the campus or district level, who supervise or have expectations for counselors. Finally, you will need the re-affirmation of the upper-level administrators to convince counselors who resist the impending changes that the changes are, indeed, what the district wants and that they need to be responsive to those changes.

Because school districts operate within a delicate political balance, recognized leaders or a majority of constituents—including parents, principals, counselors, teachers, students, superintendents, other administrators, and board members—have to be willing to ''sign on'' to the new program vision. The more you prepare them at this stage of the process, the stronger your support in the difficult times of actual implementation will be.

Now that the program structure has been selected and student competencies have been listed, it is time to seek a guidance program policy statement. The fact that the advisory or steering committee have already endorsed the program helps because they can take the program structure and student competency list to their constituent groups, educate them, and solicit feedback. However, it also is highly desirable to have your board of education adopt a guidance program policy that affirms the structure of the desired program. We have had districts adopt the program definition as the basic policy. The policymakers state the priorities for the program, such as serving students with needs for developmental, remedial, or preventive help, the relative priority of each of the four program components, and the priorities for student skill development. You may find some of the data gathered in your study of the perceptions of the current guidance program useful as a rationale for the needed changes. You also may find the "Resolution on Guidance and Counseling (4.1.26)" adopted by the Delegate Assembly of the National School Boards Association in April, 1986 useful. It stated:

> NSBA encourages local school boards to support comprehensive guidance and counseling programs, kindergarten through grade 12, staffed by professionally trained counseling personnel. NSBA also urges local school boards, state education agencies and the federal government to support activities aimed at improving the education of school counselors, the development of exemplary guidance and pupil service models and research which examines the effectiveness of such programs.

Step 4: Establish Parameters for Resource Allocation

With your program broadly outlined and basic policy support established, you are now ready to define in concrete terms the desired design for the district's comprehensive guidance program. Questions that need to be asked now are: How do we want to make best use of the counselors' talents? What does the desired program balance mean in terms of counselors' time? Which student groups should have top priority, second, third, and so on? Which student competencies should be emphasized?

At this point a "Which came first, the chicken or the egg?" issue arises: Should the desired outcomes and program design dictate the allocation of resources, or should the allocation of resources dictate the shape of the program? In an ideal setting, the identified student and community needs would justify the allocation of sufficient resources to provide a complete, comprehensive program for meeting those needs. In a real setting there are, no doubt, more needs and desired outcomes than the school or district is able to attend to, given feasible resource allocations. This is part of the challenge of "remodeling your program while you are living in it." You are probably not creating a program from scratch with the potential for unlimited resources.

You must make recommendations based on current resource allocations with some projections or requests for expanded resources. In our experience, school counseling staffs first have had to redirect their current resources and have had to be prepared to use augmented resources appropriately. Thus, at this point you make resource allocation decisions based on the priorities and realities of your schools. For example, you have identified what a fully implemented guidance curriculum would contain; however, if there is time in the students' schedules for only one guidance lesson per week (or month, or grading period), then the full guidance curriculum cannot be implemented at first. Decisions need to be made as to what topics have top priority so that the lessons that are taught are the most important.

Another example: There is a finite amount of time that school counselors have in a school day/week/year. In the current situation, there probably is not enough counselor time to implement fully all four program components of the comprehensive guidance program as desired. Thus, priorities for the use of counselors' available time must be suggested to set realistic goals for the program. In order to set priorities for use of the counselors' talents and time, the highest priority student competencies should be identified.

Define Counselors' Role

Before making concrete recommendations concerning the school counselors' role, it is important to remember the unique contributions that school counselors can and do make to students' growth and development. Counselor role expectations need to be specified; that is, job descriptions for school counselors and other related guidance department personnel need to be written. This process requires knowledge about what school counselors are educated to do. The clarification of counselors' talents accomplished in the assessment of the current program provides an excellent backdrop for ensuing decisions as to how counselors' time can be best used.

Because standard counselor job descriptions have not served us well in the past, we recommend that you consider drafting position guides. The position guide offers more detail than the standard list of 9 or 10 duties found in most traditional job descriptions. The position guide includes sections that describe the primary function of the job, the major responsibilities involved, illustrative key duties, organizational relationships, and performance standards (Castetter, 1981). Using the comprehensive guidance program model, the school counselors' position guide would state that counselors are expected to teach the guidance curriculum; assist students to develop their individual plans; counsel, consult, and refer students and others in response to their specific problems and needs; cooperate with other school staff in needed support of their programs; pursue their own professional growth; and develop and implement an effective guidance program. (See the sample position guide in Appendix D.)

Define Others' Roles

Now is also an appropriate time to redesign or reaffirm the job descriptions of the other guidance department personnel such as registrars, career center technicians, counselors' secretaries, office aides, and peer facilitators. Ultimately, all personnel who work in the guidance program must have their roles defined, including teachers who act as advisors or who teach guidance or psychology classes, and community volunteers who augment the guidance staff in specific guidance activities. Again, we recommend that you *write* the job descriptions for each of the positions so that differentiation of the various roles and multiple responsibilities are clear to all concerned.

Because human resources are basic to the guidance program, you may find it useful to consider who else in addition to the school staff is available to help deliver the guidance program. One of education's chronically untapped resources is community members; hence, an inventory of community members who may be willing to serve is an important part of a community resource list. The most dramatic examples of community-assisted guidance programs have been provided in career education programs. For example, business, industry, and labor groups, service club members, and the like are often willing to speak on occupation-specific or employment realities. Also, parent and grandparent groups have been used to provide role models of caring adults for elementary school children. PTA leaders can be used to lead parent education groups, using the National PTA and March of Dimes publication, *Parenting: The Underdeveloped Skill* (1986).

Determine the Desired Balance Between Program Components

An important consideration in designing your program is to assign time to each program component. This is a critical issue because of the traditional add-on nature of guidance. In the past, as new issues/concerns were addressed in the school, duties were added without much thought as to the time these duties would take to complete. A comprehensive guidance program is not an add-on program; it is a 100% program. The program structure is established and the time available to staff is allocated so that across all staff available, the time allocated to the program components equals 100%. Because of differences across grade or grade grouping levels, allocations of time for individual staff members may be different. Also, the allocation of time may vary from school building to building and district to district, depending on the needs of the students and communities.

To help establish the desired time allocations for the program components of the comprehensive guidance program, we have found that the steering committee or school-community advisory committee can provide direction. We also have worked with separate groups of counselors, principals and other administrators, and parents, but this is cumbersome. Consensus between the groups is hard to achieve when each group cannot hear the deliberations of the other groups. On the other hand, if you are in a district in which the major emphasis is on helping individuals determine their own best mode of operation, you might use a process whereby the counseling and guidance staff make recommendations that, in turn, are brought forward to the decision-making or advisory groups by the counselor leaders. The leaders would present the rationale of their constituents; but they must also have the authority to compromise and to develop consensus on behalf of the staff.

As implied above, you need to implement a process that will lead the group(s) to consensus because most likely you will not find unanimity among the decision makers. The Northside Independent School District project used its steering committee and applied a modified Delphi process to reach a decision about the allocation of time across the program components. The committee first was asked to establish priorities for component resource allocation. Their decision is reflected in Figure 5–1. (Please compare/contrast it with Figure 4–8.) Then committee members, who had become educated about the program model, were asked as individuals to write down the percentage of counselor time that they considered ought to be appropriated to each of the four program components. Each member then posted his or her percentage allocations on blank sheets of easel paper that had been hung on the walls of the meeting room. These postings are displayed in Figure 5–2.

Note the ranges of time. The steering committee as a whole considered the ranges and apparent "median" ratings, and deliberated and debated. Consensus on the percentages for each category was then reached. At a subsequent meeting—after some "percolating" time—the final balance in terms of percentages was considered and agreed upon. The balance that was established as desired by the district is presented in Figure 5–3 (Northside Independent School District, 1986). These figures were used to suggest allocations of staff time for Northside's desired program; they became the template against which the current program assessment data were compared and contrasted.

Another district, St. Joseph, MO (Hargens & Gysbers, 1984) established the percentages displayed in Figure 5–4 as those desired for the allocation of time for the program components.

Establish Priorities for Basic Guidance Skills/Domains

It is important to have both the counselors and the consumers of the guidance program establish priorities for the competencies that students will acquire as a result of their participation in the guidance program. Helping all students in a school building or a system make progress toward acquiring competencies contained in the 15 goals—or 12, or however many you have agreed upon in your

Figure 5–1
Northside Independent School District
Desired Guidance Program Priorities
(Data Generated By Steering Committee, January, 1984)

	Priority/School Level		
Component	Elementary	Middle	High
Guidance Curriculum	1	1	2
Individual Planning	2	1	1
Responsive Services	2	3	1
System Support	4	4	4

Figure 5–2
Individual Committee Members' Appropriations of
Counselor Time/Component

	Elementary	Middle	High
Guidance Curriculum	40 40 40 35 40 50 40 40 40 30 60 45 65	40 35 30 30 30 30 30 40 30 15 30 50 50 50	25 10 20 15 35 40 35 25 20 10 30 20 30 40 50
Consensus:	40	30	25
Individual Planning	20 25 35 30 30 20 20 20 10 10 20 10 10	20 25 30 25 30 40 30 25 20 30 15 25 15 15	30 35 40 40 25 20 20 30 40 40 30 35 30 20 20
Consensus:	25	30	30
Responsive Services	20 20 25 15 15 20 20 20 40 40 20 25 15	30 25 30 25 30 15 25 25 30 40 25 30 15 15	30 40 25 20 20 20 30 30 20 40 30 35 30 20 15
Consensus:	25	25	30
System Support	10 10 10 15 15 10 10 10 20 30 10 10 10	10 15 10 10 10 15 15 30 20 15 30 15 20 20	20 10 10 30 20 20 20 15 10 10 10 10 10 20 15
Consensus:	10	15	15

Figure 5–3
Northside Independent School District
Desired Guidance Program Balance

	% Counselor Time/School Level		
Component	Elementary	Middle	High
Guidance Curriculum	40	30	25
Individual Planning	25	30	30
Responsive Services	25	25	30
System Support	10	15	15

Figure 5–4
St. Joseph School District
Desired Guidance Program Balance

Component	% Counselor Time/School Level		
	Elementary	Middle	High
Guidance Curriculum	25	20	15
Individual Planning	10	20	30
Responsive Services	55	45	30
System Support	10	15	25

model—presents an overwhelming challenge if you are just beginning to implement a competency-based comprehensive guidance program. This challenge is compounded because you also are accepting accountability for helping students with developmental, preventive, and remedial needs. Thus, priorities as to which competencies are to be included at any given time in the program need to be established.

The goals for student competency development can and should be ranked according to their overall importance for all students. You also may wish to suggest the importance of various goals (and the competencies involved) by different grade or grade-grouping levels. The sequence for helping students reach these goals needs to be agreed upon as well; for example, many groups have agreed that helping students know and understand themselves is prerequisite to their learning to know and understand others. This process of setting priorities becomes complicated, but the various approaches usually produce some consensus in terms of overall top priorities for attention, and as you move to more specific implementation plans, you will have a sense of where to begin and where to end. Figure 5–5 presents the goal priorities established by Northside Independent School District (1986). These skills are still stated in very broad terms; they are comparable to "domains" as defined in chapter 3. If you are in a smaller setting and can manage the attendant tasks, this is an appropriate time to conduct a student and community needs assessment to ascertain priorities. In a larger district setting or a multi-building setting, however, the competency statements are still too broad to be used as an assessment of students' needs. (Ideas on assessing needs are presented in chapter 6.)

Step 5: Specify Student Outcomes

In previous work you established the domains, goals, and competencies for student development for which the guidance program and counseling staff are

Figure 5–5
Priorities for Student Skill Development

Recommended Program Design

In order to have a comprehensive and appropriately balanced program, the following priorities for allocation of resources need to be considered as goals for campus programs.

Priority Rankings Assigned to Skills

	Importance	Sequence	Level for Emphasis
1. understand and respect themselves	1	1	E
2. understand and respect others	2	2	E
3. behave responsibly in school	3	3	E
4. behave responsibly in the family	9	6	E
5. behave responsibly in the community	9	10	M
6. make wise choices	3	3	M
7. manage change successfully	7	8	M
8. solve problems	5	5	M
9. use educational opportunities well	8	9	M
10. communicate effectively	6	6	M
11. plan for personally satisfying and socially useful lives	11	11	H
12. prepare for personally satisfying and socially useful lives	12	12	H

accountable. You organized competency statements around the goals. At this point, you need to specify your intended outcomes by grade level, grade groupings, or school level. This simply means breaking the competencies into their subparts and establishing outcomes appropriate to the age levels of the students served by the program activities. The outcome lists for the life career development model presented in chapter 3 result in specific statements. These expand quickly from the basic list of 15 goals. For each grade level there are 13 competencies or 195 competencies, K–12 (listed in Appendix C).

Again, we stress the need to be parsimonious in identifying outcomes for which you will be accountable. Although you will be basing the actual number you use on the assessment of your student needs relative to these outcomes, seeking too many outcomes will make the program unworkable. The allocation of counselor time to the different program components has a direct bearing on what outcomes you are able to assist students to acquire. As the program development efforts proceed, every one of these outcomes becomes an aim of some lesson, unit, or counseling session. In the comprehensive guidance program, every activity has a student objective and every activity's objective must relate to an outcome that is on this list. The boxed material entitled "Conceptual Flow" presents an example.

CONCEPTUAL FLOW

Domain 1:	Self-knowledge and Interpersonal Skills
Goal A:	Students will develop and incorporate an understanding of the unique personal characteristics and abilities of themselves and others.
Competency:	Students will specify those personal characteristics and abilities that they may value.
Student outcome:	Fifth-grade students will identify a variety of things that they value.
Activity objective:	The student will identify six things he or she values.

The task of specifying competencies by grade level, grade-grouping, or school level is one that counselors need to do. The work group that defined the broader list of goals and competencies should either continue with this task or provide leadership to an expanded group of counselors working on the outcomes list. It is instructive for all the counselors to have some experience in developing at least a portion of the list. It helps them think in student outcome terms so that when the shift is made to the activity development phase of the project, they are used to thinking in terms of specific student behaviors.

When it is near completion, the list of outcomes should be reviewed and ratified by the total counseling staff and by all others—the steering committee or the administrative staff—who are providing leadership to the program change efforts. The total list of outcomes will be a bit much for others than counselors to review, but the counselors need the opportunity to think through every piece of the outline. Too, the review by administrators and others allows people with different frames of reference to consider the specifics of the guidance program. In this way outcomes that are potentially unpalatable to some community members or outcomes that have been overlooked and are seen as important can be identified and addressed at the beginning.

Step 6: Specify Activities By Components

The next step is to define the program components in finer detail by describing the primary emphases and the major activities included in each. Each component of the desired program should include activities that are performed effectively in the current program and identify new activities that are envisioned to meet the program goals better.

Guidance Curriculum

For the guidance curriculum, the Northside school district staff identified as curriculum strands the basic student competencies that were established for the comprehensive program (see Figure 5–5). These described the *scope* of the guidance curriculum. Next, priorities for guidance instruction were established. This process serves to help counselors know the topics to be taught at particular school levels and, because there are time limitations for teaching students, the competencies that must be addressed. The *sequence* for assisting students to learn the competencies was also established. This may merely entail restating the student outcomes specified for each grade level in the previous effort. However, if in the previous substep you expressed outcomes by grade spans or school levels, you now need to clarify what is to be taught at each grade level. Again an example from the life career development model helps portray this. The scope and a sequence for the Kindergarten guidance curriculum in this model is depicted in Figure 5–6.

Having done that, the next step is to group the outcomes into units for instruction. Heretofore the organizer for your development of student competencies has been the domains. As you identify specific outcomes for each grade level and sequence them, some natural groupings for learnings from the different goal areas probably will emerge. For instructional purposes, you will probably want to teach these by logical units rather than in the order specified in your outline of competencies. For example, the units that emerge from the kindergarten outcomes in our example above might be, first, a unit on "self" that focuses on the first 4 of the competencies as sequenced above; second, "decision making," addressing the next 2 competencies; third, "others," the next 3; fourth, "school," competencies 10 and 11; fifth, "community and work," competencies 12 through 14; and finally, "future."

Figure 5–6
Kindergarten Guidance Curriculum Scope and Sequence

Kindergarten students will

1. describe their appearance
2. describe ways they care for themselves
3. describe areas where they are self-sufficient
4. describe growing capabilities
5. describe choices they make
6. realize the difficulty of making choices between two desirable alternatives
7. recognize that they listen to and speak with a variety of people
8. describe people and activities they enjoy
9. describe their work and play relationships with others and their favorite activities
10. describe those things they learn at school
11. describe their daily activities at school
12. recognize the town, state, and country in which they reside
13. describe the work activities of family members
14. mentally project adults into work activities other than those they do presently
15. describe situations that are going to happen in the future

Individual Planning

For individual planning identify the major activities that assist students to make their personalized plans. In the schools and districts with which we have worked, these activities focus on students' educational and career plans. If your program is so directed, you also might have activities that help students make plans that relate to their personal and social lives. These major activities also must be related to the broad goals of the guidance program. An example of the activities and the skills they relate to as delineated by Northside Independent School District is provided in Figure 5–7.

As you can see, these are activities traditionally found in guidance and counseling programs. Decisions need to be made as to the priorities for the time spent within this component. Assisting students to complete successfully their elementary and secondary education is usually a priority for school counselors, with the transition grades receiving the highest priority; however, college, post-secondary vocational/technical, and career planning fall in this component as well. At the elementary level, orienting primary-grade children to school and helping upper-grade children adjust to the increasing demands of the academic curriculum by developing effective, personalized approaches to studying and time management may have priority. Where counselor case loads are larger than the 100:1 ratio suggested by those who would have school counselors work with individuals in a one-to-one relationship, this component will need to be built

Figure 5-7
Individual Planning System:
Activities and Student Skills

Activity	Student Skills
Orientation	Use well their educational opportunities in school
Educational Planning	Plan/prepare for personally satisfying lives
Preregistration*	Make wise choices
Registration*	Manage change successfully
Dissemination and interpretation of standardized test results	Understand/respect themselves
Career/vocational planning	Plan/prepare for personally satisfying/ socially useful lives
Application of other skills taught in guidance curriculum	(As identified through local needs assessment)

*Overlaps with system support.

around group activities. The group activities will need to be designed to assist individuals to develop personalized plans and should provide for one-to-one assistance as follow-up.

Responsive Services

For responsive services, identify the topics that students, their teachers, and parents present most frequently so that a systematic means for attending to them can be established. What problems interfere most often with the students' personal, social, career or educational development? How many students need counseling, consulting, or referral? What percentage need preventive help, small group counseling or brief family interventions? What percentage need remedial help, one-to-one counseling or referral? Which parents, teachers, and administrators need consulting help?

In the Northside project, a subcommittee of the guidance steering committee asked the Northside Independent School District counselors to list the topics they found themselves responding to over the course of the year. The steering committee established priorities for the counselors' attention to these topics from the school district's point of view. Again, each of these topics is related to the competencies the counselors strive to help students master. Clarifying this relationship from the outset assists counselors to specify appropriate student objectives for their counseling activities. The list of topics, the grade levels at which they were identified, and their priorities are presented in Figure 5-8 (Henderson, 1987).

Figure 5–8
Responsive Services: Topics, Skills, and Priorities

Grade Levels	Recurrent Topics	Skills
K–12	1. Academic failure	Use well their educational opportunities in school
K–12	2. Child abuse	Behave responsibly in the family
K–12	3. Divorce/single parents	Behave responsibly in the family
K–12	4. Grief/death and dying/loss	Manage change successfully
MS/HS	5. Suicide threats	Understand and respect themselves; solve problems
MS/HS	6. Sexuality issues such as appropriate dating behavior and wise date selection; pregnancy; VD	Understand and respect themselves; solve problems
K–12	7. Tardiness/absences/truancy/school phobia/dropping out	Use well their educational opportunities; plan and prepare for personally satisfying and socially useful lives
K–12	8. Discipline/behavior problems	School-related: behave responsibly in school;
K–12	9. Peer problems	Understand/respect themselves/others
K–12	10. Alcohol/drug/inhalant abuse	Understand and respect themselves
K–12	11. Family situations	Behave responsibly in the family
K–12	12. Information seekers	(Varies with different information needs)
K–12	13. Application of other skills taught in guidance (1) academic problems (2) behavior problems (3) social problems	Solve problems

The information was surprising in two ways: First, there were not that many topics—12 in all, and, second, there was much similarity between the lists the elementary and the secondary counselors submitted. These two factors made the job of becoming better at helping students handle their problems more manageable. Inservice training could be focused on these issues. Exemplary practices could be developed and shared. Northside counselors feel that one of the side-benefits of this massive redesigning effort has been learning that there is not as much of a difference between the programs at the three levels—elementary, middle, and high—as they had believed. The programs are shaped differently, but students' needs are similar and counselors' skills and interests are similar.

System Support

Providing the detail to describe and define system support divides this component in two parts. One part defines the *support* that the guidance program needs *from* the system. The other part defines the *support* that the guidance program provides *to* other programs, such as elementary and secondary education, special, gifted, vocational, and compensatory education, and the testing program.

The level of *support* needed for the guidance program *from* the system needs clarification. The various activities counselors participate in require policies and administrative procedures, staff and program development opportunities, reasonable levels of budget provisions, adequate facilities and equipment, appropriate staff allocations to implement the desired program, and public relations support. At this stage these requirements may be more of a "wish list" than a statement of realistic choices, but later when specific implementation plans are made, constraints are considered. These items are discussed more fully in chapter 6 because many are keys to the actual implementation of the newly conceptualized program.

The first step in establishing the desired or needed *support* from the guidance program *to* the other programs is to develop the list of major activities that the guidance staff participates in—if this has not already been accomplished in the assessment of your current program. The second step is to make recommendations as to which of these tasks are appropriate for counselors to do by asking the question: Is a master's degree in guidance and counseling needed to accomplish this task? If the answer is no, then it becomes the responsibility of the counselors or the school-community advisory committee to make recommendations as to what other departments are served by and thus are responsible for the tasks. Considering these factors at this time will help later as you consider ways to handle activities that need to be displaced. This concept and the issues involved are discussed more fully in chapter 7. Priorities for possible displacements, however, can be suggested at this point. Figure 5–9 (Northside, 1986) displays the order of priority established by Northside ISD for counselor support to other programs. It is based on the lists originally generated in the assessment of the current program; that is, it ranks what the counselors were then doing and is not a statement of what they should do. In theory, displacements should start with the activities listed at the bottom and continue until the nonguidance tasks are either displaced completely, shared equitably, or streamlined.

Figure 5-9

System Support: Programs and Priorities

Elementary	Middle	High
1. Consult with staff and parents	1. Consult with staff and parents	1. Consult with staff and parents
2. Student referrals	2. Preregistration	2. Preregistration
3. Test administration and interpretation to staff	3. Test interpretation to staff	3. Test interpretation to staff
4. School climate	4. Student referrals	4. Staff development
5. Staff development	5. School climate	5. School climate
6. Special education	6. New student registration	6. Curriculum planning
7. Gifted education	7. Record keeping	7. New student registration
8. Preregistration	8. Referrals to special education	8. Record keeping
9. Discipline management	9. Curriculum planning	9. Schedule changes
10. Curriculum planning	10. Schedule changes	10. Student referrals
11. Compensatory programs	11. Master schedule development	11. Admission, review, dismissal committee meetings
12. Accreditation	12. Vocational education	12. Vocational education
	13. Attendance/discipline	13. Other special programs
	14. Other special programs	14. Test administration
	15. Test administration	15. Discipline management

The Decision-Making Process

As you have gathered in reading the above sections, providing the detail to describe your desired program design is no small task. Again, the resources you use in this task will vary depending on the program redesign mechanism you are using. We recommend that you use the counselors from the steering committee to do or lead the bulk of this work. The same principle applies here as in earlier steps: The more involved more counselors are, the smoother the needed transitions will be. In any case, leader counselors need to ensure that the recommendations made are supported by the steering committee. The committee needs to assist in making the hard decisions, such as the priorities for displacing unwanted system support activities; but in many cases they need only to be educated as to what the priorities are that will become internal operating rules for the guidance department, such as determining who else on a campus can count the test booklets after administering standardized tests.

You need to be aware of topics that are of particular importance to the non-counselors on the steering committee and attend to these appropriately; for example, your high school principals might be attached to the traditional conferences held with individual 12th graders as to their post-high school plans. You need to make the effort to ensure that they understand the time these conferences take relative to the benefit in terms of student outcomes achieved. Any decision that will result in changing the shape of a major activity needs to be carefully considered by the committee. A helpful rule of thumb might be that if one committee member wants to discuss an issue, you better give it fair hearing. Even if none of the other committee members are particularly interested in the discussion, there will be others outside the committee that hold that position as well, and ultimately that discussion will recur.

As an agenda guide, you need to discuss each of the above topics—from selecting basic program structure to making recommendations regarding the levels of support needed by the guidance program—in separate meetings. The group will still be struggling to understand the basic concepts, thus making the necessary decisions is not easy. Allowing them to focus on one topic area at a time helps you in the long run, although it may extend the time you take on this step. As it can take up to a year to assess your current program, it can take a year to select your desired program design. That design, however, as stated earlier, becomes the goal statement for everything that follows, so it must be done thoroughly and with sufficient deliberation (argument) to ensure support as you move into implementation.

Step 7:   Write Down and Distribute the Description of the Desired Program

Having established the design of the desired program, the last task is to put in writing all the decisions you have made. If you are the leader of the program improvement efforts, this task is yours alone. As with any written publication, the document must portray a cohesive whole, have a logical sequence, and be written in a consistent and concise style; thus, one writer is mandatory. As stated earlier, the written description depicts the basic structure that you have decided on and becomes the working document for you and your staff henceforth. It replaces the former guidance program handbook or plan.

We recommend the write-up contain at least five parts: the structural components, the position guides, the program components, the recommended design/ resource allocations for the program, and appendices.

The *structural components* section includes the statements that express the philosophical basis of your program. The final versions of the rationale, the assumptions, and the program definition are included. In addition, the list of student competencies that are to be developed through the guidance program are presented. Listing the specific grade-level outcomes is probably too lengthy for this section of the document, but these may be listed fully in the appendices.

The second section of the program description document includes the *position guides* developed to describe the various jobs guidance program staff perform. These guides are not only for the elementary, middle/junior, and senior high school counselors, but also for any counselor specialists you have in your school/ district such as vocational, special, or compensatory education funded counselors, and for head counselors. Job descriptions also should be included for other staff members who have been identified as having roles integral to the delivery of the guidance program. Finally, if you are using or plan to use community volunteers, their positions also should be described here.

The third section includes the more detailed descriptions of the *program components*. It includes the list of strands in the guidance curriculum, the major activities that make up the individual planning system, the recurrent topics that are the focus of the responsive services component, and the specific activities identified in system support. Also included in these subsections are the priorities established, the recommended mode of delivery for each component (i.e., if small group counseling has been suggested as the preferred mode for the responsive services component, if classroom-sized groups have been defined as preferred for guidance curriculum, and so on), the recommended allocation of resources to this component (especially that of the school counselors' time), and statements of expectations regarding evaluation of the overall components' impact on students, each activity's effectiveness, and the competencies utilized by the professional staff.

The final section of the write-up contains detail about the recommended *design/ resource allocations* for the program. These statements describe the appropriate balance among the four components, the priorities for the clients to be served, and the competencies to be sought. This section presents numerically what the program *should* look like to be considered comprehensive and well balanced. For example, in addition to the priority skills ranking (see Figure 5–5), Northside

ISD stated the desired allocation of the counselors' time in terms of the best ways to use the student school day (see Figure 5–10—Northside, 1986), and in terms of the time spent in serving their various clients (see Figure 5–11— Northside, 1986). The recommended days per year and hours per day per component have provided guidelines for counselors as they plan their weeks, months, and year, and have helped program monitors understand in a tangible way what is desired for the program to be considered effective. Finally, the statements of priorities are used most heavily in the next step, planning the transition to the comprehensive guidance program.

After you have written the program description and have had it typed and printed, you need to have the steering committee or the school-community advisory committee, the upper-echelon administrators, and the counselors review it in detail. We suggest that you view this as the last chance for input before complete, final adoption. For this final review you need to use strategies that will assure you that everyone has read and considered the document. With the steering committee, this might mean one meeting spent discussing the overall product of their labors.

Each counseling staff member must be held accountable for reading the document and must be provided an opportunity to discuss it. A strategy used successfully with counselors has been to schedule an inservice education day during which the counselors from the steering committee have explained each of the sections, particularly those describing the four program components. If you then prepare an agenda for discussion and train the head secondary and elementary counselors in its use, you provide a means for counselors to consider the full scope and depth of the program design. With the discussion agenda in everyone's hands, small groups of counselors can be asked to consider the major tenets of each section of the document and to voice support or disagreement with each concept. Specific items of confusion or concern can be identified at this time.

The final revision of the document needs to be completed and presented to the school district board of education for adoption. In some districts board members read these documents in toto and then ratify them. In others, members are presented an overview of the program and priorities, and are then provided copies for review at their discretion. In yet other districts, board members are satisfied with a presentation and the knowledge that the documents are available should they choose to review them.

Finally, complete distribution to relevant parties needs to be made. At minimum, every counselor needs to have a copy of the document, as does every school principal. Other administrators need copies on a "need to know" basis; for example, if you are using vocational funds to support part of your guidance program, then your district's vocational director needs a copy. You may also wish to consider publishing sections of the document for those who need only portions of it; for example, the personnel department must have copies of the

Figure 5–10
Desired Percentages for Allocation of Counselors' Time During Student School Days

Curriculum	Elementary	40% 2½ hrs. per day 73 days per year	High School	25% 1½ hrs. per day 44 days per year
	Middle school	30% 1¾ hrs. per day 51 days per year	Vocational	25% 1½ hrs. per day 44 days per year
Individual Planning	Elementary	25% 1½ hrs. per day 44 days per year	High school	30% 1¾ hrs. per day 51 days per year
	Middle school	30% 1¾ hrs. per day 51 days per year	Vocational	30% 1¾ hrs. per day 51 days per year
Responsive Services	Elementary	25% 1½ hrs. per day 44 days per year	High school	30% 1¾ hrs. per day 51 days per year
	Middle school	25% 1½ hrs. per day 44 days per year	Vocational	20% 1½ hrs. per day 35 days per year
System Support	Elementary	10% 30 min. per day 14 days per year	High school	15% 1 hr. per day 29 days per year
	Middle school	15% 1 hr. per day 29 days per year	Vocational	25% 1½ hrs. per day 44 days per year

Note: Based on a 6-hr. student day, 175-day student year. Figures are per counselor.

Figure 5–11
Desired Percentages for Allocation of Counselors' Time By Client

	ES	MS	HS
I. Students			
A. Developmental			
1. Guidance			
a. Group	40	30	30
b. Individual			
2. Testing			
B. Preventive	15	15	15
C. Remedial	10	12	15
TOTAL	65	57	60
II. Adults			
A. District administration	5	5	5
B. School staff	15	18	15
1. Principals			
2. Regular teachers			
3. Counselors			
4. Special ed.			
5. Other			
C. Parents	12	15	10
D. Outside agencies	2	3	5
E. Community	1	2	5
TOTAL	35	43	40

position guides, the instructional staff will want copies of the curriculum-related sections, and so forth.

Concluding Thoughts

At this point, the blueprint for your new program is drawn; the vision of what you want is depicted in concrete terms. The steering committee members and the counselors are apt to think (again) that the work is done. However, in terms of the improvement process of the guidance program, you have established only the objectives to be accomplished. What remains is planning the transition to the desired program and its actual implementation. Thus, as you distribute the program description, you must at the same time be prepared to outline the next steps in the program development efforts. The momentum that has been generated for change must now be channeled toward making plans and implementing changes systematically. The details of how to accomplish these phases of the program improvement process are provided in chapters 6 and 7.

References

Castetter, W.B. (1981). *The personnel function in educational administration*. New York: Macmillan.

Hargens, M., & Gysbers, N.C. (1984). How to remodel your guidance program while living in it: A case study. *School Counselor, 32*, 119–125.

Henderson, P.H. (1987). A comprehensive school guidance program at work. *TACD Journal, 15*, 25–37.

The National PTA and March of Dimes. (1986). *Parenting: The underdeveloped skill*. Chicago: Author.

National School Boards Association. (1986). *Resolution on guidance and counseling (4.1.26)*. Alexandria, VA: Author.

Northside Independent School District. (1986). *Comprehensive guidance program framework*. San Antonio, TX: Author.

CHAPTER 6

PLANNING THE TRANSITION TO A COMPREHENSIVE GUIDANCE PROGRAM

Chapter 5 described the steps and issues involved in delineating the design for a comprehensive guidance program. Delineating the design is an important phase of the change process because it describes and specifies the directions for change that will be required to install a comprehensive guidance program. Unfortunately, some administrators who wish to make program changes stop after the designing phase. They conclude, wrongly, that if directions for the desired changes are clear, the desired changes will occur. We believe, however, that for the desired changes to occur, those changes need to be planned. Planning how you will make the transition to a comprehensive guidance program is vital.

In addition, careful planning is required because of the complexity of actually implementing the program. Although some implementation tasks are completed at the district level, much of the actual program implementation occurs at the building level. Thus, two levels of planning are required: planning for district level as well as for building level implementation. As these two levels of planning occur, remember that they interact. Some building changes cannot be made without district changes occurring first. Also, some district changes cannot be made without building level initiatives preceding them. In general, the district initiates policy changes that building personnel can implement. Sometimes, however, building level tryouts of new activities and procedures are required before district policies can be established.

Chapter 6 describes in detail four steps involved in planning the transition to a comprehensive guidance program.

Step 1: Specify changes;
Step 2: Plan your program improvements;
Step 3: Begin building-level program improvement efforts; and
Step 4: Expand your leadership base.

Step 1 involves making decisions about the specific changes that are required. The desired program description (chapter 5) serves as a template to lay over the top of your current program so that similarities and differences can be seen. What should be adopted directly from the comprehensive program model? What current activities should be maintained? What components of the program model not presently available need to be created to fill gaps in the current program? Your answers to these questions will provide the information you need to plan your program improvements in step 2. If you are working in a large school district, you will need to make plans to implement the program at the building as well as the district level; thus, step 3 details developing plans for building-level program improvement. In step 4, if you are the director of the program, we encourage you to expand your leadership base to include, in a small system, all the counselors, or in a larger system, more of the counselor leaders. As you prepare for implementation, the more ''grass roots'' leaders you have available, the more effective your transition will be. You also will have the benefit of their advice and counsel in making the transition you are planning workable in this phase of remodeling and revitalizing your guidance program.

Step 1: Specify Changes

The first step in planning the transition to a comprehensive program entails specifying the needed changes. To do this you will need to compare and contrast your current program with the program you desire, establish goals for change, and identify ways to bring the changes about. When you have completed this step, you will have specified the changes that are wanted and will be ready to begin the process of making or helping others make the required changes.

Compare and Contrast Your Current Program With Your Desired Program

Having studied your current program and having established a design for the program you want, you have the information you need to compare and contrast the two. The goal is to identify places where the programs overlap, but, even more important, where there are gaps that may need to be filled. You will also identify some places where the design of the current program goes beyond the design that is desired. You will be asking and answering the question: Is there a discrepancy between what you want your guidance program to accomplish and what your guidance program is accomplishing currently?

We advise you to conduct this discrepancy analysis from your data for both the current program and the desired program. If you have followed our suggestions in chapter 4, you have information about student competencies, about resource allocation (particularly the appropriation of counselors' time and talents), about the makeup of the program components and the balance of resources applied to them, and about the clients served. Careful analysis of this information provides you the data you need to specify needed changes.

Northside Independent School District used this process. Here is what was done. Some of the data gathered regarding the design of its current program were displayed in chapter 4 (see Figure 4–6). Similar information was presented from the design for the desired program in chapter 5 (see Figure 5–2). In Figure 6–1 these data are presented side by side. The information is presented in terms of percentages of counselors' time that is/should be spent in delivery of the four program components.

In terms of the program components, the discrepancy analysis between what is and what should be yielded the following information:

Compares favorably (appropriate amount of time spent):
  Individual planning: middle, high
  Responsive services: elementary, high
Gaps (too little time spent):
  Guidance curriculum: elementary, middle, high
Spillovers (too much time spent):
  Individual planning: elementary
  Responsive services: middle
  System support: elementary, middle, high

Figure 6–1
Northside Independent School District
Appropriation of Counselors' Time: Percentage/Program Component

	Current	Desired
Guidance curriculum		
Elementary	7	40
Middle	8	30
High	5	25
Individual planning		
Elementary	37	25
Middle	29	30
High	27	30
Responsive services		
Elementary	28	25
Middle	31	25
High	28	30
System support		
Elementary	20	10
Middle	32	15
High	40	15

In addition to analyzing the hard data collected in the current program assessment, an analysis of the more subjective data gathered is useful too. In gathering the perceptions of the current program, some themes probably emerged. Having now agreed upon what is wanted from your desired program, other people's opinions about what was good and what was missing from the current program will give you more information upon which to base your decisions for change. The subjective information regarding outcomes sought, clients served, and resources used also needs to be analyzed as to how your current program compares and contrasts with the desired program. It is useful to categorize your analysis in the same manner as you did your analysis of hard data: "compares favorably," "gaps," and "spillovers." For example, it might be that most people surveyed felt that the high school guidance program served the college-bound students adequately, did not serve the "average" students sufficiently, and invested too much time in serving individual students with difficult personal problems; the first is a subjectively stated favorable comparison, the second identifies a gap, and the third, a spillover from the desired design.

You also need to study the degree of congruence between your objective and subjective data in relationship to the improved program you envision. The ideal is for the hard data and subjective data to be as congruent as possible and for your current and desired programs to match for each component of the program, the clients served, counselors' functions, and so on. If your objective and subjective data are congruent but the two designs do not match, you have descriptive information from the subjective data upon which to base your recommendations for change. For example, if your objective data tell you that counselors spend too much time in system support and the program's users feel that the counselors function too much like clerks, you have a rationale to support the recommendation to decrease the time spent in the system support component. If your objective data and subjective data are not congruent but the two program designs match, you have identified a need for public relations efforts. For example, if your counselors *are* spending an appropriate amount of time responding to students with personal problems but your consumers do not perceive this, you know you need to educate your consumers. At the same time, the subjective data might alert you to the reality that the counselors are, for example, responding to students with personal problems on a one-to-one basis, but that more group work is desirable so that more students with problems could be served.

If your objective data and subjective data are not congruent in an area where the current and desired programs do not match, then the decisions you make depend on whether the subjective data represent a favorable or unfavorable opinion and on whether the mismatch in program design is a gap or an overflow. If the subjective data about the current program are favorable, our advice is to leave well enough alone until you have begun to implement your desired program. If the subjective data represent the opinion that you are not doing something that

proportionate amount of time, you need to educate the opinion
can implement needed changes. For example, if high school
gh school counselors are not spending enough time changing
current assessment data tell you they are, you need to help
out the disproportionate investment of valuable talent in an
t use counselors' education and talents to effect appropriate
principals need assistance to see the problem. Counselors
data to their principals because they have examples and
it will put life and meaning into the data.

itively or subjectively, the places where your current pro-
ly with the desired program tells you and the staff what
t program. That provides a morale booster for the staff,
ly quite anxious about ongoing or proposed changes. It
good foundation upon which to build.

in the design of your current program vis-à-vis the desired
ain points to two kinds of changes that may need to be made. The gaps either mean you are simply not doing enough of what is desired or not doing it at all. For example, in the Northside discrepancy analysis, there was a 20% gap in the use of the guidance curriculum component at the high school level, a 22% gap at the middle school level, and a 33% gap at the elementary school level. Thus, a change recommendation was to *augment* the current guidance curriculum efforts. In the same district's study of counselors' use of their special knowledge and skills, it was learned that no time was spent by middle school counselors at most schools in career guidance activities. Thus career guidance activities might be a new dimension to be *added* to the program at those middle schools.

Identifying where the design of your current program goes beyond that of the desired program also points to two kinds of potential changes. You may be doing too much of what is desirable, or you may be doing something that is seen as inappropriate for the guidance program or a waste of counselors' time and talent. For example, in the Northside analysis—as in that of most schools and districts with which we have worked—much more time than was considered desirable was being spent in support of other programs (one part of the system support component). For others to really understand what this means, you may need to go beyond the current assessment data and gather more specific data to help bring the real problems and issues into focus. In Northside another survey was conducted in addition to the current assessment to further specify what system support tasks counselors actually were doing. In the analysis of that data it was found that whereas some tasks were appropriate for counselors—test result interpretation, behavioral observations of students being considered for special education referral—they were absorbing too much time. Other tasks, however, were inappropriate for counselors—counting test booklets, making logistical arrangements for annual admission, review, and dismissal committee meetings for special education students. Thus, recommendations regarding the first set of tasks involved ideas for *streamlining* the counselors' involvement (keeping them involved but reducing time spent); recommendations regarding the second set involved *displacement*. Specific strategies for augmenting, adding, streamlining, and displacement will be discussed in chapter 7.

Establish Goals for Change

Having clearly identified discrepancies between the current program and the desired program, you are ready to draw conclusions. This entails studying each set of discrepancy data and identifying the gaps and spillovers. The following conclusions from the Northside study were drawn from contrasting current and desired program designs:

Program Design

- Too little time is spent in curriculum at all three levels.
- Too much time is spent in individual planning at elementary level.
- Too much time is spent in responsive services at the middle school level.
- Too much time is spent in system support at all three levels.

The guidance program leader develops the list of conclusions. This list needs to be presented to the steering and the school-community advisory committees, the counselors, and other administrators to enable them to see the specific problems that need to be addressed. It is from this list of conclusions that recommendations for change are drawn.

Recommendations for change are restatements of the data-based conclusions into "should" statements. Related to the example above, recommendations for change from Northside are presented in Figure 6–2.

Another step in the process is to assign priorities to the recommendations. Some school districts with whom we have worked have chosen to do this by identifying changes that "need" to be made and those that they "want" to make. Whether you choose to state them as needs and wants or whether you list all of them in order of priority is up to you. Because the process we have outlined generates rather lengthy lists of recommendations for change, listing changes in priority order makes the list more manageable.

Identify Ways to Effect the Changes

Now that the issues have been identified through discrepancy analysis and explicit recommendations for changes have been made, all staff and others involved in the program development effort need to identify ways to attain the recommendations and to make the changes. We recommend that those involved—the steering committee, the school-community advisory committee, the counselors, the administrators, and other staff—brainstorm ways to make the

Figure 6–2
Guidance Program Change Goals

In order to attain the desired comprehensive, balanced guidance program for Northside ISD, it is recommended that counselors and administrators work together to:

at the elementary level:
- increase the time spent by counselors in curriculum
- decrease the time spent by counselors in individual planning
- decrease the time spent by counselors in system support

at the middle school level:
- increase the time spent by counselors in curriculum
- decrease the time spent by counselors in responsive services
- decrease the time spent by counselors in system support

at the high school level:
- increase the time spent by counselors in curriculum
- decrease the time spent by counselors in system support

---

changes. It is best to involve everyone who will be affected by the changes; this process allows them to sense the feasibility of the changes and sets their thoughts in motion as to how recommendations might be carried out.

The steering committee should be the first to do this—preferably at the same meeting where the recommendations for the changes are developed—as a reality check. It allows committee members to consider whether the recommendations they are making are feasible. The steering committee also ought to help design the process for presenting the change recommendations and soliciting ideas about how to make the changes from the appropriate staff. If your building/system is large enough, it is advisable to use the steering committee members to conduct the brainstorming meetings with the rest of the staff. These meetings ought to include enough people so that true brainstorming can occur, that is, that many ideas can be thrown onto the table for further consideration.

In the case of Northside, the counselors and administrators from the steering committee conducted meetings with each of the three different principal groups: elementary, middle, and high school. The counselors conducted the meetings with the other counselors. Each group was presented with the discrepancy information relevant to their own level and were guided through the brainstorming process for each discrepancy and resultant recommendation. They responded to the question, ''How could this be done?'' For example: How could counselors spend more time in the guidance curriculum component? How could they spend less time in the system support component? The ideas generated for increasing high school guidance staff time spent in guidance curriculum are provided in

Figure 6–3. Complete lists of ideas generated in the Northside meetings on these two topics for each of the school levels are included in Appendix E.

The data from separate meetings such as these can then be aggregated and presented to the steering or school-community advisory committee to do the second half of the brainstorming process—applying judgments to the myriad suggestions. The committee, then, draws from these ideas to develop the list of items that need to be done to bring about the desired changes. The groups who brainstormed the suggestions need to see the notes from their various meetings so that they know their ideas were heard and are being considered. These lists also are useful in the future when specific changes are being implemented.

Thus, as you conclude this step, you have a clear and concrete picture of how your current program needs to change. You have formulated recommendations for the changes you are getting ready to implement, so that you will know you have achieved what you want when you get there. And, you have begun to identify ways to effect the desired changes. You are now ready to plan your program improvements.

Figure 6–3
Northside Independent School District
Results of Brainstorming Ways to Reduce Discrepancies between the Current and the Desired Guidance Program

STEERING COMMITTEE IDEAS:

High School Level

To increase time spent in curriculum
- work with groups (vs. individuals) to disseminate information, e.g., junior and senior credit checks, test score interpretation
- become involved with clubs, organizations, and other extracurricular activities, through assignment if necessary
- increase time spent in group activities
- set yearly calendar that will facilitate counselor's keeping on task for group activities
- get into the classroom—be a visible part of the educational team

All Levels

To increase time spent in curriculum
- define program expectations, monitor implementation
- develop curriculum resources
- provide staff development for counselors
- communicate program to and enlist support of administration and faculty
- design systematic delivery system (calendar, timeline, individual vs. group)

Figure 6–3, *continued*

HIGH SCHOOL PRINCIPALS' IDEAS
To increase time spent in curriculum—
times to conduct curriculum activities:

- advisories
- 4th period study hall
- on-campus suspension class
- coverage for teachers at conventions
- club schedule
- identify and work with classes that have needs, e.g., lower level academic classes
- different methods of assigning counselors to case load/job responsibilities
- priority: students on campus now, not for their future
- inservice for teachers on such topics as behavior management, listening skills
- planned for the year, consistent
- calendar

HIGH SCHOOL COUNSELORS' IDEAS
To increase time spent in curriculum

- group guidance to teach decision-making skills, self-esteem
- do away with parent notes on schedule changes
- more inservice with teachers, e.g., with freshmen teachers to help freshmen become successfully involved in school
- more time in 9th-grade advisories
- freshmen advisory: guidance in the first month of school; orientation to high school, study skills, attendance, 4-year plan revision, involvement
- 9th graders' orientation to Career Center
- more time interpreting OVIS
- need facilities to do group guidance
- more use of advisory to have small groups with all students
- "brown bag" sessions
- make "official time" for counselors to go into classrooms; ideas: restructure school day periodically, more faculty involvement with credits, clubs, etc. Principals' verbal support, sell ideas to key teachers or department heads
- counselors need planning time
- priorities: feeling good about themselves, decision-making and study skills

Step 2: Plan Your Program Improvements

At the district level, the steering committee or the school-community advisory committee and the guidance program leader should devise a master plan of action for accomplishing the district-level tasks. A list of "tasks to do" can be developed from the suggestions resulting from the brainstorming sessions previously described. Then an action plan for accomplishing these recommendations needs to be written.

List What Needs to be Done to Implement Changes

From the various lists of ideas generated in the discrepancy analysis of the current and desired programs, the guidance program leader and the steering or school-community advisory committee needs to develop a list of "things to do" to facilitate the implementation of the comprehensive guidance program. The list should be an action-oriented list, not a list of vague wishes, and the actions should be feasible.

The list may be rather long. Districts we have worked with have generated a range of 25 to 40 items that needed to be done before complete implementation could become a reality. This does not mean that all tasks have to be accomplished before some changes can be made, but it does mean that policymakers have to be realistic about their expectations for the new program implementation. A partial list of such actions from Northside, to help you envision what it might take, is included in Figure 6–4.

As you can see, these are major tasks to accomplish. Also by scanning the list, you can see that there are categories of items: for example, those that relate to staff development, to resource development, and to product development. Other categories might be those that relate to policy development and program development. To ensure the completeness of your list, you may want to group the list by the categories of resources used in the original program assessment: human resources: talent, time, ratio, assignments; financial resources: budget, materials, equipment, facilities; political resources: policy, identification of program supporters. Grouping by categories will help you and the steering committee make the next set of decisions: What to do first.

Develop Your Master Plan

Needless to say, all of these "to do" activities cannot begin at once. Some depend on the accomplishment of others. Thus, the next step is to list the "to do" activities in the chronological order in which they are to be done. Chronology is guided by consideration of whether certain tasks are prerequisite to other tasks. Consider whether tasks are developmental or experimental, and whether they are feasible to do at this time or if they might be difficult to accomplish. If they are tied to other, larger processes—such as district budget development—they must be done at times relevant to those processes. A part of the Northside "Master Plan" is displayed in Figure 6–5. The first four items were related to the development of the district's budget for the next fiscal year and were also of top priority. The budget is submitted for consideration by the superintendent by May 1; thus the research work needed to be done in March and April. The *Framework* obviously needed to be finished before it could be presented to the board of education; the board needed to approve the program description before it could be presented to the counselors with authority.

Figure 6–4
Recommended "To Do's" To Accomplish the Comprehensive Guidance Program

Develop guidance program component guides;
Develop system for assisting local campuses to design their
  guidance programs;
Establish communication mechanisms;
Design relevant counselor staff development program;
Design relevant counselor evaluation system;
Provide program development time for counselors;
Establish campus departmental budgets for guidance department;
Assess costs associated with implementation of program and
  develop an appropriate budget (district);
Review and make recommendations to ensure adequacy of
  guidance facilities;
Modify counselor staffing formulas as recommended;
Hire technical assistants at secondary schools;
Review and recommend extended contracts for counselors;
Establish parameters for counselor access to students;
Develop a public relations plan;
Explore use of other-than-local funding sources; and
Develop job descriptions for guidance department clerical staff.

Figure 6–5
Master Plan for Implementation of NISD's Comprehensive Guidance Program
(In chronological/priority order)

Task	Deadline
Make recommendations regarding extended contracts	3/25/85
Make recommendations regarding counselors' preference lowered caseload v. technical assistant	3/28/85
Make recommendations regarding priorities for implementing lowered caseloads: elementary, middle, high	3/28/85
Send memos to principals regarding campus guidance department budgets	4/5/85
Develop counselors' position guides for inclusion in *Framework*	5/1/85
Complete *Framework*; prepare for board presentation	6/1/85
Plan *Guide* development process	5/1/85
Seek approval/funding	5/15/85
Conduct leadership training	6/30/85
Develop recommendations for minimum standards for facilities/equipment for principals	8/1/85
Plan/implement inservice sessions for counselors on minimum expectations (*Framework*)	8/30/85

Plans of action to accomplish the major tasks also might need to be developed to facilitate the efficiency of those responsible. A plan of action includes several parts: identification of the tasks to be done, the order in which they must be done, the person(s) to do them, the time for accomplishing them, and a statement of how you will know they have been done—identification of the end-product or result. Using one example from the Northside ''Master Plan,'' a sample plan of action format is presented in Figure 6–6.

Whatever format you use, you need to specify what needs to be done in what order and by whom. If you are the guidance program leader, this gives you your job-related mandates for continuing the project you have been working on. You also have to identify the areas where the members of the steering committee can help you and where you and the counselors are on your own.

Step 3: Begin Building-Level Program Improvement Efforts

At this point the guidance program improvement project becomes a two-tiered one. Up to now you have been working from the frame of reference of the school system. Building-level counselors and administrators have been involved more or less on a voluntary basis, except for responding to the project's data-gathering needs. If you have followed our advice, many of the counselors and some administrators have been involved in the work groups. Those counselors who envision the new program as the wave of the future or the answer to their dreams have probably already experimented with new activities.

When the statement of the district's minimum expectations for the guidance program is adopted, responsibility shifts to the local school buildings in the district; their programs must be changed to meet these minimum expectations or go beyond them. What you should have been saying to the building-level counselors and administrators all along, as they raised the usual concerns regarding district mandates, is that there will be room for tailoring the desired program to local community needs. It is at this time that that statement becomes the challenge. The counselor(s) and administrator(s) in each building must redesign their program to better align it with the district program and also to ensure meeting their students' and local communities' highest priority needs.

Assist Building Staff to Prepare for Change

If you are the guidance program leader, you will need to assist the staff as they face this challenge. They need help to internalize the desired comprehensive guidance program as described. They need to be familiar with the planning model they will be asked to follow. They need to assess their current program relative to the district model and to identify local needs and establish priorities for meeting those needs. Finally, they need to design the desired program for the building based on the desired district model. Sound familiar? It *is* the same

Figure 6–6
Plan of Action

Major Task	Enabling Tasks	Person Responsible	Date to be Completed	Resources Needed	Comment
Make recommendations regarding extended contracts	1) Develop questionnaire	1) Director of guidance	1) March 1	None additional	
	2) "Train" steering committee counselors and principals to conduct survey with cnslrs/prins using questionnaire	2) Director of guidance	2) March 5		
	3) Place on meeting agendas	3) Steering committee, Principals, & Counselors	3) March 5		
	4) Make presentation; conduct surveys	4) Steering committee, Principals, & Counselors	4) March 6–13		
	5) Tally results by school level (Elem; MS; HS)	5) Director of guidance	5) March 20		
	6) Prepare report and make recommendations	6) Director of guidance	6) March 25		

process you have just been through at the district level. The basic difference is in the level of specificity, and of course, that difference depends on the size of the district.

At the campus level, each counselor needs to begin to think in personal terms, saying "*I* spend X hours a week in counseling," "*I* spend X hours a week in clerical tasks," and so on. "At the building level, the 20 students who are contemplating suicide and need responsive services are somewhere in *these* hallways." "At the building level, if a guidance activity is selected for third graders, *I* am the one who will or will not implement it." There is no longer room for "That's a good idea—for someone else" kind of thinking. Each counselor needs to become an instrument of change.

Understand the Desired Program Design and Description

It has probably taken you some time to reach this point—up to a year or more—so the counselors have had time to understand the concept of the *comprehensive program* and to know about the major impending changes—such as developmental guidance, small group counseling, and more emphasis on career development. The proper *balance* for the district program has been decided. Now, each counselor needs fully to understand the new program structure.

We recommend that, after a formal presentation and the distribution of the written comprehensive program description, small group discussions be held with the counselors to clarify any misconceptions, correct misinformation, and ensure as much as possible not only that they have read it, but also understood it. The most logical small groups should be used—a building staff, a cluster of elementary counselors, and so on. By "small groups" we mean 5 to 10. The guidance program leader needs to be present at as many of these discussions as feasible, because the shifting of focus to the building level in anticipation of moving from planning to implementation represents a milestone in the project.

The strategy mentioned in chapter 5 and used in Northside involved the use of a "discussion agenda." The director of guidance developed a form that identified key topics and issues addressed in the comprehensive guidance program guide. Head counselors were assigned to discuss the agenda with their staffs. The director explained the issue points and the rationale behind the choices made. The counselors were given 2 weeks to read the guide, write responses to the discussion agenda, and discuss these items in building staff meetings. Each head counselor wrote a summary of the building discussion; when the director came to the next staff meeting, those items became the focal point of the discussion. The director also collected the completed forms because several topics surfaced that needed to be addressed further. The summary information was discussed with all head counselors at one of their meetings. By the end of this process the counselors could legitimately be expected to know the district guidelines for the comprehensive guidance program.

As a final step, the counselors were asked to conduct a meeting with their building administrators to summarize the program description and to suggest what it might mean to the building program. Because the principals had already been made aware of the document by the director, this was the opportunity to enlist the building administrators' support for the development of the building plan.

Understand the Planning Model

The responsibility for developing the building plan belongs to the building staff. It is therefore important to ensure that building counselors understand the planning process and to establish mechanisms to facilitate it. At this point, we suggest that the counselors be educated about the steps in the planning process that you would like them to use. Again, depending on the size of the district, the planning model may not need much elucidation if most counselors have been involved in the development of the district plan, but if the district is large, at least one round of inservice education about the planning process may be required. Figure 6–7 displays the comprehensive planning model used by Northside.

In addition to benefiting from the experiences of the district as a whole, the building staffs have the benefit of the district's theoretical base as written in the rationale, assumptions, and definition. The district program description also portrays the model for the program structure and lists student competencies to be addressed in the program. Thus, the challenge to the building-level staff is to study how their current program compares and contrasts with the district's desired program, and to assess the needs of their students and the local community in terms of the broad parameters established for the district program.

We also recommend that the building counseling staff lead the guidance program development effort, but that they involve others as well. Representatives from the faculty, the student body, parents, the administration, and any other group of "significant others" should be involved. If you have a school-community advisory committee, use it. In fact, we recommend that the advisory committee continue functioning even after you have achieved the changes you are working for in order to give you continued advice and counsel. We believe that a program always benefits from advice and counsel from its constituents or collaborators, but remember that the guidance staff and appropriate administrators need to remain the decision makers of the implementation and management of the guidance program.

Begin Planning by Assessing Current Program Status

The "current status" study of the building program consists of the same steps needed in the district study. These were fully described in chapter 4. Most likely,

Figure 6–7
Guidance Department
Northside Independent School District
Building Planning Process

The purpose of the local planning effort is to provide a comprehensive and balanced program that is

- consistent with the district's minimum expectations;
- tailored to meet local needs; and
- such that principals and counselors can be held accountable for it.

The *Building Comprehensive Guidance Program Plan* is developed as a result of an assessment of local student, school, and community needs and an assessment of resources available to the building. The plan portrays how the resources will be applied to meet the priority needs of the program's clients' goals and how the effectiveness of the program will be evaluated.

The 12-step process is outlined below.* The forms for reporting the plan are provided by the district.

Phase I: Planning
Step 1: State the *theoretical basis* of the program. The district has expressed the philosophy of the program in the *Framework*. A campus may choose to augment the statement to reflect the campus philosophy.

Step 2: Specify the *program development* model. The district's "Guidance Program Development Project" and the "Building Planning Process" outlined herein reflect the model. The program is to be developed through the ongoing process of planning, designing, implementation, and evaluation.

Step 3: *Assess* the *needs* for assistance in achieving the outcomes desired for the students, teachers, staff, and parents as a result of program efforts. The desired student outcomes provide the basis for the needs assessment. The desired student outcomes are listed in the district's program *Framework*.

Step 4: Assess the *resources available* for use in guidance program implementation. Resources include the time, knowledge, and skills of the counselors and other guidance program and community personnel, as well as the activities and strategies used in the program components, materials, equipment, facilities, budget, and so on.

Step 5: Establish *program goals*. The goals state in general terms how the program resources will be applied in assisting students, teaching staff, and parents achieve the outcomes identified as most needed and most desired.

Figure 6–7, *continued*

Phase II: Designing

Step 6: Specify student and other client *performance objectives*. The objectives state specifically who will behave differently and how as a result of the program efforts. Client performance objectives are specified for each program component and by grade level.

Step 7: Select *program strategies*. There are a variety of strategies that can be used to assist clients in meeting the performance objectives. In this step specific activities are selected for implementation and the yearly *calendar* for activity implementation is set. Required and suggested activities for each component are described in the program component *Guides*.

Phase III: Implementation

Step 8: Develop a *plan of action* for implementing the program strategies. The tasks required to effect each strategy are detailed and assigned.

Step 9: *Develop staff*. If new or renewed knowledge or skills are needed to ensure effective implementation of the program strategies, they are attended to prior to/at this time. Staff development is a responsibility shared by the individual, the campus, and the district. If an individual needs professional development, he or she should pursue it. If several individuals on a campus or a number of individuals in the district need similar knowledge or skill development, the campus or the district, respectively, should provide the staff development opportunities.

Step 10: *Implement* the program strategies and *monitor* their effectiveness. Formative evaluation techniques are suggested in the program component *Guides*.

Phase IV: Evaluation

Step 11: Conduct *formative* and *summative evaluation*. Based on the evaluations of the strategies implemented, the campus guidance department assesses its effectiveness in accomplishing the goals established in Step 5 and its overall success in assisting clients reach the needed and desired outcomes identified in Step 3.

Step 12: *Communicate* evaluation *results* to campus and district administration and others as appropriate. These results form the basis for the next year's program plan as well.

---

*These steps are an adaptation of a program development model published by the American Institute for Research, Palo Alto, CA. (1978).

the building data are available from the original assessment, so at this time the task is not to collect the data, but to study them in light of the now-established desired program design. Building guidance staff members should be cognizant of their currently available resources and how they are used. You will recall that we discussed three kinds of resources: human, financial, and political. Human resources included not only the number of guidance program staff, but also the specialized talents of each, their case loads, assignments, and time available as well as the appropriation of that time to the various functions and activities of the program. Financial resources included budget, materials, equipment, and facilities. Political resources included policy support as well as support by individuals within the system and the community.

At this point, the guidance activities conducted in the current building program need to be arranged according to the comprehensive guidance program components, and the competencies that they assist students to attain need to be specified. A listing of clients the building program serves needs to be made, not by names of specific individuals, but by categories and by numbers; for example, it is important to know how many or what percentage of students in the building receive "preventive" or "remedial" assistance, how many or what percentage of faculty receive consultation services, how many parents have sought consultation or referral services, and so on. Every bit of concrete data that can be gathered regarding the current program needs to be assembled, so that as the building staff develops its plan for change, it is grounded solidly in reality. A premise here is that the design of the current guidance program had emerged in response to the most immediate and most visible student, teacher, and parent needs. Thus the current program provides an "informal" assessment of these needs from these perspectives.

Assess Perceived Student and Community Needs

Assess Perceived Student Needs. Some program planners do this task before any other step in the planning process. Although this assessment can be done first, we do not believe the results will be as useful as those of one done during this phase of the program improvement process. A major reason we recommend waiting until this phase is that it is not until now that you have identified the student competencies for your program. And, in the type of assessment we are proposing, student competency statements become, in effect, the needs assessment items. In fact, this part of the designing process could just as well be called an inventory of student competencies—an inventory of where students are in competency development and where they would like to be in their competency acquisition.

To illustrate how the competencies you have chosen can be converted to needs assessment items, examples are provided in Figure 6–8. From the competencies

Figure 6-8
Competencies as Needs Assessment Items

First grade	
Competency:	Students will describe how exercise and nutrition affect their mental health.
Needs assessment:	I can tell how exercise and eating habits make a difference in how I think, act, and feel.
Eighth grade	
Competency:	Students will analyze effective family relations, their importance, and how they are formed.
Needs assessment:	I can tell why good family relations are important and how they are formed.
Eleventh grade	
Competency:	Students will evaluate the need for flexibility in their roles and in their choices.
Needs assessment:	I can explain the need for flexibility in my roles and in my choices.

presented in chapter 3, we selected one competency from grade 1, one from grade 8, and one from grade 11.

The actual assessment can be done using a card-sort approach or a questionnaire format. The card-sort approach provides direct interaction with students, but it takes more time to administer and score. The questionnaire format is easier to administer and score, but it does not provide the direct contact with students some may desire. To show you what a needs assessment questionnaire using converted competencies looks like, we chose a section of one used for grades 10, 11, and 12. (See Figure 6–9). The section of the questionnaire we chose is on life-career planning competencies.

It is common to describe needs assessment as a way of determining the discrepancy between what exists and what is desired. If this practice is observed rigidly, only contemporary needs will be recognized, and the needs of the past, or those that already have been met, may be overlooked. When asked to respond to a needs statement, individuals would be justified in asking whether it makes a difference if the statement represents a need they feel is important but is being satisfied, or if it is a statement that represents an unmet need. For program planning, it is important to know the needs that are being met as well as the needs that deserve additional attention.

An additional means for considering met needs is to review the needs being met in the current program. It is likely that current program activities grew out of a prior informal or formal needs assessment. If students' evaluations of these

Figure 6–9
Life Career Planning

To fill out this questionnaire, students were asked to complete the following steps.

Step 1:   *Read each sentence carefully.* Each one describes things students are able to do in order to demonstrate learning in that particular area.

Now make a decision. Are you able to do what the sentence describes? Are you not able to do what the sentence describes?

Fill in the circle that shows what you think.

If you think you are able to do what the sentence describes . . .

fill in circle *a*   ⓐ   ⓑ | ⓒ

If you think you *are not* able to do what the sentence describes . . .

fill in circle *b*   ⓐ   ⓑ | ⓒ

Step 2:   *Choose the five sentences on each page that describe what you would really be interested in learning to do.* Some of the statements will really interest you and some will not. *In the second column (circles are lettered c), fill in the circle for each of the five statements that you feel you need to learn how to accomplish.*

For example, if you feel you would really be interested in learning to analyze how characteristics and abilities develop, you would mark as follows:

I CAN 1. describe and analyze how an individual's characteristics and abilities develop.

ⓐ   ⓑ | ⓒ

The statements below are about things you can do to show you are preparing yourself for the future and are able to make decisions about what you want to do in your life. Review your instruction sheet carefully. Then fill in the circle that shows what you think about that statement.

I CAN
1. evaluate the importance of having laws and contracts to protect producers.   ⓐ   ⓑ | ⓒ
2. provide examples of decisions I have made based on my attitudes and values.   ⓐ   ⓑ | ⓒ
3. analyze the decision-making process used by others.   ⓐ   ⓑ | ⓒ
4. distinguish between alternatives that involve varying degrees of risk.   ⓐ   ⓑ | ⓒ
5. evaluate the importance of setting realistic goals and working toward them.   ⓐ   ⓑ | ⓒ

Figure 6–9, *continued*

6. describe my rights and responsibilities as a producer.	ⓐ	ⓑ	ⓒ
7. explain and analyze how values affect my decisions, actions, and life styles.	ⓐ	ⓑ	ⓒ
8. identify decisions I have made and analyze how they will affect my future decisions.	ⓐ	ⓑ	ⓒ
9. analyze the consequences of decisions others make.	ⓐ	ⓑ	ⓒ
10. explain how my values, interests, and capabilities have changed and are changing.	ⓐ	ⓑ	ⓒ
11. speculate what my rights and obligations might be as a producer in the future.	ⓐ	ⓑ	ⓒ
12. summarize the importance of understanding my attitudes and values and how they affect my life.	ⓐ	ⓑ	ⓒ
13. use the decision-making process when making a decision.	ⓐ	ⓑ	ⓒ
14. provide examples and evaluate my present ability to generate alternatives, gather information, and assess the consequences in the decisions I make.	ⓐ	ⓑ	ⓒ
15. assess my ability to achieve past goals and integrate this knowledge for the future.	ⓐ	ⓑ	ⓒ

activities indicate that they are valuable, then it is a good assumption that they are meeting a relatively important need.

The opportunity to respond to a relevant sampling of needs is another important point. Simply stated, How can a need be identified if no one presents the statement? Limited coverage, insignificant choices, or redundancy may distort a needs survey. We recommend that you develop your own needs assessment survey from the list of competencies you have established. However, because some states (for example, Missouri) have developed statewide needs assessment surveys (Missouri Department of Elementary and Secondary Education, 1981), check to see if your state has one relevant to your school district and community.

If your district is similar to those with which we have worked, more needs (competencies) will be identified than the program resources can provide for; thus, one purpose of a needs assessment is to determine priorities for needs (competencies). Also, whereas there will be common needs (competencies) across a school district, there also may be differences as dictated by the needs of particular buildings in a district. If you are uneasy about or inexperienced in developing such surveys, you may find it advantageous to use an adopt-adapt strategy; that is—selecting and modifying needs statements from existing instruments rather than constructing new ones. Be sure, however, to include a needs statement for each competency for which your program is accepting responsibility.

A final point to keep in mind is whose perceptions of students' needs should be assessed. The answer is those of anyone involved in the educational process, including those receiving education. This includes students, educators, parents, community members, employers, and graduates.

Students: This group should receive top priority in any needs assessment. Who knows more about students than students? Students can tell you what they need as a group and as individuals. They will also let you know whether or not the current program is meeting their needs.

Educators: Assessing this group will give you their perceptions of student needs as well as perceptions of their own needs.

Parents: This group will help you identify what they feel their children should learn from school experiences. Including them in the needs-assessment process offers them an opportunity for involvement in planning the guidance program. As a result of their personal involvement they may be more willing to offer their support.

Community members: Included in this group are individuals who are not employers; yet, they support the school financially. Information from this group may give a somewhat different perspective to the information gained from an assessment of parents.

Employers: Those who are responsible for hiring graduates of your school system or for hiring students still in school have definite ideas about the outcomes of education they expect. Including employers in the needs assessment process will give the school an opportunity to know what employers expect as well as offering the employers a chance to know more about the guidance program.

Graduates: An assessment of this group can provide information about the effectiveness of the guidance program for those who are applying their skills in post-high-school pursuits. They can help identify areas that are of the most benefit as well as areas that need strengthening.

Because of time and resource limitations, you may not be able to assess all of these groups about student needs. If you must restrict the number of groups to be assessed, students and educators should receive attention first by virtue of being the most immediately involved. It may be that you could assess students and educators the first year and members of the other groups during following years. It is important, however, that each of these groups be assessed at some point in the periodic needs assessment process.

Assess Community Needs.   It is important to remember that although students are the primary clients of the guidance program, there are other clients whose perceived needs must be surveyed as well. Teachers, parents, administrators, and other specialists are all clients in one way or another. Ideally, the survey of their needs also should be related to the student competencies you are seeking to develop or enhance. An example would be to ask teachers to respond to items in terms of their needs for assisting students attain the desired competency. Using the same examples as we did for the student needs assessment above, a sample of teacher items is presented in Figure 6–10.

It is important, also, to assess staff needs for system support activities. This needs assessment can be focused in two ways. You can assess your clients' needs for system support for activities performed in the current program, or you can assess their perceived needs for the proposed activities of the desired program. If the latter is your aim, this assessment cannot be done at the building level until after the desired program has been established. At this time, however, it may be relevant to assess perceived needs for current activities or those you are thinking of doing—using the district's suggested activities. If conducted in the appropriate context—for example, in conjunction with the assessment of student needs—you will probably help build a powerful case for divesting the guidance department of some of the typical quasi-administrative and clerical tasks. Staff assessment will identify their perceptions of the need for counselors to do such tasks as "senior credit checks" or "bus duty supervision." You will also identify tasks to be displaced or streamlined, such as recommending students for above-

Figure 6–10
Teacher Needs Assessment

First Grade
  Student Competency: Students will describe how exercise and
                              nutrition affect their mental health.
  Teacher Need: I need assistance in helping students learn to
                              tell how exercise and eating habits make a
                              difference in how they think, act, and feel.

Eighth Grade
  Student Competency: Students will analyze effective family relations,
                              their importance, and how they are formed.
  Teacher Need: I need assistance in helping students learn why
                              good family relations are important and how
                              they are formed.

Eleventh Grade
  Student Competency: Students will evaluate the need for flexibility in
                              their roles and in their choices.
  Teacher Need: I need assistance in helping students learn to
                              explain the need for flexibility in their roles and
                              in their choices.

or below-average level course offerings or coordinating the testing program. Finally, you will identify the topics that you need to address in faculty and parent workshops and consultation sessions.

Articulate the Design of the Desired Building Program

Armed with the district's model for a properly balanced and comprehensive guidance program, with data regarding your students' and other clients' needs, and with concrete information about the design of your current guidance program, the building guidance staff, with the assistance of the building school-community advisory committee, must now design their desired building guidance program. The desired design must be in writing, for all the reasons explained heretofore, must be clearly relevant to the community's needs—both students' and adults'— and must be realistic in terms of the resources available to the building.

The building description of its desired program should include the same parts as does the district program description. There should be a statement of the *rationale* for the building program, using local needs and demographic data that support its unique design. The *assumptions* should mirror the district's philosophical statement, but in addition be localized to incorporate the philosophy of the building and its surrounding community. The program *definition* should likewise mirror the district's definition, but provide specific detail for the desired structure and balance of the program. The competencies students are to attain as a result of participating in the school's guidance program need to be listed. A summary of the resources available to the building program needs to be included; this includes the description of the guidance staff and their unique talents and skills.

Each of the components in the delivery system needs to be spelled out in detail. The section on the *guidance curriculum* should include the student competencies to be addressed in units and lessons taught at each grade level and should reference the materials to be used. The building staff need to follow Gelatt's steps for selecting activities described in chapter 7. The number of guidance learning activities per grade level should be specified. How guidance lessons are infused into other educational programs also needs to be described.

The activities and services that compose the building's *individual planning* component need to be specified. The activities for each grade level as well as the outcomes they address need to be stated. The materials used as well as other resources available need to be referenced. The results for students and the means by which parents are involved also should be described.

The *responsive services* write-up should detail the information gleaned from assessing students' needs for special assistance. The number and topics of small group counseling services as well as a description of a counselor's case load of individuals should be provided. The consultation services and mechanisms used for referral should be listed. Although this is perhaps the hardest component to describe in advance, typical priority topics or student needs can and should be identified, and the approximate number of students, parents, and teachers who typically benefit from these unique services can be provided. These appraisals help you anticipate the number of activities that will need to be offered, and the amount of counselor time that will need to be provided to ensure adequate attention to these needs.

The *system support* component needs to be specifically written to clarify what the guidance department staff program does to support other programs and to itemize the support they need to ensure appropriate delivery of their own program. Support to other programs should be listed by program—state the activity, and briefly describe the counselor(s)' role(s) and responsibilities. Support needed from the building administration and staff should include such items as policy and procedural assistance; budget, equipment, and facilities needs; support for specific staff development opportunities; and building public relations activities.

An important consideration in writing the description of the program that is desired for your building is the format you will use to present the program. As you have no doubt gleaned from the discussion above, the write-up must be as specific as you can make it, complete with the listing of materials and other resources you will use in program delivery. A committee of counselors from the various school levels of your district needs to be formed to establish the format to be used by all buildings. Districts we have worked with have chosen different formats. It is important, however, that the format make sense to the counselors and to others who will be reading and using the program design. It is also essential that all buildings use the same format to be able to judge the quality of programs across the district and to ensure some consistency across the district. A format that was used to summarize program activities is presented in Figure 6–11. This format served as a vehicle for identifying all activities provided for a certain competency (skill), a specific set of student clients (grade level; developmental, preventive, remedial), or for a particular program component. The counselors found it a relatively easy and understandable vehicle for displaying their repertoire of activities.

Once the program for a building has been written, building counselors can work with their administration and faculty to show them what the guidance program for their building is. The appropriate roles for the counselors can be clarified. Current activities can be judged as appropriate or inappropriate for the use of counselors' time. The counselor:student ratio can be evaluated, and if it is not appropriate, the principal can be enlisted in the struggle to improve it. Where better procedures are needed for delivering system support activities, a building team can be charged to develop them. Having established what is desirable, building staff can build guidance program budget requests and renovate

Figure 6–11
Sample Format to Summarize Building-Level Program Activities

Building Name: _____

COMPREHENSIVE GUIDANCE PROGRAM
Identification of Activities

STUDENT SKILL: _____ GRADE LEVEL: _____

Student Need Level: Developmental   Preventive   Remedial
(Circle One)

Program Component: Cuidance Curriculum   Individual Planning
                                                System
(Circle One)
                      Responsive Service   System Support

INTENDED OUTCOMES: _____

_____

_____

_____

PROGRAM ACTIVITIES & RESOURCES: _____

_____

_____

_____

_____

_____

facilities. With a concretely drawn vision in hand, the building staff, in collaboration with the district staff, can work together to specify and implement the changes needed to attain the desired building programs.

With the development of the design for each building's desired program, the designing phase of the program redevelopment efforts is finished. You are ready to make the transition to program implementation. Before we move on to suggestions for making the transition to the new program, however, it is time to consider expanding the leadership base for the program development efforts.

Step 4: Expand Your Leadership Base

If you are the district guidance program leader and are approaching implementation of a redesigned program, you will benefit from expanding your leadership base at this point. To date, leadership has been provided by the counselors on the steering or school-community advisory committee. In addition, there are other designated leaders of counselors—the building level head counselors, who have had some responsibility for the program improvement efforts and who will have much more responsibility as you move into building program redesign. Thus, at this juncture the leadership base should be expanded in two ways: Increase the number of program development leaders by augmenting the number of counselors involved in program development activities; and enhance the building leadership role of the head counselor. In some cases, the program development leaders are head counselors, but by establishing two different categories of leaders, some options are provided in selecting leaders for program development. Thus, the program development leaders are those who assist in implementing the new program and new program activities; they are the program innovators. The head counselors are the managers of the program as implemented; they are the program maintainers.

Regarding the selection of leaders, the guidance program leader for the district needs to be cognizant of the strengths and weaknesses of the designated, formal campus counselor leaders, the head counselors, and needs to identify potentially successful program development peer leaders in order to build a strong leadership team for program implementation. With both sets of leaders ''in hand,'' then, the tasks each group will do need to be specified. Group members have to be trained to do the tasks and must have opportunities to use their designated roles. The efforts they make need to be recognized and reinforced.

Head Counselors. In anticipation of the positive leadership that will be needed from them, the head counselors need to have their roles enhanced and supported. As mentioned above, the head counselors in each building are probably already in place, so identifying them is not a challenge, whereas becoming familiar with their operational style may be. Also, if the guidance program leader has the chance to participate in the selection of new head counselors, he or she needs to work diligently and skillfully with the principals to ensure the selection of someone who is aligned with the new program. In our experience, building principals want someone who will be loyal to them and to their school, but they will leave the assessment of the individual candidates' guidance and counseling expertise to the guidance leader. Principals also want someone who will provide good leadership to the building program and who will work to make their building program the ''best in the district.''

If you are the district guidance program leader and if you have not already begun to assist the head counselors to play their roles more fully, you should begin at this time. Many districts with which we have worked have not spelled out the responsibilities of the head counselor. If your district does not have a specific job description for the head counselor, one needs to be developed. If you are starting from scratch, you may want to consider the position guide developed in Northside school district and provided in Figure 6–12. We suggest, however, that you begin the development of their job description with the head counselors themselves. By being asked what they do that is unique to their role, they not only develop an investment in the job description, but they begin thinking of themselves as different from and leaders of the campus staff. They need to be identified as the on-campus program managers and supervisors of the guidance staff.

Having specified head counselors' responsibilities, you need to assist them to develop the skills they need to carry them out. If they are not internalizing the new program concept, you need to help them do that. You can help them through programmatic discussions in head counselor meetings and by modeling for them during building staff meetings. They, too, want to do the best job they can, and can benefit from a role model.

Given the lack of specialized training for head counselors and the dirth of literature on the subject, they probably need inservice education and training on staff supervision. We will discuss this in more depth in chapter 8, but most head counselors we have worked with have sought help in learning such basic skills as how to conduct effective meetings, how to provide constructive criticism, how to build a team, and how to help staff set appropriate goals.

If the district is large enough, or if there are neighboring districts/schools with which to cooperate, the head counselors enjoy providing a support system for each other, that is, being a "team" of their own. This provides them a support group that serves to enhance their growth as building leaders. They need to be supported as they try out new strategies and as they carry out the guidance

Figure 6–12
Head Counselor Position Guide

Title:	*Head Counselor (Middle & High School)*
Primary Functions:	as a member of guidance department staff, fulfill the role of school counselor as described in the position guides; as the leader of the guidance department, effect the continuous improvement of the guidance program and personnel.
Major Job Responsibilities:	(1) implement the campus comprehensive guidance and counseling program and specifically provide services to meet the special needs of his/her caseload (MS: 400, HS: 200); (2) administer the campus guidance program; (3) manage the guidance department staff; (4) contribute to the development of the district's guidance program, policies, and procedures.

Figure 6–12, *continued*

Key Duties:

(1) implement the campus comprehensive guidance and counseling program and specifically provide services to meet the special needs of his/her caseload: please refer to the appropriate level position guide.

(2) administer the campus guidance program: lead the development and implementation of the campus guidance program consistent with the district and school goals and objectives; prepare request for and utilize allocation of department budget; conduct campus guidance department meetings; represent the guidance department to the administration and to other department coordinators; supervise the maintenance of student records and other guidance department procedures.

(3) manage the guidance department staff: supervise the department staff; assist the principal and director of guidance in observations and evaluations of staff; assist the principal in selection of new counselors; assist the principal and director of guidance in providing staff development programs.

(4) contribute to the development of the district guidance program, policies, and procedures: represent the campus staff at the district head counselor meetings; communicate and promote implementation of district policies and procedures.

Organizational Relationships:

is supervised by the principal and the director of guidance; supervises and coordinates the work of department staff, professional and paraprofessional; collaborates with administration; cooperates with district and campus instructional staff leaders.

Performance Standards:

A head counselor's performance is considered satisfactory when:
(1) the principal and director of guidance concur and the head counselor's level of competence is reflected as such on the "Northside Independent School District Head Counselor Evaluation Form"; and
(2) evaluation of the Annual Guidance Program Plan–High School indicates overall effectiveness of the program.

program leaders' assignments. As discussed previously, they should be held accountable for the on-campus discussions of the district program framework and other topics related to the new program. As districtwide mandates are given for implementing new program activities, head counselors should be held accountable for seeing that they are performed.

And, finally, the head counselors will need to have their authority supported in their newly defined roles. As they supervise and monitor their staff members, their leadership must be recognized, and the central office guidance program leader should model this recognition for the counselors. Head counselors' effectiveness will mirror the amount of authority that is delegated to them. In this arena, the principal's role is key also. The principals want their department heads to be effective; it makes the principals' job easier. The more work that is done through the head counselors and with the principals, the clearer the head counselors' responsibilities for campus program operation will be.

Program Development Leaders. Depending on the size of the district and the representation on the steering committee, it is probable that the number of program development leaders will need to be expanded by involving more counselors as improved program implementation approaches. Program development leaders should be chosen from counselors who are visibly supportive of the new program directions, have enough vision to be able to anticipate the benefits of the improved program, and are either informal or formal leaders of other counselors.

To identify these individuals, the steering committee counselors should be consulted. They need to feel comfortable with the new leaders as the steering committee counselors will have responsibility for bringing these new leaders "on board" and working with them. Their recommendations do not have to be binding, but their thoughts and concerns need to be attended to. Again, it depends on the size of the district, but even in reasonably small districts counselors may not know each other from one building to the next. The person with primary responsibility for the program development efforts is the one with the broader perspective.

Having identified the counselors that are going to be brought onto the program development leadership team, time must be taken to ensure that they feel comfortable in their understanding of the comprehensive program concept. That they were selected because of their initial understanding and support of the new concept helps, and initiation does not take a great amount of time but it does need to be done. At the same time, the expanded group needs to be built into a cohesive team of workers. This is accomplished by clarifying the roles and tasks that they need to help accomplish. The model that worked effectively in Northside was to develop subgroups of experts for each component; that is, subcommittees were formed for each component—a curriculum committee, an individual planning committee, a responsive services committee, and a system support committee. Each committee had representation from each of the school levels—elementary, middle, and high school. Thus the total group also could be divided by level grouping, which was later useful for certain activities. Each committee's major responsibility was being the voice of its particular component to their colleagues.

A task for the committees to accomplish that is worthy of consideration is to coordinate the collection of current practices that are good examples of implementation of the various components. For example, the curriculum committee collects sample guidance lessons and units that assist students at various grade levels to reach the priority competencies; the individual planning system committee collects samples of activities that help students develop personalized educational or career plans; the responsive services committee collects samples of exemplary counseling, consulting, and referral practices. When compiled, these collections become resource guides for all counselors to use as they add to their programs.

The program leadership team then have the data they need to become true experts in the implementation of the components at the relevant school levels. After being trained in the component definitions and after reviewing and selecting the multiple exemplary practices, they are equipped to disseminate these ideas to their colleagues. We also have found that they benefit from training in leadership skills so that they can present themselves as peer leaders.

The more the team members are used as leaders, the more depth their role takes on. If they are collecting materials for resource guides, let them plan the guide formats and their own processes for collecting the materials and for acknowledging other counselors who are taking strides in the new direction. Provide them the opportunities they need to communicate with their colleagues; that is, call meetings as they need them, support their efforts with the rest of the counselors, and so on. They operate from the power that is delegated to them; this delegation must be clear to the total group of counselors.

Resource guide development is not the only task that a program leadership team can take on. As you approach implementation of the new program, many innovative or pilot efforts will need to be tried. Such efforts might be curriculum writing, experimenting with new activities (including the use of teacher advisory systems like the one described in chapter 3), or developing a recommended protocol for a campus response to a student suicide. Program leaders might take on the responsibility for designing the district's staff development plan. Whatever the project, the same principles apply. The team leaders' task needs to be clearly given, their expertise carefully developed, and their authority clearly recognized.

Finally, if motivated and professionally committed individuals have been selected, and if they have been given a meaningful task to do, they will be working hard at something that their colleagues may still be dubious about. It is imperative that their work and their worth be reinforced. Rewards for professionals, according to Hurst (1984, p. 84), may come from any of six motivators: "Achievement (what you believe you did), Recognition (what others think you did), Work itself (what you really do), Responsibility (what you help others do), Advancement (what you think you can do), Growth (what you believe you might do)." Program leaders feel a sense of achievement in completing each task that is part of their charge; for example, when the position statements or resource guides are published. They receive recognition by their very selection to be a "program leader;" this is maintained as they present new concepts and ideas to their peers. We have found that encouraging them to make presentations at local, state, and national professional growth conferences is not only good for the emerging leaders, but it also helps others learn from what they are doing. If the new program leaders have been selected as we suggested from the ranks of those who believe in the new program concept, the work they do to better understand the new program and to help implement it is rewarding to them. If part of their charge is to help their colleagues learn about and implement new program strategies, the leaders are vitally responsible for the successful implementation of the program and for the effective performance of the rest of the counseling staff. Program leaders can be helped to *feel* like leaders and to envision themselves as the head counselors and guidance supervisors/administrators of the future. Program innovators that we have worked with consistently talk about how much they are learning from their experiences; they are eager to grow and find new opportunities, such as program improvement, as fuel for their own professional development.

Guidance Program Leader's Roles and Responsibilities

This phase of the guidance program improvement project results in a shift in overt leadership from the steering committee or the school-community advisory committee to the guidance program leader. If you are the leader, the district "master plan for program improvement" becomes the responsibility of your office. You also are responsible for helping building staffs plan their improved programs. Again, you have program management and administrative tasks and staff leadership and supervision tasks to accomplish.

Like in the prior phases, as the guidance program leader you must continue to be the prime mover. Although we describe the steps as though they are taken one at a time, in reality many activities go on simultaneously; for example, while you are developing the master plan, you are also helping buildings assess their current program, and you will be training your new leaders and providing supervisory inservice to head counselors. Again, it is up to you to keep each part of the project moving along a constructive course. You must use every opportunity to reinforce positively the individual change efforts the counselors make. You are probably the only individual in the district who "sees" the whole picture, although by this time the expanded program leadership team and the head counselors are beginning to see a lot of it too—provided you keep them informed.

There are some tasks in this project phase that in all likelihood only you can do. You need to compile and present the discrepancy data; that is, display the data and note the conclusions. You need to maintain an open discussion climate as staff members brainstorm ideas for discrepancy reduction. You need to write the district master plan and select and train the co-leaders. You need to be prepared to use the expanded or redirected resources that begin to flow to the guidance department as soon as the steering committee makes its recommendations for changes. If ratios improve, you will be hiring more counselors, and your selection criteria must be tailored to identify those who will fit into the new program. If your department receives a higher budget allocation, you need to be prepared to spend it. If you are allowed facility improvements, you need to have your blueprints ready. If counselors' contracts are extended, you need to have your inservice training or program development activities ready to implement. This is the part of the project that is most fun, but it too represents challenges for you.

By now many of those you work with, including fellow administrators as well as counselors, are beginning to "get" the program concept. This, too, is exciting; but, you may find the counselors frustrated that they have not yet been freed of all the undesirable system support activities and the administrators frustrated that counselors are not yet seeing all their students more often. You need to transform these frustrations into the energies that will *cause* the needed changes.

We have learned that people want to see the changes they desire, but are reluctant to change their own behaviors that others want changed. You probably will—and possibly should—feel at this point that you are constantly swimming upstream—explaining rationale, defending recommendations—but each constructive change begets another. Ultimately, the momentum for change takes over and you will be able to relax somewhat. At this time you are moving into the *implementation* phase of the program improvement project.

References

Hurst, D.K. (1984). Of boxes, bubbles, and effective management. *Harvard Business Review*, *62*, 78–88.

Missouri Department of Elementary and Secondary Education. (1981). *Missouri comprehensive student needs survey*. Jefferson City, MO: Author.

National Consortium Project. (1978). *Developing comprehensive career guidance programs*. Palo Alto, CA: American Institutes for Research.

PART 3—Implementing

CHAPTER 7

MAKING THE TRANSITION TO A COMPREHENSIVE GUIDANCE PROGRAM

Having organized for change, adopted a comprehensive program model, assessed the current program, established the design for the desired program, and planned the transition, as the guidance program leader you are now ready to make the transition. You also are ready to develop mechanisms to maintain the program once it is in operation. This is one of the most crucial phases of the entire program improvement process. The questions to be answered include: How is the transition to a comprehensive program made? What activities remain from the current program? What activities need to be displaced? What activities need to be added? Five steps are described that help answer questions such as these.

Step 1: Implement the master plan for change;
Step 2: Focus on special projects;
Step 3: Facilitate building-level changes;
Step 4: Monitor changed program implementation; and
Step 5: Plan and implement public relations activities.

Chapter 7 opens with a discussion of the tasks involved in implementing the "Master Plan for Change." Recommendations concerning the staffing patterns and the financial and political resources required to operate a comprehensive guidance program are presented. Then, the change strategy of focusing on special projects is introduced. Attaching the guidance program improvement process to federal, state, and local priorities can provide the energy, motivation, and support to carry the overall improvement process to completion. Next, chapter 7 describes how to facilitate the building-level changes required to fully implement the district comprehensive guidance program at the building level. In addition, chapter 7 describes how to institute a districtwide system for monitoring program changes and overall program implementation at the building level to ensure that the program does not revert back to its original, traditional operation. Monitoring systems, ways to reinforce staff who are making progress, and mechanisms for making program adjustments are described. In addition, chapter 7 presents ideas about planning and implementing, with district leadership, public relations activities to make sure that students, teachers, parents, administrators, and the public at large are aware of the remodeled and revitalized comprehensive guidance program. Finally, chapter 7 delineates the roles and responsibilities of guidance program leaders in the transition process.

Step 1: Implement the Master Plan for Change

In developing the ''master plan'' (chapter 6), the guidance program leader identified the major tasks that needed to be done, developed an order for doing them, and identified people who would be involved in their accomplishment. The tasks that need to be done, their degree of feasibility, and the specific timeframe for each building or district may be different; for example, if the school system is currently ''into'' curriculum writing, then guide development fits right into already established district priorities. If the system's thrust is staff development, then the recommendations for inservice training, job description development or supervision, and evaluation improvement might be the most feasible to accomplish.

However, there are some recurrent recommendations that need attention for the program actually to change. Regardless of the particular timeframe, the guidance program leader might want to consider some of the following ideas for the improved use of human, financial, and political guidance program resources as the master plan for change is implemented. These ideas are presented below in outline form and are explained in detail on the pages that follow.

Human Resources

1) Modify counselor staffing formulas (ratios)
2) Develop counselors' job descriptions and develop job descriptions for guidance department clerical staff

Financial Resources

3) Establish budgets for guidance departments at the district and building levels
4) Explore use of other-than-local funding sources
5) Develop guidance program component *Guides*
6) Review and make recommendations to ensure adequacy of guidance facilities

Political Resources

7) Update policies and procedures
8) Implement displacement/streamlining of nonguidance and counseling activities
9) Recommend guidelines for support from building administration
10) Work with resistant staff members

Human Resources

Modify Counselor Staffing Formulas (Ratios)

Having outlined the program's basic structure and the desired levels of service to students and other clients, it is possible to use this information to suggest the ratios needed to conduct the program as desired. For example, using the Northside ISD desired program figures, the formulas displayed in Figure 7–1 could be used to recommend appropriate ratios at the elementary, middle and high school levels.

Elementary counselors have been added in rather dramatic numbers in the program development projects we have worked with. The elementary guidance programs are developmentally based and thus are already closer to the desired program as defined by these districts than are secondary programs, which are traditionally entrenched in system support—quasi-administrative/clerical tasks (Peer, 1985). No district with which we have worked has stated that counselors *as supporters* of the system should have top priority in the program; all of the districts have assigned high priority for all school levels to the guidance curriculum.

All this is to say that ratio improvement is one of the more difficult tasks to implement; it is extremely costly, and there must be some evidence that the counselors themselves are willing to provide services to all students. Once that intent has been established and some effort has been applied in that direction, justification for improved ratios is more credible. At the same time, being such a large cost item, ratio improvement is tied to the district's overall budget development procedures. The guidance program leader must be armed and ready and be prepared to implement the improvements in stages. We advise you to continue to implement other more feasible changes and not wait until ratios are improved to begin.

Develop Counselors' Job Descriptions and Develop Job Descriptions for Guidance Department Clerical Staff

Identifying the various human resources available to the guidance program brings with it the need to define the roles and functions of the various personnel to ensure appropriate use of their education and talents. The counselors' job description has already been described in the position guide format discussed in

Figure 7–1
Elementary Counselor Ratio Recommendation

Desired program design:
   Curriculum: 40% × 70 = 28 slots

   Ind'l plng: 25% × 70 = 17 slots

   Resp serv: 25% × 70 = 18 slots

   Sys supp: 10% × 70 = 7 slots
Program activity slots = 30 minutes each (average)
Student school day = 7 hours
7 hours yield 14 activities per day
14 activities × 5 days/week = 70 activity slots/week

To implement *Guidance Curriculum* as desired:
$$\begin{array}{r} 28 \text{ slots} \\ -12 \text{ for planning*} \\ \hline 16 \text{ classes**} \\ \times 25 \text{ (average \# students/class)} \\ \hline 400 \end{array}$$

400 students per counselor is the ratio needed to implement the guidance curriculum.

To implement *Responsive Services* as desired:
             18 slots
60% for preventive level, small group counseling
40% for remedial level, individual counseling

$$\begin{array}{r} 18 \\ \times .6 \\ \hline 11 \text{ groups} \\ \times \;5 \text{ students @} \\ \hline 55 \text{ students} \end{array} \qquad \begin{array}{r} 18 \\ \times .4 \\ \hline 7 \text{ students} \end{array}$$

55 students + 7 students = *62 students* in responsive services case load
   Responsive services attends to 15% of population on the average
   62 is 15% of *413 students per counselor*

Thus, 400:1 is the recommended ratio for elementary counselors in order to implement the program as designed.

---

*2 slots per week @ 6 grade levels.
**Each class is to be guided one time per week.

Middle School Counselor Ratio Recommendation

Desired Program Design:

Curriculum: $30\% \times 35 = 10.5 = 11$ slots

Ind'l plng: $30\% \times 35 = 10.5 = 10$ slots

Resp serv: $25\% \times 35 = 8.75 = 9$ slots

Sys supp: $15\% \times 35 = 5.25 = 5$ slots

Program activity slots = 1 hour each (average)
Student school day = 7 hours
7 hours yield 7 activities per day
7 activities × 5 days/week = 35 activity slots/week

To implement *Guidance Curriculum* as desired:

$$\begin{array}{r} 11 \text{ slots} \\ - \ 2 \text{ for planning*} \\ \hline 9 \text{ classes per week per counselor**} \end{array}$$

$$\begin{array}{r} 18 \text{ classes} = \text{curriculum case load} \\ \times 27 \text{ (average \# students/class)} \\ \hline 486 \end{array}$$

486 students per counselor is the ratio needed to implement the guidance curriculum.

To implement *Responsive Services* as desired:

9 slots
50% for preventive level, small group counseling
50% for remedial level, individual counseling

$$\begin{array}{cc} \begin{array}{r} 9 \\ \times .5 \\ \hline 4.5 \text{ groups} \\ \times \ 9 \text{ students} \\ \hline 40.5 \text{ students} \end{array} & \begin{array}{l} 9 \\ \times .5 \\ \hline 4.5 \text{ students} \\ (8\text{--}10 = \text{average} \\ \text{size group}) \end{array} \end{array}$$

40.5 students + 4.5 students = *45 students* in responsive services case load
  Responsive services attends to 15% of population on the average
  45 is 15% of *300 students per counselor*

Thus, 393:1 is the recommended ratio for middle school counselors in order to implement the program as designed.

*Planning: teachers—1:6, counselors, 2:9.
**Each class is to be guided every other week.

High School Counselor Ratio Recommendation

Desired Program Design:

Curriculum:	25%	$\times$ 35 =	8.75 =	9 slots
Ind'l plng:	30%	$\times$ 35 =	10.5 =	10 slots
Resp serv:	30%	$\times$ 35 =	10.5 =	11 slots
Sys supp:	15%	$\times$ 35 =	5.25 =	5 slots

Program activity slots = 1 hour each (average)
Student school day   = 7 hours
7 hours yield 7 activities per day
7 activities $\times$ 5 days/week = 35 activity slots/week

To implement *Guidance Curriculum* as desired:

$$\begin{array}{r} 9 \text{ slots} \\ - \ 2 \text{ for planning*} \\ \hline 7 \text{ classes per week per counselor**} \end{array}$$

$$\begin{array}{r} 14 \text{ classes} = \text{curriculum case load} \\ \times 27 \text{ (average \# students/class)} \\ \hline 378 \end{array}$$

378 students per counselor is the ratio needed to implement the guidance curriculum.

To implement *Responsive Services* as desired:

11 slots
50% for preventive level, small group counseling
50% for remedial level, individual counseling

$$\begin{array}{r} 11 \\ \times .5 \\ \hline 5.5 \text{ groups} \\ \times 9 \text{ students} \\ \hline 49.5 \text{ students} \end{array} \qquad \begin{array}{l} 11 \\ \times .5 \\ \hline 5.5 \text{ students} \\ (8\text{--}10 = \text{average} \\ \text{size group)} \end{array}$$

49.5 students + 5.5 students = *55 students* in responsive services case load
   Responsive services attends to 15% of population on the average
   55 is 15% of *366 students per counselor*

Thus, 375:1 is the recommended ratio for high school counselors in order to implement the program as designed.

---

*Planning: teachers—1:6, counselors, 2:9.
**Each class is to be guided every other week.

chapter 5. We recommend that position guides be developed for every full-time, permanent guidance department staff member. More concise job descriptions can be developed for others, including volunteers. Specific job descriptions are prerequisite to any staff expansion. Community speakers, clerical aides, and peer counselors all need to have their jobs described. These job descriptions not only help clarify the functions that new (and old) staff members are expected to implement, but they also help administrators see the justification for augmenting the guidance staff. Indeed, to justify a new staff position, a thorough job analysis of existing related staff positions is required.

Financial Resources

Establish Budgets for Guidance Departments at the District and Building Levels

In the assessment of the current program, one of the tasks was to review the financial resources available. In the review you may have found that the financial resources were described in terms of a well-defined budget in which all of the money spent on guidance, including salaries, was part of the budget. Or you may have found that money for only such items as testing materials and a few other guidance resources was included. Or perhaps there was no budget at all. Within the budget policy guidelines for the school/district, the task is to establish a budget. To do that, consider such major categories as those displayed in Figure 7–2.

Prerequisite to any resource expansion is to ascertain the costs of implementing the recommendations. The guidance program leader will need to develop a *cost analysis* for each of the items for inclusion in the district departmental budget— or in other budget categories if that is where the item fits. The total amount, presented all at once, could be overwhelming, so our advice is to prepare these cost analyses on an item-by-item basis. Thus, as each recommendation is brought forward for consideration, the guidance program leader can present the dollar figures associated with it. For example, if implementing the improved ratios recommended above entails adding counselors to the staff, it is the guidance program leader's responsibility to know how much those additional staff positions will cost. Having specific cost information available allows the guidance program leader to anticipate others' concerns about the increased expenditures and to be prepared to defend the allocation of additional dollars.

Explore Use of Other-Than-Local Funding Sources

A majority of the funds for the program probably comes from local and state sources. There are, however, funds from other sources. Federal legislation is one source. Federal funds available to augment the comprehensive guidance program include those that support vocational education, special education, compensatory education, and special topics of national priority such as drug abuse

Figure 7–2
Budget Categories

1. Personnel
   a. Counselors
   b. Secretarial/clerical
   c. Guidance administrators
   d. Fringe benefits
2. Materials
   a. Student materials
      1) Texts and workbooks
      2) Audiovisual materials
      3) Testing materials
      4) Reference materials
      5) Career/guidance center materials
      6) Testing materials
   b. Professional resource materials
      1) Professional library books
      2) Journal subscriptions
      3) Training materials
3. Supplies
      1) Office supplies
      2) Computer-assisted guidance equipment supplies
      3) Instructional supplies
4. Capital outlay
      1) Equipment and maintenance
      2) Furniture
5. Professional development
      1) Meetings and conferences
      2) Consultants
6. Travel
7. Communication
8. Research and evaluation

prevention education. Federal employment and training legislation also may have guidance funds available for schools.

Most federal funds are distributed by the state department of education. If the guidance program leader is not already familiar with these sources, a visit with the state's guidance consultants would be a rewarding experience. They will be able to tell you about federal and state monies that may be available for guidance programs. Keep in mind that most of these sources will not fund an entire program. They do, however, provide dollars for such aspects of a program as counseling disadvantaged or drug-using students, augmenting a career center, or implementing a vocational assessment program. Also, keep in mind that most of the time access to these funds is through a proposal or the development of a written plan. With the comprehensive program already designed, such a proposal or plan is readily developed because the program context and student needs already have been established. The proposal writer has to extract only the portions of the total program that are of interest to the funding source to present the plan.

Develop Guidance Program Component Guides

A major task in making the transition to a comprehensive guidance program is to choose the guidance activities and materials that will assist students to develop the competencies that have been decided upon. Describing the specific activities that make up the program and having adequate program materials is prerequisite to successful implementation of the program. Counselors must have tools to assist them in their changed roles. Whether such guides are written for use in a building's program or for an entire district makes a difference in the approach to this task, but the end products will be similar. The guides describe the activities used in the implementation of the comprehensive guidance program components. In developing the guides, new activities may be created, or activities may be collected that have been used successfully in a building. Suggestions for developing guides for the four comprehensive program components are provided below.

Guidance Curriculum Guide.   A curriculum guide provides the description of curriculum units and specific lessons. We suggest that the guidance program leader use the curriculum writing expertise that is available—instructional supervisors if the district has them, the administrator in charge of curriculum development or instruction, or regional consultants in curriculum writing. The leader must also keep in mind that there will probably not be a one-on-one match between a specific activity or resource and a specific competency. Often a single guidance activity may result in the achievement of a number of student competencies.

To illustrate how an activity may be written and to show its relationship to the goals and competencies of the guidance curriculum suggested in previous chapters, an example is displayed in Figure 7–3. The example is from the Self-knowledge and Interpersonal Skills domain of the life career development model and relates to goal A for the fifth grade. You may wish to consider this format for your own activity descriptions. Note that the activity is described on one page and follows a straightforward outline that defines the basic activity. Counselors are encouraged to develop the lesson plan according to their teaching style.

Individual Planning Guide.   An individual planning guide describes in detail activities and procedures to help students apply information and develop their personalized plans. These write-ups exemplify the refocusing of some current activities from ''system support'' activities to student outcome-focused activities that help them make their educational plans. For example, the objective for preregistration of secondary level students can be changed from ''students will

Figure 7–3
Sample Activity and Format

Domain I
Goal A
Grade 5
Performance Indicator 2

COAT OF ARMS

Domain I:	Self-Knowledge and Interpersonal Skills
Goal A:	Students will develop and incorporate an understanding of the unique personal characteristics and abilities of themselves and others.
Competency:	Students will specify those personal characteristics and abilities that they value.
Performance Indicator 2	Students will identify a variety of things that they value.

Activity Objective:
The student will identify six things he or she values.

Materials:	Coat of arms, pencil
Time:	One session of approximately 30 minutes
Directions:	Have each student fill in an outline of a shield with the following for a personal coat of arms:

Box 1: Draw a symbol to represent your greatest success.
Box 2: Draw a symbol to represent your family's greatest success.
Box 3: Draw a symbol to show a place you dream about.
Box 4: Draw symbols to show two things at which you are good.
Box 5: Draw a picture to show what you would do if you have one year to live and would be a success at anything you do.
Box 6: On one-half of the box write two words you would like used to describe you; on the other half write two words you would not like used to describe you.

circle course numbers on course selection cards'' to student learning objectives, such as ''10th graders will select an 11th-grade course of study that is an appropriate next step toward their educational/career goals.'' The activities that might be envisioned as a unit include interpretation of career interest and aptitude assessments, information exploration in the guidance center, review of the high school graduation and college entrance requirements, revision of the students' ''High School Four-Year Plans,'' and, finally, preregistration for the 11th grade year—the circling of the numbers on the cards. Or, the objective for an elementary school Career Day can be changed from "the school staff will provide X number of career speakers" to "3rd-, 4th-, and 5th-grade students will list the educational requirements for five careers that relate to their identified career interests." The guidance program activities provided to assist students attain the objective might include a career interest inventory, a guidance lesson on the relationship between levels of education and levels of occupations available in various job clusters, and Career Day speakers who describe their educational histories as they relate to their occupations.

Responsive Services Guide. A responsive services guide can provide a description of the topics and modes—such as counseling, consultation, or referral—the counselor uses in response to students', parents', or teachers' problems. Counseling session plans and the overview of a planned series of counseling activities can help other staff members as well as less experienced counselors benefit from the ideas used in activities. *Changing Student Attitudes and Behavior Through Group Counseling* (Myrick & Dixon, 1985) or *Brief Family Interventions in the School Setting* (Golden, 1983) are examples of such descriptions.

Including a list of the community referral sources counselors use in the building or across the district also enhances the implementation of this function. Developing this list not only provides the names of outside source people who have cooperated effectively with school counselors in the past, but it can also provide a vehicle for gathering consistent information about these sources' areas of expertise.

Describing Exemplary Activities

To begin the task of guide writing we suggest using the results of the current program assessment already completed. Take those current activities and materials you feel are in keeping with the improved program that has been designed—those that have the potential of helping students to develop the chosen competencies—and place them in the appropriate component and grade-level grouping.

If, as guidance program leader, you are working in a single school or in a small district setting, this may be easily accomplished; however, if the setting is larger, you may need to implement a process similar to that done in Northside Independent School District. This approach was developed after a group of 12 counselors from the district—4 from each school level—spent a week, the district's typical allotment for curriculum writing, to develop the units and lessons to teach decision making to grades 4–12. The work was more closely aligned with textbook writing than with typical curriculum guide development efforts. In addition, that district had identified 15 guidance curriculum strands; the counselors—and the director—concluded that they could not wait 14 more years to have the curriculum guide completed, to say nothing of the guides for the other components. It also was not realistic to expect the district to hire the counselors as a curriculum writing team for a year or whatever it took to accomplish the tasks.

The counselors decided to collect "exemplary practices" that were currently performed in district buildings, write them up in consistent formats, and categorize them by program component. They found this to be an excellent vehicle for crossfertilization of ideas. By working with counselors from different school levels, the pooling of ideas helped everyone learn about each other's programs and was a major step toward an articulated, K–12 program. It had the additional benefit of helping all participating counselors see how what they were currently doing fit into the new program concept.

The scope of this activity would vary with the size of the district guidance program. No matter how large or how small the program is, however, the guidance program leader should attend to the details of the guide writing. In Northside, the compilation of ideas into guides took 3 years to accomplish. Once guides are published they have a permanency that provides part of the foundation upon which the new program can rest. It is important that this foundation be solid.

In Northside, a work committee was used to develop the formats to be used in the guides, such as lesson plans, activity plans, and counseling session outlines. In turn, the work committee trained the rest of the counselors in how to complete the forms. When counselors submitted their "promising practices" in the prescribed format, they were ready for typing for inclusion in the guide. The work committee screened the inputs and selected the best practices. The difference between these guides and those developed in the small district is that these become illustrative examples that a building program can use as a pattern, as contrasted with those that represent actual descriptions of a particular building's guidance activities.

Developing New Activities

After a list of activities that are currently being performed successfully in the building or district program has been compiled, there still may be gaps where there are no exemplary activities for some student competencies, so that new activities need to be developed. Gelatt (1975, pp. 19–22) outlined four steps in selecting guidance activities and resources. First, as he suggested, all imaginable activities and resources are surveyed. Next, all the possible activities and resources are listed. Then a list of desirable activities and resources is drawn up, and finally, choices are made of the preferred activities and resources. To assist individuals with the first step, Gelatt identified two major groupings of activities and resources: instructional and guidance procedures, and direct-indirect interventions. He provided the examples displayed in Figure 7–4 in each of the groupings.

Figure 7–4
Examples of Activities and Resources

I. INSTRUCTIONAL AND GUIDANCE PROCEDURES

  A. Reading printed materials
    1. Narrative materials
    2. Programmed materials
    3. Cartoon booklets
    4. Kits
  B. Observing
    1. Live demonstration
      a. Peer student models
      b. Cross-age models
    2. Live dramatizations
    3. Films
    4. Filmstrips
    5. Slides
    6. Videotapes
    7. Any one or all of the foregoing observational media followed by guided practice, supervised either by the models or by counseling personnel
  C. Listening
    1. Radio
    2. Sound recordings
      a. Records
      b. Audiotapes
  D. Interacting individually or in groups with
    1. Counseling personnel
    2. Community resource persons
  E. Practicing behavior under simulated conditions
    1. Simulation games
    2. Simulated work
    3. Role playing
    4. Behavioral rehearsal
  F. Gathering personal assessment information
    1. Responding to instruments measuring personal characteristics
    2. Collecting information from people
    3. Self-assessment activities
  G. Participating in computer-supported programs
  H. Using on-line computer technology

II. DIRECT-INDIRECT INTERVENTION

  A. Direct interventions—learning activities employed directly with students
    1. Developmental activities
      a. *Orientation-in*: Orienting students for a new school level, a new educational system (for example, individualized education), an innovative guidance program, or a new specific school setting

Figure 7–4, *continued*

---

    b. *Personal assessment*: Helping students understand and develop their own abilities, interests, physical attributes, personal and social behaviors and values, and preferences related to available career opportunities

    c. *Personal-choice opportunities*: Assisting students to consider choices in each of the areas of behavior

    d. *Personal problem-solving skills*: Enabling students to make wise decisions and plans and to use the information gained in personal assessment and personal choice opportunities

    e. *Formulating and pursuing personal goals*: Assisting each student to formulate and to pursue his/her goals and plans for achieving these goals

  2. Prescriptive activities

    a. *Within-school learning experiences*: Working with one or more students having learning, social, or personal problems

    b. *Orientation-out prescribed learning experiences*: Providing prescribed learning experiences for students at critical times—for example, beginning a new job, dropping out without specific plans, enlisting in the military

B. Indirect interventions—services provided on behalf of students

  1. Interventions implemented through providing assistance to assess and possibly to modify

    a. Aspects of the educational setting and system

    b. School personnel

    c. Home and neighborhood factors

    d. Community resources (for example, health, social, and welfare agencies; business and industries)

  2. Interventions implemented through guidance-related

    a. Research

    b. Evaluation

In step 2 of Gelatt's outline—listing all possible activities and resources—the task is to narrow down the list of all imaginable activities and resources to those that seem possible, to those that could be carried out. The key point in step 2 "is *not* to eliminate activities and resources you could do but may not want to do" (Gelatt 1975, p. 23). Next, in step 3, the task is to list all desirable activities and resources. Here is where local constraints and personal values come into play. Possible activities and resources can be reviewed in light of such things as

Magnitude: How much of the total school population or program will be affected?
Complexity: How many other changes will it incur?

Convenience: Can it be developed and operated locally, or will it require outside consultants?

Flexibility: How rigidly must the method be followed in order to be successful?

Distinctiveness: Is it new and different?

Interaction with other programs: Does it stand alone or require other programs to be involved for success?

Readiness: Can it be applied immediately?

Cost: What are initial costs and future funding needs?

Content: Is the content an innovation or a redo of an old method? (p. 26)

Steps 1 and 2 that Gelatt suggested can be accomplished by a work committee of counselors. We would advise using the steering committee counselors or the other counselor leaders that have been identified and whom you would like to involve further. All the counselors should review the products of these steps. Steps 3 and 4—listing the desirable and choosing the preferred activities and resources—should involve all counselors in the district because each counselor has personal values to be considered.

The guidance program leader and the guidance staff are now ready to choose the materials that will best help the students attain the outcomes identified previously. At the elementary level a plethora of commercial materials is available to support the guidance curriculum, and even to some extent the individual planning and responsive services components, but even then the use of the materials needs to be carefully related to the student competencies and the activities used to help students achieve and apply them. At the secondary level not as many commercial materials are available, so activities and related materials may need to be developed locally to implement the guidance curriculum, individual planning, and responsive services components.

Review and Make Recommendations to Ensure Adequacy of Guidance Facilities

Ensuring adequate guidance facilities and equipment may be difficult considering the costs that may be involved. However, now that you have identified the desired program design and have chosen guidance activities for the program components, you also are aware of the facilities required. For example, if classroom guidance is to be an essential part of the developmental program, a guidance classroom may be deemed essential; if counselors are expected to conduct small group counseling, an adequately sized room is needed; if a guidance center is to be the hub of the program, a large classroom is needed; and so on. Space in growing districts may be at a premium, but in schools and districts where enrollment is declining, the facilities acquisition challenge may not be as great.

Whatever the situation, however, an important task is to review the physical facilities available to the current program and to identify your needs for augmentation or modification. The reason that physical facilities are so important is that they often provide students with their first and sometimes lasting impression of the guidance program. Staff and parents also gain impressions about the guidance program and the work of the counselors through the program's physical facilities. If a guidance office has many filing cabinets prominently displayed containing student records, and, in addition, has the master schedule on the wall, it does not take long to know what the counselors do. If, on the other hand, the counselor's office or classroom is decorated with posters exemplifying the need for sound decision making, good interpersonal skills and so on, the program priorities may be perceived differently.

Attention to the type and the use of physical space and equipment of a comprehensive guidance program often is neglected in the change process. Unfortunately, what attention is given remains fixed to the traditional ways of organizing guidance. To make the guidance curriculum, individual planning system, and responsive services function effectively and to provide appropriate support to other programs, a new way of organizing guidance facilities is needed.

Traditionally guidance facilities have consisted of an office or suite of offices designed primarily to provide one-to-one counseling assistance. Such an arrangement frequently has included a reception or waiting area that serves as a browsing room where students have limited access to some displays or files of educational and occupational information. Also, this space typically has been placed in the administrative wing of the school so that the counseling staff can be close to the records and the administration.

The need for individual offices is obvious because of the continuing need to carry on individual counseling sessions. There is also a need, however, to open up guidance facilities, to make them more accessible to all students, teachers, parents, and to community representatives. One approach to make guidance facilities more usable and accessible is to reorganize traditional space into a guidance center.

A comprehensive guidance center can bring together available guidance information and exploration resources and make them easily accessible to students. The center can be used for such activities as group sessions, self-exploration, and personalized research and planning. At the high school level, students can gain assistance in such areas as occupational planning, job entry and placement, financial aid information, and postsecondary educational opportunities. At the middle school/junior high school level, students can gain assistance in such areas as career planning, high school educational opportunities, community involvement, and recreational opportunities. At the elementary school level, students and their parents can gain information about the school, the community, and parenting skills, and read books about personal growth and development. An area for counseling with toys can be provided.

Although the center is available for use to school staff and community members, it should be student-centered, and many of the center activities should be student-planned as well as student-directed. At the same time, the center is a valuable resource for teachers in their program planning and implementation. Employers, too, will find the center useful when seeking part-time or full-time workers. Viewed in this way, the impact of the center on school and community can be substantial.

If community members and parents are involved in the planning and implementation of the center and its activities, their interest could provide an impetus for the involvement of other community members. When parents and other community members become involved in programs housed in the center, they gain firsthand experience with the educational process. Through these experiences new support for education may grow.

The guidance center should be furnished in as comfortable a way as possible for all users. Provision should be made for group as well as individual activities. Coordinating the operation of the guidance center should be the responsibility of the guidance staff. All school staff should be involved, however. We recommend that at least one paid paraprofessional be employed to ensure that clerical tasks are carried out in a consistent and ongoing manner. Volunteers also may be used.

Although such centers are seen more and more at the secondary level, the concept is useful at the elementary and postsecondary levels as well. Salmon and Selig (1976) discussed the center concept in the elementary school and provided a number of examples of activities that could be included in such a center. The postsecondary focus could be much the same as that of the secondary program. Reardon and Burck (1977) described procedures and methods to establish such centers in postsecondary institutions, as did Beaumont, Cooper, and Stockard (1978).

Equipment needs are identified by a similar process to that used for facilities. In the current program assessment, you surveyed the equipment available. Having now identified the major material resources, you can now specify related equipment needs. For example, you may learn that bulletin boards, filmstrip or movie projectors, or VCR players would be useful. Again, this information allows you to analyze the costs involved and to develop your budget request. The request is substantiated by the clearly stated relationship between equipment, facilities, and the program design.

Political Resources

Update Policies and Procedures

Another task to be completed to implement the new program is an update of the policies and procedures that govern guidance as they appear in the district policy and procedural handbooks (those you identified in assessing the current program.) Some of these changes may be merely editorial or cosmetic; some, however, will be major changes in procedures and will not be easy to effect. The former changes are those that merely translate board policy to administrators; the latter are those that will need to be negotiated, particularly those that describe how the guidance department interacts with and supports the programs of other departments.

In analyzing how the current program compares and contrasts with the desired program, you have documented something you already knew: A number of activities for which you are responsible are not guidance activities at all or are, at best, only tangentially related to guidance. They have become a part of the guidance program over the years, perhaps by someone's design but more likely by default. As you also know, no matter how these activities became part of the program, once they are established, they are difficult to remove. And, what is worse, these responsibilities consume the valuable time and resources needed to conduct the actual guidance program.

Displace/Streamline Nonguidance and Counseling Activities

In identifying discrepancies between the current and desired programs (chapter 6) you identified gaps in your current program design as well as spillovers, where your current program resource appropriation went beyond what was desired— such as where counselors were spending too much time on certain activities. As you will recall, for those activities in which it is desirable that counselors spend less time, the recommendation to *streamline* the counselors' investment was made. Activities from the current program that do not fit into the desired program become targets for *displacement*. The *displacement strategy* entails replacing undesired or inappropriate activities or duties with desired guidance program activities, that is, *augmenting* or *adding* desirable activities. Many activities to be displaced or streamlined are those performed in support of other programs.

Counselors already should have listed the activities they perform that need displacing/streamlining and agreed as to those activities that *are* appropriate. Negotiating to displace activities will require solidarity among counselors, a clear picture of needed guidance activities, and solid data to provide a rationale for the displacement. Besides the data gathered in the staff time analyses, other data gathered in the assessment of the current program can support the recommendations for displacement. One example given in chapter 4 was the study of "quasi-administrative or clerical tasks" done in Northside. You also need to consider at this point whether streamlining or displacing an activity is the result of district policy or practice, or if it is a building-specific problem. If the practice is districtwide, district decisions need to be made to change the situation. If, however, it is a building problem, it should be solved at the building level with district support.

In describing the current program, you identified ways the guidance department provides support to the overall educational program. If you have followed our suggestions, you have identified these by specific program. It is not unusual for guidance departments to provide support for regular educational programs by referring students to special programs, implementing orientation and articulation activities, participating in curriculum planning, assisting in the development of accreditation reports, preregistering students for next years' courses, consulting in the development of the master schedule, and making student schedule changes. It also is not unusual for guidance departments to provide support for other programs such as testing, discipline management, gifted education, special education, and vocational education. In the Northside study you will recall that the activities performed in support of these various programs was consuming, depending on the level, 30% to 40% of the school counselors' time districtwide. In addition to the total time absorbed by these activities, there were many tasks of a clerical, quasi-administrative, or other nonguidance nature that counselors were performing. For example, counselors were scheduling the admission, review, and dismissal committee meetings, writing principals' annual reports, and counting the credits that high school students were accumulating toward graduation. Those tasks and many others were targeted for displacement.

The question of who handles displaced activities if the guidance staff does not is an issue that is not often discussed but should be. Identifying who should spend time on these activities or how else the activity might be accomplished becomes the responsibility of the counselors seeking to divest themselves of the tasks. If the counselors suggest a reasonable plan, their chances of effecting the displacement are increased substantially. Such questions as—Who is the primary beneficiary of the activity? Who has the knowledge or skills to conduct the activity? How can the task be delegated to as many people as possible so as to be least wasteful of any individual's time?—need to be asked and answered. The answers to such questions suggest the displacement recommendations.

At the district level, agreements can be made between the guidance program leader and those of other departments that would facilitate the shift in responsibility for these activities to the related department staff. If you have other department administrators on the steering committee, you will benefit from their understanding of the primary mission of the comprehensive guidance program and the new expectations for counselors. It is not easy to figure out who else will add these usually burdensome tasks to their calendars because other staff will not volunteer for them eagerly. If, however, the administrators know that counselors are not just saying, "It's not my job," but rather are saying, "But my job is to guide and counsel students," these transitions can be managed. Again, these changes will not be made overnight nor magically; they fit into the "hard-to-do" category and require clarity of direction and persistence from the guidance program leader.

Examples of typical nonguidance support tasks high school guidance departments do are credit checks, scheduling, and cumulative record keeping. Credit recording and checking reflects the basic mission of the school: teaching and learning. The primary beneficiaries of this service, then, are students and teachers. In a teacher-student advisory system, the credit checks are an all-staff responsibility, not a time-consuming activity for one relatively small group of staff members. Also, by giving some of the responsibility to the students, counselors enable them to monitor their own progress toward graduation and thus to be more in tune with their own status. Scheduling or student registration is the means of distributing students into teachers' classes. Again, it is a total school function. By using a university-type scheduling system, the vast majority of scheduling can be accomplished in one day if the entire staff and the various departments work together. Scheduling does not have to be done one student at a time by guidance staff over a period of 3 to 4 months—and then, in our experience, done again in September through massive numbers of schedule changes. Other suggestions might be that gifted education teachers accept primary responsibility for the assessment of potential gifted program participants, or that vocational education teachers be responsible for collecting the information needed for the Vocational Education Data System (VEDS) report. New procedural guidelines for implementing these changes should be written and published by the district personnel involved.

We are sure that you have already identified the activities that need to be displaced, but to illustrate how the displacement strategy works, consider an example from the Northside project. In the Northside staff time analysis, it was learned that the middle school counselors spent 7.1% of their time on administrative tasks related to special education and 2.1% of their time in group guidance. In further study of the detail of time spent on special education, it was found that much time was spent in the annual review meetings where Individualized Educational Plans (IEPs) were developed for students already enrolled in special education. The counselors felt that their time was not well used in these activities as the special education staff were more knowledgeable than they about the individual needs of the students. It was negotiated with the district special education administration that the special education staff would consult with the counselors prior to and after the annual reviews and that the counselors, thus, would not need to spend unnecessary hours in the IEP development meetings. The time saved was made available for the middle school counselors to conduct classroom guidance—the guidance curriculum. At each building, the counselors involved worked out the communication procedures with the special education staff and developed their classroom guidance schedules.

Some displacements will entail the hiring of additional staff. Often the case can be made for hiring less expensive staff to free the counselors for activities that their guidance and counseling education has prepared them to do. For example, often counselors are asked to maintain the cumulative student records, to become the school registrar. Those of you who have this responsibility know that it is time-consuming. The answer to this problem is to work toward hiring a registrar or at least sufficient clerical personnel to do the job.

Augment Activities

As we mentioned at the beginning of this discussion, at the same time as the counselors are seeking to rid themselves of tasks that are inappropriate considering their education and training, it is helpful if, at the district level, some mandates for new or improved guidance and counseling activities are issued. This helps individual counselors to make it clear that they are not just giving up some tasks, but that they are being held accountable for other, more appropriate guidance tasks. These new mandates must be related to the program improvements that are sought, but they might also be related to the activities being displaced. For example, if counselor involvement in test administration is being streamlined, it might be politically smart to include a systemwide mandate that counselors improve their efforts to assist others to use test results appropriately. If counselors are displacing the task of developing lists of students who might be retained, they could be mandated to provide specialized counseling for students who are failing two or more courses. If counselors are being taken out of the role of disciplining students, they could substitute workshops for parents on effective parenting skills.

Recommend Guidelines for Support From Building Administration

Guidelines may need to be written for building administrators to suggest appropriate levels of support for their guidance programs. These might entail statements about adequate facilities for counselors, as well as adequate budget appropriations for guidance department supplies. Statements also might be made about work schedules for counselors; for example, what their expected work hours are, including recognition of lunch hours and preparation periods. Some tasks identified for displacement may be handled in this manner, especially those that have become common practice at the building level but are not rooted in district policy. Examples include stating that elementary counselors should benefit from the secretarial services available at the school and not be required to do their own typing; recommending that new middle school students begin the registration process in the administrative office and be referred to the guidance department after such items as verification of address and immunizations are taken care of; and recognizing that the standardized testing program provides useful information to faculty and administration as well as counselors and thus test administration is a shared responsibility of all building staff members.

Work With Resistant Staff Members

By now it will be clear that there are counselors and other guidance staff who understand the new program and are eager for its implementation. And, by now, it will be clear that there are counselors and other staff members who resist the changes that are called for. The resistors probably fall into several categories: those who have not yet quite grasped the program concept; those who disagree with the educational-developmental basis of the program, preferring the psychological-crisis oriented services approach; those who are skeptical as to the validity of the changes; those who do not believe the changes will ever occur; those who are worried about their own competence for meeting the new mandates; and those who do not want change, period.

We recommend that the guidance program leader continue open dialogue with the counselors and other guidance staff about their concerns. As the change process continues to unfold, however, more and more of their concerns, anxieties, and fears will be addressed. Changes do not happen overnight, and the concept does become clearer with time. The superintendent *is* in support of the program; inservice training is provided. We also recommend that the guidance program leader identify and find ways to acknowledge those who do support the changes and the efforts that lead in the right directions. We will discuss this point more extensively later in this chapter.

Step 2: Focus on Special Projects

The educational reform efforts of the mid-1980s have brought change to many aspects of the educational system. Once you have established the design that is wanted for the guidance program, the guidance program leader is encouraged to focus on special projects that help incorporate recommended reforms into the guidance program. The energy provided by the educational reform or other professionwide movements can facilitate some of the changes that need to be accomplished. New directions from the federal, state, local community, district, and building level could be mirrored by special emphases within the guidance department. Such changes keep counselors abreast of changes in the total educational system and help maintain their position on the educational team, that is, other staff who have to change see that counselors have to change also. Such changes also have the side benefit of helping counselors avoid having change forced upon them that may be inappropriate to the directions of the new program. For example, many of the current reforms have increased the paperwork/accountability burden of the school staff, such as noting students' mastery of required instructional outcomes. If the counselors have to attend to changes of their own, they can better avoid being assigned to complete some of the paperwork tasks that belong to teachers or administrators; if the counselors are visibly augmenting the guidance curriculum component, for example, fellow staff members will see more readily that the counselors do not have time to do such notations for them.

Federal and State Priorities

The review of the history of guidance and counseling provided in chapter 1 demonstrated the impact of federal priorities on the development of our profession. As well, contemporary guidance program changes can and should relate to the current *federal* emphasis on "at risk" populations. Surely, children and youth who are "at risk" because of drug and other substance abuse, educational disadvantagement or academic failure, premature sexual activity, or adolescent depression are priority clients for school counselors implementing the responsive services component of the comprehensive guidance program. That these clients have federal priority provides rationale for their needing counseling services and for the guidance department to receive some of the funds appropriated for special programs to meet their needs.

Current *state* level educational reforms have focused on improved instructional methodology, improved curriculum, improved student achievement, and improved student discipline. These emphases have caused the development of new teacher appraisal/evaluation systems, new requirements for lesson planning, efforts to better facilitate the achievement of "academic excellence," and increased emphasis in vocational education on preparation for a highly technological work world. There has been a renewed interest in minimum competency tests and standardized achievement measures. Mandates for improved student discipline include systems that provide consistent and logical consequences for student misbehavior and require more parental involvement for students who "act out."

Each of these efforts can be used to enhance and support needed changes in the guidance program. The actual specifics of reforms vary from state to state and according to local priorities and needs; nonetheless, some common themes point to directions for counselors. New systems for assisting teachers to use current teaching methodology include clinical supervision strategies of observation and feedback, refined appraisal/evaluation models, and professional growth plans. The same strategies can be used for counselors and are discussed more extensively in chapters 8 and 9. Asking counselors to write their plans for counseling sessions and guidance lessons is a companion piece to asking teachers to develop better lesson plans. Districts across the country are using school improvement planning techniques and developing long-range plans. Counselors and guidance departments too should be asked to clarify their plans for the year by submitting calendars or using a goal-based improvement approach. This fits nicely into the comprehensive program concept.

Curriculum development in other disciplines provides counselors with the opportunity to write the guidance curriculum and to provide for infusion of guidance curricula in the more traditional curricula. For example, in addition to the guidance dimension within the mental health curriculum strand in the traditional health and science curricula, the social skills outcomes that are part of the guidance curriculum can be easily infused into the social studies curricula; communication skills can be infused into the language arts; and problem solving can be infused into science and math.

The renewed emphasis on testing calls for counselors to renew their units on test-taking skills for students and to help teachers use test results responsibly. This provides counselors the opportunity to shift their role from being test administrators to being consultants in appropriate test utilization. Similarly, improved discipline management programs rest heavily on guidance content. Counselors can seize this area of high priority to administrators and work collaboratively with them in helping students learn new ways to behave responsibly and to make decisions through activities in the guidance curriculum. Both of these emphases give counselors clear priorities for providing students with special services; students who fail to meet minimum academic standards and students who consistently misbehave often can benefit from effective small group or individual counseling.

District Priorities

With or without impetus from federal or state sources, school districts typically have priorities of high interest to their school boards or to their superintendents. School board members are often interested in academic excellence reflected in the number of scholarship winners, or in "back to the basics" of the schools' mission that can include the "basic" of responsible behavior. District administrators are challenged by declining or expanding enrollment; both have implications for teacher morale. Counselors can be visible in their role of helping others—as well as themselves—cope healthily with change. "Wellness" programs are emerging and bring with them a potential interest in mental health. These activities are "system support" of the best kind: that which uses the expertise of the guidance and counseling field.

Community Priorities

Influential community groups, such as the PTA, the chamber of commerce, and service clubs (e.g., Lions and Kiwanis clubs) have priority projects that can bring positive visibility to improving the guidance program. The PTA is interested in youth problem topics such as suicide prevention. Lions Clubs are actively working to combat drug abuse and to help children care for their personal safety. In some areas locally elected public officials are concerned about child abuse. Economic development groups are interested in career development programs. Guidance program reformers are advised to listen to the priorities of these groups; where their interests dovetail with guidance goals suggests priority areas for guidance efforts as well.

Building Priorities

Major events in school buildings can highlight the need for specific changes in the guidance program. Accreditation self-studies and visits provide opportunities to make recommendations for improving the guidance program. Visible student problems—teen suicides, drug "busts"—demand counselors' attention. Principals have goals for their schools. Counselors should collaborate with their administrators by showing them how the comprehensive guidance program supports the development of strategies to help attain the school goals. Principals' goals quite often include such items as holding high expectations for students, working to enhance the self-esteem of students, and improving the interpersonal relationships among the staff. Counselors can and should share parts of these goals. Needless to say, the more counselors' and principals' goals have in common, the more support counselors will have.

Finally, individual counselors or counseling staffs have special talents, interests, and areas of expertise. Some high school counselors are expert in helping teenagers deal with grief and loss; some elementary counselors are creative in using popular toys as materials in developmental guidance programs. By capitalizing on these, the guidance program leader can not only give appropriate recognition to those counselors, but also provide for the development of special projects that, when successful, can be shared with other buildings.

Step 3: Facilitate Building-Level Changes

If the school district has a guidance program leader, that individual can assist the building counselors make needed changes by establishing systems that help them focus on those changes. Two such mechanisms are described next: first, having building staffs commit to goals for program improvement and develop action plans for achieving those goals; and, second, having building staffs develop transition and implementation plans similar to those developed at the district level. If counselor leadership is at the building level, school counselors and their principals can use the strategies described next.

Use a Goal-Based Program Improvement System

An effective means for helping building staff make the transition to a comprehensive guidance program is the use of a goal-based program improvement system. Goals help individuals focus their energies on changes they and others perceive as important, and make change manageable. In the circumstance we are describing—remodeling and revitalizing your program while you are living in it—the thought of striving to implement all the changes at once can be overwhelming. Focusing on a handful of goals is conceivable to most people;

being allowed to develop their own strategies for attaining those goals allows counselors a sense of autonomy and comfort in making the needed changes.

In Northside, the goal areas are established at the district level. The district initiates the goal-setting and action planning processes, but each building is provided latitude in choosing specific implementation strategies that fit its needs or specialties. Establishing the goals for high priority skill development, clients, or activities and the process of goal-setting, action planning, monitoring, and evaluating progress toward the goals provides a consistency of focus across the district. These efforts serve to effect the continuity of newly implemented programs, allow for the continuation of dialogue between counselors from different buildings about change efforts, and give direction for inservice training and staff development activities.

Goal Setting

In reviewing the current guidance program and the desired guidance program, you discovered some discrepancies, as we discussed in chapter 6. These discrepancies are the logical targets of and point to the goals for program improvements. The number of goals people are asked to consider depends on the number of discrepancies found, the size of the discrepancies, and the priorities the district or building has set. A handful of goals are probably enough for a counselor to strive for in one year. Goals should be delineated for program improvements and for performance improvements. A sample of a memo used in Northside Independent School District to assist counselors to attend to meaningful goals is presented in Figure 7–5. (It should remind you of Figure 6–2; the difference is that in this instance the goals are presented to individual staff members as challenges to each to do something to help repair the discrepancies between the current program design and that of the desired program.)

These goals are broad and leave each counselor or building staff with choices. What they do "to improve the quality of time spent in responsive services" and how they do it is left to them. Couselors may strive to decrease individual counseling time by initiating small group counseling, or systematically consulting with teachers, for example. An example of more specific goal targets is presented in Figure 7–6.

These goals establish more specific activities for counselors to implement at the building level, but leaves the implementation plan to them. They are asked to conduct group counseling for targeted populations, but the actual design of the counseling series is left to them. In both cases the counselors specify the student outcomes and also objectives for their new activities; they plan their own strategies and methods of evaluation based on local needs and their own resources.

Counselors are asked to set their own goals to be reviewed by their immediate supervisor. Where there is more than one counselor in a building, the guidance department as a whole should have goals also; for example, the department will develop an annual plan for expanded implementation of the guidance curriculum.

Figure 7–5
Goals Memo

To: Counselors
From: Director of Guidance
Re: Program and Performance Goals

Below are listed general goals that have been identified for *program* and *performance* improvements. Please pick two from each category to focus on for this school year, and specify the improvement you envision on the action planning form that is attached.

Program Goals
- to increase time spent in *curriculum*/developmental guidance
- to decrease time spent in *responsive services*/to improve quality of time spent in responsive services
- to decrease time spent in *system support*
- to decrease time/improve quality of time spent with school *staff*
- to increase time spent with *parents*

Performance Goals
- to improve group guidance skills
- to improve counseling skills
- to improve consulting skills
- to improve program planning/evaluation skills
- to improve referral skills

The individuals' goals within the department should be related to each other's, and all counselors on a staff should be cognizant of their colleagues' goals. This helps to develop a support system that is useful in helping the counselors meet success in striving for their goals.

We also recommend that building principals sign off on the goals to indicate not only their awareness of the counselors' endeavors, but also their approval. The head counselor or, in buildings where there is no such designated department leader, counselors should meet and discuss the goals with the principal. This ensures that the guidance goals are consistent with the general building goals and provides a vehicle for enlisting the principal's support in goal attainment. The goals should ultimately be submitted to the district office for review by the administrator responsible for guidance.

Action Planning

Once specific goals have been established, each counselor and each department should develop action plans for meeting these goals. This process was outlined in chapter 6. As mentioned previously, action planning encourages forward and realistic

Figure 7–6
Counselors' Goals Memo

To: Elementary School Counselors
From: Patricia Henderson, Director of Guidance
Re: Counselors' Goals, 1986–87

The goal-setting process implemented for the past several years worked well to help focus the guidance program improvement efforts. The districtwide goals for 1986–87 are listed below. Please discuss these goals with your principals and add others that are in response to the needs of your campus community.

1. To continue to contribute to students' education by effectively teaching guidance curricula outlined in the Comprehensive Guidance Program *Framework*.

2. To respond to campus-identified high priority student-clients through effective group counseling. "High priority student-clients" may include students who are underachieving or who are behaving irresponsibly.

3. To respond to campus-identified high priority parent-clients through systematically implemented parent consultation or parent education.

4. To decrease student-contact-time spent in clerical/quasi-administrative tasks by identifying personal "time-eaters" and minimizing the time spent on these.

5. To provide a better balanced guidance program by systematically planning the year's acitivities to adhere as much as feasible to the district-outlined and campus-specified comprehensive program design. (Planning assistance will be provided by the Director of Guidance.)

6. To increase the effectiveness of counseling and guidance activities by clear articulation of the counselor's theoretical base.

As in previous years, we will be discussing the strategies you identify as appropriate for striving to attain your goals. A copy of the revised Planning Form is attached. Please submit a copy of your "Guidance Program Improvement Planning" forms to me by *September 15.*

Approved: _____
                J.E. Rawlinson, Associate Superintendent

cc. Elementary School Principals

---

thinking. It sets in motion a series of decisions and plans that actually help implement the strategies. A sample planning form is provided in Figure 7–7.

Once counselors' goals have been identified and counselors have committed themselves to implementation strategies, the guidance program leader has a means of monitoring counselors' progress toward these goals. This process is discussed in more depth a little later on in this chapter.

Develop Building-Level Implementation Plans

To make the transition to the comprehensive guidance program at the building level, several sets of plans must be drawn up: plans for change, action plans, and program plans. The building "plan for change" is similar to the district's "master plan for program improvement." It includes a list of tasks that must be accomplished in order to fully implement the desired program. "Action plans" outline the actions to be taken in order to accomplish target goals or to implement specific change strategies. The "program plan" is a description of the actual activities that need to be accomplished to deliver the comprehensive program components.

Develop Building Master Plan for Change

A building "master plan for change" needs to be developed. Building guidance staffs have identified areas for change based on the student and community needs assessment, and based on the comparison of their current guidance program with the expectations expressed in the district program description. The former suggests the content and client priorities, the latter the program shape and counselor function priorities. At this time the building guidance staff make decisions about and clarify in writing the parts of their current program that need augmenting, streamlining, or displacement, and the kinds of activities that need to be added to their current program.

Develop the Building Action Plan

Next the building guidance staff lists its priorities for change and writes the building plan of action for accomplishing the desired changes. The plan of action includes taking actions and performing tasks, identifying the person responsible to see that the task is accomplished, establishing the timeframe for its accomplishment, and clarifying the evidence that it has been done. For example, if, in order to access students in a junior high school, guidance curriculum time must be negotiated with the academic teachers, several tasks need to be accomplished before the counselor can infuse the guidance learning activities into the various curricula: (a) The counselor must have lesson objectives planned, (b) the principal's support must be enlisted, (c) a meeting with the academic department chairs needs to be established, and so on. To accomplish each of these tasks successfully, plans must be made.

A point needs to be made here: The changes must begin with reallocation of the resources currently available and in anticipation of new resources that will probably be allocated. Counselors must resist the mentality of waiting until everything at the system level has been done. This is where the give-and-take nature of the process is most evident. Only so much change can occur at the building level within the current resource allocation, but those changes need to be made. For example, if a principal wants counselors teaching or developing guidance lessons for use in a homeroom-type situation and perceives counselors

Figure 7–7
Guidance Program Improvement Planning Form

GUIDANCE PROGRAM IMPROVEMENT PLANNING

School: _____

Name: _____

Principal/Head Counselor Signature: _____

Date: _____

USE A SEPARATE FORM FOR EACH GOAL

PLANNING
(To Be Completed by September 1)

EVALUATION
(To Be Completed by Contract End—June)

Goal:

Program Objective/Strategy	Tasks to Accomplish	Timeframe	Level of (1–5) Accomplishment	Student/Others' Outcomes

Overall Assessment of Level
Of Accomplishment:

1	2	3	4	5
(Not Achieved)				(Fully Achieved)

Counselor's Signature: _____

Principal/Head Counselor: _____

Date: _____

as sitting in their offices spending undue amounts of time with individual students, the counselors should devise ways to attend to the principal's goal. It is conceivable that if they managed their time with the consideration that the principal has an important priority for them, the lessons could be developed. The principal, then, would be more apt to believe that the counselors use their time efficiently when they ask for other considerations.

Often the success of system-level resource expansion depends on the evidence of maximum resource use at the school level. Spending all the money appropriated for buying program materials is an obvious example. On the other hand, once buildings have established their local plans, the district can identify and target problems and solutions identified in several buildings. If several building guidance program plans seek to augment the guidance curriculum through use of ''homeroom'' periods, a districtwide group might be formed to work together to develop appropriate guidance learning activities.

Develop the Building Program Plan

At this time, the building staff should describe their specific program plan for the upcoming year. In establishing the desired program for the building (chapter 6), activities were described for each component. This plan will not only list those activities and the related outcomes, but will also project the timeframe in which they will be done. It will include the activities being maintained and those intended to be added to the program, reflecting the goals that have been established.

Now that a desired balance has been established for the organization of the building guidance program, decisions have been made concerning the student competencies that have priority for achievement, and appropriate guidance activities and resources have been chosen for the program, the next step is to establish timetables and activity schedules. This is another one of those important steps in the program improvement process because it provides still another opportunity for the guidance staff to make their program visible—visible in the sense that others can see the totality of the program and the resources and time required to carry it out. This step is also important because of the discipline required to develop timetables and activity schedules. It forces you to think through carefully how the program will unfold before it is implemented.

A format for portraying the yearly program plan is displayed in Figure 7–8. The calendar provides at a glance an overview of the program plan.

This calendar format is simple and graphically displays the balance of the program, but it does not provide all the information desirable. Activities should be described elsewhere in enough detail so that a reader could know what the program is accomplishing and how. The actual program plan should reflect a realistic application of the program resources—time, talent, materials, facilities, and so on.

Figure 7–8
Program Activities/Component/Month

NISD Guidance Department CALENDAR for 198_____–198_____

Campus: _____

	CURRICULUM	INDIVIDUAL PLANNING	RESPONSIVE SERVICES	SYSTEM SUPPORT
Aug.				
Sept.				
Oct.				
Nov.				
Dec.				
Jan.				
Feb.				
Mar.				
Apr.				
May				
June				
July				

Design New Activities.

Having developed the yearly program plan, the building staff is strongly urged at this time to make final their plans for any new activities that are to be performed to implement more fully any of the program components. Once the school year has begun it is difficult to take the necessary time to plan thoroughly a new activity to ensure its being done with quality. It is imperative that new activities be done well so that the success of the activities is reasonably assured. Most likely, in order to add new activities, you will have displaced some traditional activities; thus, others will be observing the merit of the new activities very closely.

We have previously discussed Gelatt's model for designing a new activity. The guidance program leader needs to be realistic about how far the budget resources will go and plan their expenditure in accordance with the program priorities. The new materials need to be ordered in ample time to receive them. Finally, the logistics of how to conduct the new activities need to be planned: not just the content plan, but the facilities that will be used, how the students will be accessed, the timeframe for the activity, and securing the necessary audiovisual equipment.

Step 4: Monitor Changed Program Implementation

By now you are well into the implementation of a comprehensive guidance program. As difficult as planning and designing the program was, it is even more difficult to maintain the momentum for change and to maintain the improvements so that the program does not revert back to its original traditional form. Systems for monitoring progress toward the established goals and for monitoring overall improved program implementation must be developed and used. Staff must continue to be encouraged to try the new activities and reinforced in their efforts. Finally, program adjustments must be made as a result of monitoring the changes.

Monitor Improvement Plans

If you have used the action planning process and the format we have recommended, the guidance program leader has a vehicle for monitoring progress toward the goals that have been set. In planning the process to attain their goals, counselors have listed the activities they need to do and have established a timeframe for doing them. Depending on the size of the district, the guidance program leader can monitor counselors' efforts according to their timeframes—a "tickler file" system will help—or reports of counselors' progress can be elicited on an announced schedule: monthly, quarterly, or once per semester. If there are head counselors, it is appropriate for the head counselors to monitor the progress of the counselors, and for the guidance program leader to monitor the progress of the head counselors and, only indirectly, the building staffs.

Monitoring does not need to be heavy-handed; most staffs will have worked hard to succeed at their new efforts and will be proud of their accomplishments. Indeed, monitoring provides the guidance program leader with the opportunity to support and reinforce their work. Also, if staff need resources that the guidance program leader can provide, the leader will be aware of their needs. If for some reason insurmountable obstacles get in staff's way or a well-planned activity does not yield the anticipated results, the guidance program leader will be aware of their hurt and will be able to encourage them to continue to strive for improvement. Changing involves risk taking. A sample of the timeframe used in Northside for the goal-setting, monitoring, and goal-attainment assessment process is provided in Figure 7–9.

Monitor Overall Program Implementation

The district has established guidelines or rules for what the desired program is and for ways to accomplish it. Methods for monitoring the content and shape of the buildings' changing programs—and, indeed, that of the district as a whole—must be used. These provide the guidance program leader with information about who is and is not working toward the desired improvements, and about what is and is not possible in the given circumstances—that is, what else outside the guidance department needs to change in order for the guidance program to be as comprehensive, balanced, and student-directed as the newly established policy states.

To monitor the changing content of the program, the guidance program leader can use some of the methods described in chapter 9, such as aggregating student outcome data or using unobtrusive measures such as cataloging the new program materials that counselors order for their programs. To monitor the changing shape of the program, the guidance program leader can continue to ask the counselors to account for their use of time through calendars or logs. We recommend that the guidance program leader use the same time accounting measures as over time they will provide graphic evidence of the shift in the program. This evidence proves to be a reward in itself for the counselors. Remember, success breeds success!

Provide Encouragement and Reinforcement

Part of the difficulty of maintaining a program stems from problems associated with trying to change staff work behavior patterns. It is relatively easy to do something new once, particularly if it is highly visible. Also, some staff members may sabotage the improvement process by going along with a new activity once, but when it is over, withdrawing their support. As a result, is is important to build into the program ways of assessing the need for reinforcement and ways to provide such reinforcement.

Figure 7–9
Timeframe for Supervisory Activities

TO: Middle School Head Counselors
             Middle School Principals
FROM: Patricia Henderson, Director of Guidance
SUBJECT: Guidance Department Supervisory Timeframe
DATE: August 22, 1986

It is recommended that Head Counselors keep records of their supervisory activities.

August–September
  Individual Goal Setting Conferences
    1. Principal with Head Counselor (by 9/15)
    2. Head Counselor with Counselors (by 9/15)
    3. Director of Guidance with Head Counselor (9/15–9/30)

October–November
  Observation of counselors

December–January
  Conferences regarding:
    1. feedback from observations
    2. progress towards goals

February
  Development of counselor performance evaluations in consultation with
    Principal and Director of Guidance
  Conduct evaluation conferences (by 3/1)

March
  Counselors develop Professional Growth Plans

April–May
  Observations of counselors

June
  Conferences regarding:
    1. feedback from observations
    2. assessment of goal attainment
    3. Professional Growth Plans
    4. tentative goals for following year

APPROVED: _____
J.E. Rawlinson, Associate Superintendent for Instruction

Because the need for reinforcement occurs over time, it is important that at least part of the staff development program be designed to provide such reinforcement. Skill building and discussion sessions that take place on regular basis are vital. Skill building opportunities can be provided by encouraging counselors in the system to share their successful new activities with others in a miniconvention type format, if the system is large enough to do this, or at local, state, or national professional growth conferences.

Discussion sessions around specific events in the guidance program can be held in regular staff meetings. Staff meetings provide counselors opportunities to talk with their colleagues about guidance and counseling issues. Glickman and Jones (1986, p. 90) cited professional dialogues as one of the critical factors in creating a successful school. They stated that: "Essentially a dialogue occurs when supervisors provide the elements of time, focus, and structure for individuals to meet and talk." Thus counselors' staff meetings are an essential vehicle to continue to encourage needed changes in addition to ensuring a basic communication of information.

On a more informal basis, birthday parties, potluck dinners, and other socials are helpful ways to provide reinforcement and form inter-building teams. When such events are planned, consider the down times that occur in any academic year. In some areas of the country, the last part of January and the first part of February need special events to brighten the season. Midyear conferences can be held on a regional basis and are usually well attended.

Make Program Adjustments

As the program unfolds, there will be times when it is necessary to make program adjustments. Keep in mind that such adjustments are fine-tuning adjustments. They are not major adjustments made as part of the initial program improvement. Those come after more thorough evaluation, as discussed in chapter 9. Any changes made in the program now should be made only after careful thought. Some changes will be obvious, as in activities that simply do not work. Others will not be obvious on the surface, but will become clear after systematic evaluation. As a rule, count to 10 before making any substantial changes. Some activities need time to take hold and as a result may not show up too well at first; for example, a shift from individual counseling to group counseling may not be appreciated at first by students who are used to individual attention, but as more students receive group counseling, its positive effects will influence the evaluation.

Monitoring and adjusting the program are the results of formative evaluation, a concept discussed in chapter 9. For now, the kinds of changes you can expect to be making most often as you fine-tune the program may include modification of timetables, modification of activity schedules, substitution or modification of activities, substitution of resources, and changes in student competencies at various grade levels.

Step 5: Plan and Implement Public Relations Activities

Now that you have a grasp of the new program and are comfortable in describing it, you are ready to plan and implement public relations activities. Because the best generator of good public relations is a good program, counselors need to feel that they are conducting the best program feasible. They need to feel secure in the priorities that have been set and feel that they can explain them to the many ''publics'' served such as students, teachers, administrators, parents, the business community, and community members at large.

Planning public relations begins with study of the data that were gathered in the assessment of the current program as to how others perceive the guidance program. Because one purpose of public relations is for people to know more about the program, the goal at this time is to help people move from what they thought the program was to what the new program structure is. To accomplish this task, we recommend that a work group be formed to assist in planning and implementing the public relations program. The work group should include not only counselors but also representatives—preferably leaders—of the publics with whom you plan to relate. It could be an ad hoc group and it may include representatives from the steering or school-community advisory committees. Ultimately, the group that will continue public relations activities, once they are undertaken, is the school-community advisory committee.

Plan Your Public Relations Program

Public relations program planning is not different from the planning used in the rest of the guidance program improvement process. You need to know where you are; perform a ''current assessment''—in this case, the perception survey. You need to know where you want to go—the ''desired'' end—in this case, the established goals for the public relations program. And, you need to know how you are going to get there; establish your plan of action that includes the public relations objectives and strategies to be accomplished and the timeframe involved.

To be systematic, public relations activities are installed as an ongoing part of the program's overall improvement and management procedures. Public relations activities that are not related in this integrated fashion to the total program may be superficial and, as a result, may not have sufficient impact. Thus, careful attention to the planning is important.

To develop your plan for public relations, consider these steps:

1. Establish goals for your public relations efforts; for example, for program consumers to be informed about, understand, and be supportive of the comprehensive guidance program.
2. Identify the target populations for your public relations efforts; for example, students, teachers, parents, administrators, referral agency personnel, community representatives/leaders.

3. Find out what these publics think about what you are doing and what they think you should be doing; for example, the specific data gathered in the current program perception survey should tell you this.
4. Establish specific objectives for each subgroup; for example, to inform all parents about the program; to gain support from some parents for the program.
5. Identify the resources available to assist in your efforts; for example, "Meet Your Counselor" pamphlets, PTA newsletters and programs, daytime radio talk shows, and school official communiqués.
6. Consider the relative impact each resource may have on the target population; for example, inviting PTA leaders to serve on the guidance advisory committee provides them an opportunity to fulfill their leadership/representative role and, if advice is taken, their support for the program has been enlisted.
7. Translate these resources into strategies to be used. Where possible we recommend using the already existing resources that have demonstrated effectiveness for reaching the target population, for example, the Administrator's Association newsletter to communicate with administrators. Where none exist, creating unique resources such as guidance department newsletters or "Counselor Corner" columns in the local newspaper is to be considered.
8. Outline the steps that will be taken in the development of these strategies and relate them to the overall plan.
9. Assign a person to be responsible for the activities.
10. Establish your timeframe.

Well-planned public relations activities are an integral part of the guidance program improvement process. Remember, an effective public relations program is sincere in purpose and execution; in keeping with the total guidance program's purpose and characteristics; positive in approach and appeal; continuous in application; comprehensive in scope; clear, with simple messages; and beneficial to both sender and receiver.

There are two purposes of public relations activities: to let consumers know how good the program is, and to change any negative perceptions they may have to more positive ones. To do this, it is important to listen for and understand the negative perceptions that some consumers may have. For example, some teachers do not know about our program and are often dissatisfied that they do not get "instant service" when they think they need it. They are not aware of our taking work home at night like they do to grade papers and plan lessons. They do not think that we are tied to a set schedule that someone else has determined. Many are not familiar with our role as student advocates; they see us in problem situations as adversaries. Also administrators may think that counselors do not work very hard. Co-administrators work evenings supervising activities, and they do not think that counselors do that. Some counselors are perceived as not being loyal to the school because they do not attend extracurricular activities. Some parents do not feel that they get the response they want, or perceive counselors as having made recommendations about their children that have damaged their educational careers. Many are not aware of our specialized training. Some in the population at large still—unfortunately—have negative bias against people with mental health problems and are skeptical about the value of psychological services. In addition, some students do not recognize or acknowledge the help they receive from counselors. They perceive us as paper-pushers who were not helpful when they perceived they were having a problem. In general, because our programs have not been well defined, people have had unrealistic expectations about counselors and the services counselors can and should provide.

Implement Your Public Relations Program

In implementing your public relations program there are two essential factors to consider: timing and quality. Public relations activities should be planned to capitalize on times when you have your audiences' attention. The quality of any activity ought to be high; you need to put your best foot forward.

We suggest that you consider conducting your public relations activities with your various target populations at those times when you are changing or working on improved activities that affect particular consumer groups. When you are asking teachers for classroom time to conduct the guidance curriculum activities, some may be reluctant to cooperate. This can be balanced by conducting effective lessons when the opportunity is provided. Teachers may be quite upset when they look for a counselor to assist them with a problem and learn that the counselor is scheduled into classrooms for guidance for a certain amount of time. This can be the ideal time to explain to them the benefits gained from developmental guidance. Administrators also may be resistant when counselors try to divest themselves of the quasi-administrative/clerical tasks that take up so much time and talent. They get weary of counselors saying, "That's not my job." If, however, they become convinced that the time saved is directly focused on helping students through the guidance curriculum, individual planning, or responsive services, this negative feeling may be dissipated. Parents who are used to the notion that counselors work one-to-one with students may be put off by group guidance activities. If group guidance is unexplained, it may further parents' feelings of not getting adequate service from this specialist for their own child. At such times, careful explanation of how many more students and parents are receiving service offset this concern.

Guidance Program Leader's Roles and Responsibilities

The role of the guidance program leader shifts during this phase to that of staff leader and program manager for ongoing successful program implementation. While the transition to the new program is being made, the roles that the leader will play in continuing leadership and supervision of the improved program are begun.

The guidance program leader keeps the momentum for change focused and alive during the transition, and in implementation maintains the focus on continuing improvement and fine-tuning of the improved program. The person responsible for program development leads the district-level changes and is the chief implementer of the district master plan for change. The leader brings in appropriate consultants to assist with the implementation of special projects. The central office guidance staff member is in a position to know what is going on at the district, state, and federal levels and has the responsibility to communicate and interpret that information to the rest of the guidance staff. The guidance program leader manages the ongoing public relations efforts.

The guidance program leader develops building planning and improvement monitoring systems to be used when the program has settled into ongoing planning-evaluating-adjusting. The ultimate accountability for program success and for performance improvement is up to the designated guidance program leader. The guidance program leader works not only to ensure that guidance department staff continue to strive for program improvements but also encourages and reinforces their efforts. It is conventional wisdom among personnel specialists that employees do what is ''inspected'' not what is ''expected''; an ''inspector'' is needed.

Some of this authority is delegated to the other designated leaders such as building head counselors or counselor cluster leaders. Those leaders need assistance in carrying out their roles effectively. As discussed more fully in chapter 8, this will probably entail direct modeling of appropriate conduct as a supervisor, and it will entail encouraging these leaders as they try leadership strategies. To ensure full implementation, we encourage the continued use of other staff leaders—informal or otherwise—to ensure healthy communication between the district-level guidance program leader and the entire guidance staff. Informal leaders are often the best vehicles for honest feedback.

Central office guidance program leaders need to establish their roles with the principals and other administrators. Because administrative responsibilities are probably shared with them, they must be educated as to the guidance department goals and priorities and their support must be enlisted for the changes and the ongoing efforts as well. Their concerns and goals need to be attended to and supported with the counselors. A goal we have not discussed fully is that of striving for open and clear communication between the building counselors and their administrators; this is sometimes problematic and deserves conscious attention. For guidance program change efforts to be successful, collaboration must occur between the counselors and the administrators. The interactive nature of educational program decision making presents challenges to both building- and district-level administrators; successful program implementation depends on taking correlated steps toward program improvement. The more these actions are orchestrated, the more effective the guidance program will be in achieving its goals for helping students learn what the program can offer.

During implementation of the newly conceptualized guidance program, it is time to focus on efforts to ensure that the guidance department staff members—professional and paraprofessional, leaders and followers—have the competencies they need to conduct the well-balanced and comprehensive guidance program that is envisioned. Chapter 8 will discuss in more detail *how* the staff leader can work to ensure that each staff member is striving to reach full professional potential, that each staff member is operating competently.

References

Beaumont, A.G., Cooper, A.C., & Stockard, R.H. (1978). *A model career counseling and placement program*. Bethlehem, PA: College Placement Services.

Gelatt, H.B. (1975). *Selecting alternative program strategies, Module 7*. Palo Alto, CA: American Institutes for Research.

Golden, L.B. (1983). Brief family interventions in the school setting. *Elementary School Guidance and Counseling, 17*, 288–293.

Glickman, C.D., & Jones, J.W. (1986). Supervision: Creating the dialogue. *Educational Leadership, 44*, 90–91.

Myrick, R.D., & Dixon, R.W. (1985). Changing school attitudes and behavior through group counseling. *School Counselor, 32*, 325–330.

Peer, G.G. (1985). The status of secondary school guidance: A national survey. *School Counselor, 32*, 181–189.

Reardon, R.C., & Burck, H.D. (Eds.). (1977). *Facilitating career development: Strategies for counselors*. Springfield, IL: Charles C Thomas.

Salmon, S.J., & Selig, M.R. (1976). The guidance learning center. *Elementary School Guidance and Counseling, 10*, 260–267.

CHAPTER 8

ENSURING SCHOOL COUNSELOR COMPETENCY

In the past, the school counseling profession has emphasized the process (skills and techniques) of guidance such as counseling and consulting. Emphasis on the content of guidance—decision making, problem solving, communicating—has, until recently, been of secondary importance. In addition, the comprehensive, developmental approach is relatively new to guidance program conceptualization and delivery. Also, new competencies are required of school counselors or, at minimum, new emphasis is being placed on competencies that traditionally have been underutilized. Thus, during the program improvement process and beyond, attention needs to be given to ensuring the competency of school counselors in developing and implementing comprehensive guidance programs. Chapter 8 describes how to do this by focusing on five steps that need to be taken to ensure school counselor competency.

Step 1: Getting ready;
Step 2: Getting the right people in the right roles;
Step 3: Providing appropriate supervision;
Step 4: Evaluating staff effectively; and
Step 5: Encouraging professional growth.

The first step focuses on becoming knowledgable about the resources required to establish programs that will ensure school counselor competency. This involves reviewing the position guides and the human, financial, and political resources available. The second step involves getting the right people into the right roles. "Right people" means people who are competent—who have sufficient knowledge, skills, attitudes, and beliefs—to handle their assigned jobs. "Right roles" means roles that the program requires to ensure effective delivery of the desired program. Collaborating between counselor supervisors and counselor educators, recruiting qualified applicants, selecting appropriate candidates for available positions, placing them in appropriate settings, and orienting them to new roles are the tasks required to accomplish the second step.

The goal of the other three major steps is helping staff members reach optimum levels of performance in their assigned positions. According to Barret and Schmidt (1986), school counselors benefit from administrative, clinical, and developmental supervision. This section of the chapter includes a discussion of the changing role of the building-level guidance department head—frequently called the "head counselor." Although specific ideas for counselor performance evaluation are discussed in chapter 9, a brief discussion is included in this chapter because we feel it is best if performance evaluation is envisioned as part of an overall system designed to encourage professional growth and development. Finally, the section on professional growth includes discussions about developing individual professional growth plans, assessing the needs for counselor competency development, forming a district master plan for staff development, and dealing with individuals who do not meet minimum professional competency standards. If you are just beginning a guidance program, you would accomplish these tasks in the order described. If the program is already operational, however, these tasks are ongoing.

Step 1: Getting Ready

Before a systematic effort to ensure the competency of school counselors can begin, performance expectations for counselors' positions must be stated, and the person charged with the responsibility of improving counselors' performance must be aware of the resources available to assist with staff development.

Base Counselors' Roles on Position Guides

As we stated earlier (chapter 5), counselors' roles should be defined by position guides. Position guides state the expectations of staff members in implementing the program. The example we used from Northside Independent School District delineates the following expectations: School counselors should *teach* the guidance curriculum, *guide* students in their individual planning efforts, *counsel* students with problems or concerns, *consult* with parents and staff, *refer* students or their parents to other specialists, and *coordinate* the work of others (e.g., faculty doing tasks previously done by school counselors, and community volunteers participating in comprehensive guidance program activities). Thus, counselors in a system that uses this position guide are expected to have the competencies needed to teach, guide, counsel, consult, refer, and coordinate effectively. Further delineation of these competecies—the related skills, knowledge, attitudes, and beliefs—is not the subject of this book. What is important for our purposes here, however, is that you be aware that ensuring counselor competency can occur only if you and your district have identified the counselor competencies required to successfully deliver a comprehensive guidance program.

Consider Available Resources

As you prepare to accomplish steps 2, 3, 4, and 5 in ensuring school counselor competency, you need to consider the resources available. Buildings, districts, and communities have the human, financial, and political resources required to ensure counselor competency. The question is: How can these resources be used effectively?

Human Resources

Effective performance in a position is a shared responsibility of the position holder and the school district. Counselor applicants have a responsibility to define themselves adequately so that prospective employers can evaluate whether they are "right" for the jobs available. Employers have the responsibility for clearly and specifically defining the positions available. Counselors have a professional responsibility to be competent in what the district has the right to expect—that is, the educational areas defined as minimum standards for certification by the state and the ethical standards defined by the profession.

Every school and district employs administrators who are responsible for the performance of the guidance department staff. The titles of such administrators vary, as do levels of authority and responsibility. Administrators may have such titles as principal, superintendent, head counselor, guidance and counseling director, coordinator, or supervisor. The roles that each fulfills on behalf of ensuring school counselor competency need to be specifically defined. The number of these administrators who may be involved and the degree of their competency in guidance and counseling will vary by the size of the school district as well as by its commitment to the comprehensive guidance program concept. Chance may also enter the picture in terms of the career paths of the administrators involved—for example, a principal who was formerly an effective school counselor may provide a different quality of administrative direction and supervision than one who has had no counseling experience; and the quality of such direction and supervision may vary depending on the principal's experiences as a school counselor.

Certain communities and geographical regions have resources that counselors may be able to use. For example, there are over four hundred counselor training institutions in the United States. Many school districts are sufficiently close to these institutions to have access to counselor educators. Other school counselors, professional counseling association leaders, mental health counselors, counseling psychologists, psychiatrists, training consultants, business/industry human resources specialists, and other specialists also may be available. In order to make optimum use of these specialists for professional development, however, their expertise needs to be surveyed and cataloged. We suggest that you compile a list of such individuals, identify their areas of expertise, the topics on which they present workshops, their professional licenses and certificates, and their fees.

Financial Resources

The financial resources available to the guidance program should make provision for the professional development of the counseling staff. Districts provide monies and opportunities for inservice training and attendance at professional conferences and conventions. Regional offices and state departments of education also provide education and training opportunities for school counselors. Larger school systems and intermediate school districts often provide professional journal subscriptions, books, and training tapes through professional libraries.

Political Resources

In this era of educational reform, there is increased support to enhance professional educators' competency and accountability. Many states' reform efforts include renewed emphasis on professional growth in the form of mandatory inservice education, professional renewal requirements for recertification, and career ladders. Even if counselors are not mentioned directly in these efforts, the movement to improve overall staff competency can be used specifically to assist counselors. For example, Texas mandated a "Model for Effective Teaching and Supervision," which provided the training of the trainers, the training materials, and the hourly requirements for teachers and administrators to be trained in the model. Counselors and counseling supervisors were not included in the mandate; however, counseling administrators were. It then became the counseling administrators' responsibility to see that counselors were also provided opportunities to learn about effective teaching, counseling, and supervision.

Step 2: Getting the Right People in the Right Roles

With the position guides written and the available resources identified, a systematic approach to staff development may begin. The first task for ensuring competency of school counselors is to have the right people in the right roles. Finding the right people requires the guidance program leader to *collaborate* with the colleges and universities in which most of the counselors are trained, to *recruit* the most highly skilled graduates to apply for available positions, and to *select* the most talented/skilled applicants to fill those positions. Helping school counselors fulfill the right roles requires the guidance program leader to *place* them properly and to *orient* them to their new assignments.

Collaboration

Most college and university counselor education departments seek to develop collaborative relationships with the school districts in their areas that are most apt to hire their graduates. Such relationships are built by the professors' seeking advice about various aspects of their training program. Many counselor education departments have formed formal advisory committees consisting of counselors and guidance program leaders from their neighboring districts. In addition, counselor educators seek advice through professional discussions and involvement in local or state professional associations for counselors. Often practitioners are invited to make presentations to counselor education classes, whereby both the students in preservice training and the professors themselves gain insight into the actual work of school counselors.

Field experiences provide a primary opportunity for meaningful collaboration between counselor educators and local school districts. Accreditation standards developed by the Association for Counselor Educators and Supervisors (1986) encourage counselor educators to include field experiences for counselors-in-training. Making these experiences effective is a shared responsibility of the college/university staff and the building/district staff. To ensure successful completion of coursework that includes fieldwork, professors need to be explicit about the experiences that counselors-in-training should have. Requiring them to counsel individuals and write up case studies, to conduct group counseling sessions with students with problems, and to teach developmental guidance lessons guarantees that counselors-in-training will have these experiences. At the same time, school counselors responsible for supervising counselors-in-training need to be explicit about the experiences they know to be valuable relative to the design of their school guidance program. Figure 8–1 provides an example of guidelines for practicum students used by Northside Independent School District to help counselors-in-training consider what experiences they would benefit from in order to learn to be effective school counselors within that district. Guidelines such as these and the related experiences that students have help the counselors-in-training to conceptualize the program and to understand the relationship between the skills and techniques they are learning and the program in which they will use these skills. For most counselors-in-training it becomes their first opportunity to explore this relationship.

Recruitment

Interacting with counselors-in-training is one way to recruit applicants. The purpose of recruitment is to develop a quality pool of applicants. The better the applicant pool, the more potential there is for those selected to become outstanding counselors. The basis for recruitment is to have a quality program and to let

Figure 8–1
Guidelines for Practicum Students
Guidance Department
Northside Independent School District

To ensure that you have experience in each of the components that constitute the District's Comprehensive Guidance Program, please consider the following as possible activities to be included in your practicum experience:

Guidance Curriculum Component
- Developmental group guiding (guiding-teaching of guidance content using guidance techniques)

Individual Planning Component
- Helping groups of students apply
    (1) skills learned through curriculum component
    (2) tests results information
    (3) career information and/or experiences
- Helping students develop educational plans

Responsive Services Component
- Counseling individuals
- Small group counseling
- Consultation with teacher and/or parents regarding children with problems
- Referring

System Support Component
- Coordinating testing
- Teacher in-service
- Special purpose testing
- Assist with pre-processing PAC referrals

Please read the
TACD Position Statement, 1982: "The School Counselor: Personal Characteristics, Work Environment, Roles and Competencies"
NISD's Guidance Program Description Materials

---

people know about it. Clearly explaining the guidance program to district faculty provides teachers who are certified as counselors or those who are planning to seek advanced training an opportunity to consider the merits of being part of the school counseling staff. Providing teachers with quality feedback about students they refer and consulting effectively with them as they face problems with students or students' parents are other recruitment vehicles. If your school or district hires experienced counselors, presenting quality programs at professional conferences and workshops also is a useful recruitment activity. Finally, the more active the school counselors in a district are in local, state, and national professional organizations, the more visible the program will be; if the quality of the school counselors' leadership and sense of responsibility is impressive, others will want to be part of the district's comprehensive guidance program.

Selection

After attracting quality applicants, the next challenge is selecting the best as candidates for school counseling positions. As we have said before, school counselor positions must be defined explicitly in order to match the applicants' qualifications with the expectations of the positions. The competencies required for the counselor positions already have been defined at the district level, but each building may have specific demands that must be made explicit as well. These demands may include needing individuals with certain personality characteristics as well as certain preferences for various guidance program functions. The goal is to assemble a balance of characteristics and competencies across a building or district staff. For example, balanced staffs may have conceptualizers and logistics specialists, leaders and followers, those who enjoy group work and those who enjoy consultation, and so on. It may also include an ethnic/racial balance parallel to that of the student body and a balance of men and women.

The process for staff selection includes interviewing applicants, considering the recommendations of people familiar with their work, and reviewing their experiences and achievements. Interviews of prospective counselors should be conducted not only by the personnel department staff but also by the supervisor or administrator who will oversee the work of the staff member. In the case of the school counselor, this means the building principal as well as the district guidance program leader. Some systems also have effectively involved the current counseling staff in the interview process. Although effective interviewing by a large group is difficult to orchestrate, some districts have all the counselors participate in a group discussion with applicants. Others have had individual counselors conduct different parts of the interview—for example, one counselor taking the applicant on a tour of the school, another explaining the guidance center, and so on. The size of the current staff and the number of candidates to be interviewed directly influence the interview format to be used.

The interview should provide the opportunity for the candidates to relate themselves to the positions that are open. An atmosphere conducive to self-expression should be established. Interview questions should lead the applicants to report as much about themselves in relationship to the position as possible in a reasonable length of time. There should be a direct relationship between the questions asked in an interview and the job requirements. Much has been written about the value—or lack of value—of the interview as a selection tool, but it is one way of allowing candidates the opportunity to provide self-reports of their experiences and abilities to fill the position competently. It also allows the employer the opportunity to gain insight about the candidate's personality.

In soliciting recommendations from other professionals who have worked with a candidate, the administrator or supervisor should ask specific questions about the quality of the applicant's experiences in relationship to the role of the school counselor in the district, such as: How effective a teacher has the applicant been? What has been the quality of the applicant's relationships with parents? Persons who give recommendations should be encouraged to provide concrete examples to support their opinions.

Finally, a review of the applicants' strengths and weaknesses as noted in their past performance evaluations provides insight as to their probable success or failure as school counselors. We believe that it is imperative for a counselor to have been an effective teacher in order to begin to be an effective counselor. Counselors should come from the ranks of the best teachers if they are to deliver a quality developmental guidance program that includes classroom guidance. Because the ability to be part of a team also is essential to delivering a comprehensive guidance program, indicators of individuals' past relationships in this regard are important. The guidance program and staff are on center stage in a school, thus potential counselors must have demonstrated that they are first and foremost good employees. Evidence of such traits as these is usually found in past performance ratings.

Proper Placement

A well-developed selection process provides the information needed about candidates selected to fill available school counselor positions. It is imperative that staff members be placed in positions that will make maximum use of their strengths and in which their weaknesses will be minimized by the strengths of others. As we indicated above, strengths and weaknesses in terms of competencies and personal characteristics need to be considered in placing individuals in specific assignments. The "chemistry" of a staff, although difficult to define, is as important to consider as are the competencies available and those required. For example, if a staff already has several highly assertive individuals, the addition of a follower would probably do more for staff balance than the addition of a person seeking a leadership position. With a clear definition in mind of the program that is desired for your building, you are better able to make judgments about who will best fit the job available.

Within a school system it is often possible to redistribute staff members to make optimum use of their talents. The same clarity regarding the competencies and personality characteristics needed in a particular work setting is required if you have the opportunity to transfer individual staff members from one work setting to another. Transfer opportunities can occur naturally in districts where growth provides new positions, or when counselors retire or move on.

Orientation

To help new counselors fulfill their roles properly, orientation to the requirements of the job itself and the context of the work setting is necessary. By orientation we mean providing them with as much information about the comprehensive guidance program as possible. New counselors receive information about the counselor role in their training programs, and about the work setting in the job application and selection process. Once placed, however, they need more specific information about their role and the appropriate use of their competencies in the program. If the new counselor previously was a teacher, it is important to remember that counselors' roles and teachers' roles are different; the transition from one to the other is not automatic. New counselors need to know how the guidance program, perhaps only globally defined to them up to now, actually operates in the building to which they are assigned. The specific acivities that define the four comprehensive program components will need to be conveyed. New counselors also will need to be informed about the structure of the building in which they will work, the principal's priorities, and the organizational relationships.

A member of the existing staff should be designated to help newcomers learn the facts they need and to ease their evolution into the new role. Helping new counselors use their unique competencies is a role for the building guidance department head. This may include helping new counselors to broaden their perspective from a classroom perspective to the school perspective, to act as a consultant to other staff members and as an advocate for students, to put the concept of the guidance program in operation, and to learn the informal power structure of a school.

Orientation should begin with formal meetings conducted by supervisors and administrators. Other topics are best handled through ongoing dialogue with the new counselor and a counselor colleague, who may or may not be the building supervisor. In some programs a "buddy system" has been used effectively. In any case, there is a lot of information for new counselors to learn, and the more systematic their induction into their new positions is, the smoother the transition will be.

Step 3: Providing Appropriate Supervision

Once the right people are in place and are prepared to fulfill the right roles, helping them perform these roles is the challenge. A regular system to encourage performance improvement needs to be established. There are three components that compose a counselor performance improvement system: supervision, evaluation, and professional development. The goal of a performance improvement system is to use procedures that will guide counselors to be accountable for helping students reach specified guidance program outcomes, and to carry out their work as defined in the counselor position guides in a competent manner.

The supervision process provides some of the data needed to evaluate an individual's performance. Supervision helps employees clarify what they are held accountable for. Both the supervision and the evaluation processes provide vehicles for identifying an individual's needs for competency improvement that can be attended to in the professional development component.

Although the primary responsibility for an individual's performance improvement belongs to the individual, others in the system can be of help. Principals, head counselors, and guidance program leaders all have expertise in different aspects of the counselor's role. Conceptualizing supervision, evaluation, and professional growth opportunities as parts of one system to enhance school counselors' professional development also provides the opportunity to clarify the roles and responsibilities of the various overseers for school counselors' performance.

Supervision provides counselors specific feedback regarding their performance in guidance program activities, assistance in attaining their established goals for program improvement, and information regarding their attention to administrative requirements. It is one means for recognizing outstanding performance and contributions and for identifying performance deficiencies. In addition, because it has been recognized that professionals seek feedback on the quality of their performance, supervision also provides a vehicle for doing that. As Glickman and Jones (1986, p. 90) stated: "The critical point is that supervision creates an instructional dialogue among and with teachers that results in planning and acting upon improvements in learning for students." Substitute "counselors" for "teachers" and the point is equally true. Thus, the essential goal of supervision is to encourage a healthy, professional dialogue between counselors and their supervisors and among counselors as a professional group.

To the question posed by Barret and Schmidt (1986):

> Should counselor supervision be categorized as a threefold process: administrative (performed by principals with a focus on employee attendance, punctuality, staff relations, outreach to parents); clinical (performed by properly trained and certified counseling supervisors with a focus on direct service delivery); and developmental (performed by program coordinators with a focus on program development, in-service training, and other system-wide concerns)? (p. 53)

we say YES!!! This categorization helps clarify the different aspects of counselors' roles that are supervised by suggesting the appropriate supervisory approach for assisting counselors in those various roles, and by sorting out the roles of the various administrators who supervise counselors.

Administrative Supervision

Administrative supervision focuses on counselors' work habits and ethics. Other tasks that might come under administrative supervision are those related to system support activities—particularly those in which the guidance program provides support to other educational programs. These may include such activities as participating in the planning of the standardized testing program, appropriately completing forms for referring students to special education, and completing required reports.

School buildings and districts use many different forms that support this supervisory component, such as daily sign-in sheets, calendars, telephone call logs, and reports of parent conferences. As Barret and Schmidt (1986) mentioned, the primary administrative supervisor for the school counselor is the building principal. Administrative supervision should be ongoing. As with other forms of supervision, feedback to the counselor should include positive and negative comments and should occur on a regular basis.

Clinical Supervision

Clinical supervision focuses on counselors' direct service delivery and on counselors' unique professional skills such as guidance, counseling, consultation, and referral. Observing counselors use their skills, as well as specific feedback regarding what was observed, is the essence of clinical supervision. A five-step process model is suggested:

1. Preobservation conference
2. Observation
3. Analysis of data
4. Postobservation conference
5. Postconference analysis

Aubrey (in Boyd, 1978, p. 306) defined skills as "behaviors that are operational, repeatable, and predictable within a delimited range of effects." The counselors' professional skills (we use the word competencies) can be delineated so as to lend themselves to this form of observation. Many counselor education programs and school districts have listed the competencies that they expect of school counselors they educate and employ. Competency lists provide the basis for observations. To illustrate, the "descriptors" used for this purpose by Northside Independent School District are provided in Appendix F.

Supervisors certified as school counselors—such as head counselors, central office guidance administrators or supervisors, or counselors assigned supervisory responsibility of their peers—should perform clinical supervision if it is to be effective. Forms that assist the supervisor to focus on specific, important behaviors are helpful in clinical supervision. They provide a vehicle for communication between the observer and the person being observed. Sample forms from Northside are provided in Appendix G.

No matter how minutely competencies are described or how refined the observation forms are, training is required to provide supervisors with the background they need to provide meaningful feedback to practitioners. Feedback should be given within 48 hours after an observation occurs so that both parties have a fairly accurate recollection of the events.

It is hard for us to recommend to you an ideal number of contacts that the clinical supervisor and counselor should have. If counselors are not unduly threatened by such observations and the related feedback conferences, then the more the merrier because professionals do value feedback to help them improve their competencies. Clinical supervision is akin to tutorial assistance; it is one-to-one, direct, and competency-focused. Counselors can benefit from clinical supervision in each of the functions required in their work—instruction, counseling, consultation, and referral. Observation and feedback about counseling competencies will not necessarily provide counselors with ideas about how to improve their consultation competencies, for example. We do recommend that observations occur at least twice a year.

Developmental Supervision

Developmental supervision, as stated above, focuses on program and staff development issues. It entails the three-phased approach of (1) collaborative goal setting for program and performance improvements, (2) monitoring counselors' progress toward those goals, and (3) assessing counselors' level of goal attainment.

Developmental supervision provides the vehicle for challenging counselors to repair discrepancies between the current and the desired program. For example, if more group counseling is desired of the program, counselors can be asked to set goals of increasing the number of groups served. It also provides the vehicle for targeting specific competency development goals for counselors. If, for example, as a result of clinical supervision or the summative performance evaluation counselor competency deficiencies are noted, counselors can set goals to repair those deficiencies. Such goals might be to expand their repertoire of response techniques in counseling sessions. In school systems where the primary supervisor of the counselors is the principal, one version of developmental supervision calls for the use of contracts developed between the counselor and the principal. In this system, the principal identifies a goal that the principal wants to reach, such as lower absence rates, and the counselor suggests strategies to attend to that goal, such as group counseling for students with three or more unexcused absences during the first semester.

Goal setting and assessing the level of goal attainment are steps that require one-to-one conversations between the supervisor and the counselor. Monitoring, however, should be done by counselor supervisors on an ongoing basis and can be effective with separate groups of counselors at a time. Monitoring provides counselors the opportunity to communicate about their successes and failures and to suggest different strategies to one another. Staff meetings provide the opportunity to do this.

Examples of forms that support the goal setting and assessment steps of developmental supervision in Northside Independent School District are program improvement action plans (see Figure 7–7 in chapter 7) and professional growth plans (see Figure 8–2).

Another approach that has been successful in Northside is using annual, monthly, or weekly calendars to guide counselors in planning their implementation of the comprehensive guidance program. Example calendar formats are provided in Figure 7–8 (chapter 7) and in Figure 8–3.

Developmental supervision is best provided by supervisors assigned the responsibility for program development. Head counselors have this responsibility at the building level and central office guidance program leaders at the district level.

Changing Role of the Building-Level Guidance Department Head

Strengthening the means by which we help counselors improve their job performance, as well as more clearly defining expectations for the guidance program, calls for the recasting of the role of the building-level guidance department head. Various titles are used to label this position such as head counselor, guidance department chair, guidance coordinator, and director of guidance; we will use "head counselor" as it seems to be the title most used. Traditionally, head counselors have served as a liaison between the guidance staff and the administration, and between the guidance department and the instructional departments. In some instances they have been expected to do the quasi-administrative tasks assigned to the guidance department such as building the testing schedule or the master schedule.

In a school that is changing its guidance program to the comprehensive one we are proposing, and is striving to use all its available resources to enhance the effectiveness of the counselors, the head counselor's job description must change. First, it is imperative that some member of the staff be designated as the head of the building guidance program. Next, a position guide appropriately tailored to address the additional responsibilities of that person must be written. The head counselor position guide used in Northside Independent School District is provided in Figure 6–12 (chapter 6). This guide states the expectations that head counselors will provide leadership to the program development efforts on their campuses, and that they will supervise the counseling staff, in addition to

Figure 8–2

Counselor Professional Growth Plan Form

COUNSELOR PROFESSIONAL GROWTH PLAN

School: _____

Name: _____

Principal/Head Counselor Signature: _____

Date: _____

USE A SEPARATE FORM FOR EACH COMPETENCY AREA

PLANNING	EVALUATION
(To Be Completed by June 1, 1987)	(To Be Completed by June 1, 1988)

Targeted Competency Area:

Objective(s):

Description of Tasks/Activities	Timeframe	Evidence of Achievement	Actual Completion Date	Verification of Achievement	Level of (1–5) Accomplishment

Overall Assessment of
Achievement:

1　2　3　4　5

(Not Achieved)　　　(Fully Achieved)

Counselor's Signature: _____
Principal/Head Counselor: _____
Date: _____

Figure 8–3
Weekly Calendar

NISD Guidance Department   for 198____–198____

CALENDAR

	MONDAY	TUESDAY	WEDNESDAY	THURSDAY	FRIDAY
7:30					
8:00					
8:30					
9:00					
9:30					
10:00					
10:30					

	11:00	11:30	12:00	12:30	1:00	1:30	2:00	2:30	3:00	3:30	4:00	4:30

the more traditional responsibilities of serving their own case load and representing the department to others. The guide also clarifies that head counselors'
authority to do this is delegated to them by the principal and the district guidance
program leader—those designated as their supervisors in the building and in the
central office.

Finally, the principal and the central office guidance program leader must
work with and for the head counselors to help them carry out their responsibilities.
The newest challenge for head counselors is the responsibility of supervising the
building-level counseling staff. The regular staff members need to be informed
as to the authority of the head counselor. The head counselors need to be provided
the skill development they need to conduct their clinical, developmental, and
administrative supervisory roles appropriately. Counselor educators can help
local buildings and districts as they retrain head counselors; the supervisory skills
that counselor educators use with students in field experiences are essentially
the same skills that head counselors need in working with their staff.

Taking this one step farther, head counselors in turn need to be supervised.
Administrative supervision of the head counselors is done by the building principal. Clinical and developmental supervision should be done by the central
office guidance program leader. Clinical supervision could entail observing the
head counselor conducting a staff meeting and providing feedback in techniques
for effective meetings. Developmental supervision would entail setting goals that
are specific to head counselors' program leadership responsibilities (e.g., instituting group guidance activities for 12th graders in which they learn their status
relative to high school graduation, and initiating a post-high school plan) and to
staff supervision responsibilities (e.g., implementing a specific team-building
strategy).

We believe that the effective use of these various modes of supervision is a
primary vehicle for ensuring school counselor competency. Each mode entails
targeting specific performance behaviors of counselors and provides mechanisms
for assessment and feedback of the accomplishment of their desired objectives.
Through these mechanisms both supervisor and counselor are forced to be concrete about strengths and deficiencies. In our experience, when professional
counselors have been assisted to see specifically what they can do to improve,
they are eager to improve.

Step 4: Evaluating Staff Effectively

Counselor evaluation is most effective when it is conducted as part of the total
performance improvement system. An approach to counselor evaluation is discussed extensively in chapter 9, but we include this brief discussion of it here
to allow you to see how it is related to the other parts of an overall performance
improvement system.

As with the other parts of an overall performance improvement system—supervision and professional development—evaluation of counselor performance rests on the expectations held for the position of school counselor as clarified in the position guide. Remember that the position guide was written based on the desired comprehensive guidance program. *There must, then, be congruence between the program, the position guide, and the procedures used for school counselor evaluation.*

The purposes of the three parts of the overall performance improvement system are related but each has a separate goal. The goal of supervision is to use the resources—that is, the supervisors—of the system to assist school counselors to reach their professional potential within the district. The goal of the professional development component is to encourage school counselors to continue to grow in their professional competency, using both school district and personal resources. The goal of the evaluation system is to rate the competency level of the school counselors from the school district's perspective, to judge how competently they are performing the job to which they are assigned.

In theory, supervision and professional development are conducted in a nonjudgmental manner, but in reality they also provide some of the data that support the judgments made in evaluation. If, for example, counselors are observed by their clinical supervisor as consistently giving misinformation to students or as consistently projecting their own values into students' decisions, the clinical supervisor is responsible for providing that information to the evaluator. The relationship can work the other way as well. If the evaluator perceives counselors not being authoritative enough with students, the clinical supervisor can explain to the evaluator the professional rationale for being nonjudgmental.

Supervision and professional growth also provide strategies for assisting counselors to repair deficiencies identified through evaluation. If the evaluator perceives that a counselor is not effective with groups of children, the clinical supervisor can observe the counselor in action with groups and provide technical assistance. In developmental supervision, the counselor and supervisor might agree that a professional development goal for the counselor would be to improve the use of instructional methodology. Through strategies provided in the professional development component, the counselor might attend workshops on effective teaching techniques. Thus, evaluation is a very important part of the overall performance improvement system. The schema for Northside Independent School District's performance improvement system is displayed in Figure 8–4. In it the centrality of evaluation is clear.

Step 5: Encouraging Professional Growth

Although professional growth is primarily the responsibility of the individual school counselor, there are many resources that a school district can and should

Figure 8–4

Counselor Performance Improvement System

	SUPERVISION			EVALUATION			PROFESSIONAL DEVELOPMENT	
	Clinical	*Developmental*	*Administrative*	*Self-Evaluation*	*Administrative Evaluation*	*Assessment of Goal Attainment*	*Individual*	*District*
COMPONENTS	observation feedback	goal setting monitoring measuring	(YOURS)				(goals objectives strategies)	
FORMS	OBSERVATION — Instruction, Guidance, Counseling, Consultation, Referral	ACTION PLANS — Program Improvement, Professional Growth	e.g. Sign-in Sheets; Conference Requests	Self-Evaluation	Performance Evaluation	Action Plans –Program, –Professional Growth	Professional Growth Plan	District's Counselor Staff Development Plan

246

provide. The needs and wants of the district need to be balanced with the needs and wants of the individuals on the staff. From the district's perspective, the purpose of providing professional growth opportunities is to provide cost-effective inservice education and training that meets the needs of the largest number of counselors in relationship to priority needs of the district and building guidance programs. From the school counselors' perspective, the purpose of participating in professional growth opportunities is to improve their professional and personal competencies in areas that they perceive as important. As stated earlier, the goal of professional growth is to encourage staff members to continue to grow in their professional competency, using both district and personal resources.

The challenge is to provide mechanisms that help both the district and the district counselors target specific competencies—knowledge, skills, and attitudes—that need enhancement. We recommend developing a process for encouraging professional growth that begins by having counselors identify their own competencies and compare them with the competencies required to implement the desired district comprehensive guidance program. From these two data sources a master plan for counselor staff development for the district is developed that identifies the competencies to be addressed for the various subpopulations of school counselors and describes how these will be addressed.

Individual Professional Growth Plan Development

As a result of clinical, developmental, and administrative supervision, and as a result of evaluation, counselors will have identified specific competencies that need to be targeted for improvement. Counselors' professional growth plans are developed in the context of their long-range professional and personal goals as well as in the context of the comprehensive guidance program. In developing their plans, counselors should be explicit about their long-range plans and be encouraged to identify the intermediate and immediate goals that will help them reach their larger goals.

Both sets of data—the specific job performance targets and the professional-personal goals—provide information to counselors as they develop professional growth plans. Counselors should be encouraged to develop such plans for a 2-, 5-, or even 10-year periods. As a district, however, you will have more than enough data to work with if you know the counselors' immediate needs and wants for competency acquisition or improvement.

In a formally defined performance improvement system, school counselors write professional growth plans in collaboration with their supervisors and submit them to the guidance administrator. A form used for this purpose was displayed in Figure 8–2. With a form such as this, counselors and supervisors (principals or head counselors) agree on a "targeted competency area," such as the implementation of effective group counseling. They also discuss appropriate objective(s) that, if met, would increase counselors' effectiveness, such as the ability to (a) articulate a theoretical base for counselor behaviors, (b) use a variety of response techniques, and (3) facilitate students' development of behavioral plans. Counselors, then, identify tasks/activities that they plan to perform to meet the objectives. The plan includes a timeframe and a statement to the supervisor about potential evidence of achievement. (The second half of the form relates to the evaluation of the counselors' accomplishment of the plan—when the tasks were completed, what documentation of accomplishment is available, and at what level they were accomplished. These are reviewed at the end of the year by the counselors and the supervisors as part of the evaluation system described in chapter 9.)

Having received the counselors' plans, counselor supervisors and administrators know what their staff members want. They are then in a position to encourage counselors to seek educational opportunities.

Assessment of the Needs for Counselor Competency Development

Knowing what the counselors *want* is only one part of the needs assessment in a plan for staff development. It also is necessary to assess counselors' needs for performance improvement in terms of the skills *needed* to implement the comprehensive program desired by the building or district. It is important to assess counselors' competencies to find out those they have as well as those they need to work on.

To assess counselor competencies the same methodology can be used that was used to assess the perceived needs of students; only the items are changed. The items to be used can be generated from the competencies that have been identified as necessary to organize and implement the comprehensive guidance program. The "descriptors" you have identified to support the observation-evaluation components of the performance improvement system provide these specifics. Using a questionnaire, card sort, or other assessment technique, the data are gathered and tabulated. Many such assessments ask counselors not only how much they need to acquire the competency, but also how important they feel it is. Figure 8–5 provides an adapted part of one such form used in the Community Collaborative Career Guidance Project conducted by the National Center for Research in Vocational Education.

From the system's perspective, the guidance supervisor—the guidance program leader—also has a viewpoint as to the importance of each competency that should be considered as the plans for staff development are made. If, in comparing and contrasting the current and the desired programs, discrepancies have been identified that seem to be related to competencies not used in the current program but wanted in the desired program, the district guidance program leader would know the importance of staff development in those competencies, whereas the counselors might not yet be aware of it. For example, if the desired program calls for more group counseling than is currently done, competency improvement in those skills would receive a high priority from the district's perspective.

Within the counseling staff not only will different groups of counselors *want* to acquire different professional competencies, but different groups of counselors will *need* to acquire different competencies. New counselors have different needs than do experienced counselors. Some experienced counselors are more competent than others and may need advanced training, whereas others need remedial training. The program improvement process itself will dictate some staff development needs. The priority needs for training head counselors will probably be different from those for staff counselors. If you have a cadre of peer leaders, they may have different professional growth needs.

Staff Development Related to the Program Improvement Process

As they proceed through the program improvement process, school counselors learn a variety of new concepts. They learn about the comprehensive guidance program, about their roles in it, and about some of the processes that it takes to implement it. The presentation of the information gathered in assessing the design of the current guidance program provides insights into the program and its facets, as does the recasting of the program that is presented in the expression of the district's basic structure. Whether you have chosen to select current examples of effective practices or ventured into innovative activities that fit the desired program, counselors learn about operational details of a comprehensive guidance program.

If, as a first step in assessing the design of their building programs counselors kept logs of their activities, they learned about their own piece of the program and watched as their data were aggregated with those of others. This helped them further internalize the program concept and provided them with insights into their own work habits. Such information, when compared with the expectations for their roles as stated in the position guides, provides counselors with ideas as to how they can add to their professional competencies. At the same time, study of the position guides of other staff in the guidance department helps all staff members understand the "chain of command" as well as the responsibilities of the head counselor and those of the various paraprofessionals.

Counselors need to learn processes related to planning such as goal setting, ranking for priority, and action planning. Counselors also need to learn about program planning and personal planning. By being involved in the program improvement process they learn about program planning. They have been involved in such program planning activities as conducting needs assessments, assessing the current program, and establishing the desired program structure. By setting goals and developing action plans for attaining those goals, counselors learn personal planning. One of the major benefits of establishing a comprehensive guidance program with clear-cut priorities is that the guidance program

Figure 8–5

Excerpt From Training Needs Assessment Form

Competency Areas and Specific Statements	Competency			Importance		
Competency Area 3 SELECTING PROGRAM'S CAREER DEVELOPMENT THEORY: Choosing a career development (and decision-making) theory on which the career guidance program will be based.						
Describe the advantages of using a theory of career development and career choice as the basis of your career guidance program.	a	b	c	d	a	b	c	d
Explain the key features such as philosophy, assumptions, propositions, and hypotheses of several theories of career development and choice.	a	b	c	d	a	b	c	d

Select, using previously defined criteria, an underlying theory for your career guidance program by choosing from or adapting available alternatives to meet the needs of clients and your organization.	a	b	c	d		a	b	c	d
State the selected theory in clear terms, defining how its components provide the basis for each major area of your career guidance program.	a	b	c	d		a	b	c	d
Communicate the theory, its importance, and rationale to team members and others who work within the program setting.	a	b	c	d		a	b	c	d
Apply the theory throughout all phases of the development and implementation of your program so that ongoing decisions are made on a clear and logical basis.	a	b	c	d		a	b	c	d
Evaluate the effectiveness of the theory, and revise it as necessary to provide a sound basis for your program.	a	b	c	d		a	b	c	d

Note: From *Trainer's Manual* by L.L. Phillips, 1979, Columbus, OH: National Center for Research in Vocational Education.

becomes manageable to the counselors. Instead of a series of days that just happen, the counselors' work year becomes a planned year. Not every minute of every day can be planned—that will never happen as long as the important responsibility of responding to students and others in crisis is present. The major events of the program can be planned, however, enabling counselors to feel a sense of accomplishment. Having control of the major parts of the program and their jobs empowers counselors and contributes to their professional pride, and consequently helps revitalize their commitment to their profession.

Counselors, especially those who are not used to thinking of the program as having any resources, need to learn the processes for effective use of resources such as budgeting, careful selection of materials, and time management. During the program improvement process counselors need to learn to use assertion and political skills; they need to see themselves as being empowered.

Once the desired comprehensive program design has been established for the building and district, and the discrepancies between "what should be" and "what is" are clear, generating as many ideas as possible for repairing these discrepancies not only provides a plethora of ideas, but also gets the counselors' creative juices flowing. Brainstorming sets in motion "How can *I* change?" thought processes.

If in the program improvement process special projects are used to enhance the program change process, some counselors may need competency development related to those special efforts. Not only will they need to learn to take risks comfortably, but they also will need to learn the competencies associated with the specific projects they are participating in. If you are experimenting with curriculum writing, for example, inservice training in curriculum development is important, as is training in the specific content area to be developed. If some buildings are trying out large group guidance activities, then competency in working with large groups is required. If you purchase materials for possible districtwide use, counselors need training in the effective use of these materials.

Once the analysis of the disparities between the current and the desired programs have been completed, and the basic directions for program change have been established, the training needs of counselors in the district can be anticipated. Because much has been learned about the teaching-learning process in recent years, counselors need updating in that process if they are to deliver the guidance curriculum effectively and maintain their credibility as consultants to teachers. They also can benefit from staff development activities that focus on instructional methodology such as task analysis, lesson design, and effective teaching practice. In addition, the new program design requires that counselors update their competencies in structured and growth group work; in effective methods of parent and teacher consultation; in brief family intervention techniques; in addressing the needs of at-risk students (such as dropouts and potential dropouts, substance abusers and children of substance abusers, unmotivated learners and those who continually fail to succeed academically, depressed adolescents and those who threaten or attempt suicide); and in incorporating career development activities in the program such as decision making, planning, and problem solving. Another recurrent need—and one that administrators support wholeheartedly—is that of acquiring time management skills. Finally, counselors need to fine-tune their public communication skills.

As the guidance program shifts to require better use of counselors' educational talents, their sense of professionalism should be enhanced. To further this feeling, workshops or study sessions on ethical standards and issues could be held. Counselors should be encouraged to belong to professional associations and to become involved in association work. When available, attainment of licensure or registry should be encouraged, with such accomplishments being publicly acknowledged.

Guidance program leaders, head counselors, or other peer leaders can benefit from learning about leadership characteristics and leadership styles. A personal benefit they gain from participating as leaders in the program is increased self-knowledge. They also can benefit from learning about situational leadership, team building, the use of power, the needed balance of both task and relationship orientation, and the roles they play in groups and leader-follower situations. If you are the guidance program leader, or if your role as program administrator does not require special administrative or supervisory certification, you too will benefit because most of this material is not included in guidance preservice education.

The head counselors will benefit from specialized training that helps them to implement their newly clarified roles better. Where you begin their inservice training depends on the individuals involved and the roles identified for them. We recommend beginning with action planning because that is basic to their work with counselors and to their responsibilities for leading the building guidance program redesign and implementation. Head counselors and peer leaders also may have needs for competencies in motivating staff members, conducting observations and providing constructive criticism, risk taking, delegating, assertion, and managing stress. In addition, they may need help in developing the skills and attitudes needed for effectively encouraging others. They may need to learn the leadership roles associated with mutual goal setting as well as those associated with effective monitoring of plan implementation. If your district organizational structure involves a team approach with the principals sharing the supervisory responsibility for the counselors, principals need to be informed to ensure their understanding of the newly designed comprehensive guidance program. Thus, the district staff development plan ought to include principals.

District Master Plan for Staff Development

Knowing what the staffs' wants and needs are for competency development is a first step. The next step is to develop a plan to meet these needs efficiently and effectively. The plan includes identifying the strategies and resources available for staff development, developing a timeframe for the staff development activities that the building or district will provide, and considering how to evaluate the effectiveness of the strategies used. Figure 8–6 displays a format that could be used for writing the staff development plan.

Choose Strategies for Staff Development

A variety of delivery methods are available for staff development including lectures, reading materials, audiovisual materials, demonstrations, programmed learning, discussions, simulations, and direct experience. Each method has costs and benefits. Making decisions about which methods to use depends on the outcome intended for the staff. Lectures typically help listeners to become aware of ideas or practices, whereas direct experiences such as internships or shadowing help participants internalize the content.

The lecture mode is traditional for inservice education. The lectures can be motivational or instructive. Consultants can be brought into the district, or staff can be encouraged to attend professional growth conferences held at the local, regional, state, and national levels. Skilled counselors should be encouraged to present at such conferences because organizing and presenting helps them refine their practices and ideas.

Reading materials include professional texts and journals. Individuals seeking growth in specific areas can use bibliographies. If the goal is for a number of people to consider certain topics, readings can be assigned and groups can be formed to discuss the content of the readings. The discussion can be focused by means of a "discussion agenda" such as that displayed in Figure 8–7 and used in Northside. Professional journal reading is a cost-effective, readily accessible, and professionally sound staff development vehicle that staff development planners typically underutilize. Where such reading is encouraged, follow-up discussions to assist the readers to process the ideas they have read are not often held, but should be.

Other vehicles for professional discussions include staff meetings and retreats. Case consultations, particularly those led by an expert consultant, provide meaningful learning opportunities as well. Feedback conferences held as a part of clinical supervision also can provide learning experiences for counselors. New counselors can learn much by observing master counselors as they demonstrate their skills in actual work settings.

Identify Resources Available and Plan Their Use

Earlier in the chapter we listed some of the resources that are potentially available to help in staff development. At this point it is important to be specific as to the expertise of the people available. Then, the expertise available can be matched with the priority needs of the staff. Some consultants are available within the school system, others will cost money. Thus, the guidance department

Figure 8–6
Format for Staff Development Plan

| Staff Category | Staff Outcome | Strategy | Timeframe | Resources | | | Evaluation Method |
				Expertise	Fac/Equip	Cost	

Figure 8–7
Group Counseling Project Discussion Agenda

High School Counselor Staff Meetings

Group Counseling Project Discussion Agenda

1. *Uses/values/limits of groups*
2. What *counseling* is/is not
3. Individual's *theoretical models*
4. Professional *processes and techniques* used in group counseling
5. *"Climate"* needed for group to succeed
6. *Forming your groups*
7. *Group process*
    Norms:
    Organization:
    Structure:
8. *Leader's role(s)/responsibilities*

budget must be considered. Once the priority needs of staff have been identified and the means by which they can pursue professional growth have been decided, it is now possible to project how much money is required to make optimum use of the resources. Ideally, every staff member has the opportunity to grow professionally in the course of a year. Thus, the resources available should be distributed with this principle in mind. At the same time means for having individuals share ideas and information they have gained is a way to spread the wealth. For example, if only one counselor from a district can attend a state or national professional conference, that counselor could give a report at the staff meeting.

One final important consideration in implementing the staff development plan is planning the use of the facilities and equipment available. Be sure to consider where the various activities will be held, what the seating capacity is, and whether the atmosphere is conducive to discussions. If plans include the use of equipment, make sure that the necessary equipment is present and that it is in working order. This may seem obvious, but all too often the excitement of the topic causes lapses in memory about meeting logistics.

Establish the Timeframe for Staff Development

Careful consideration should be given to when staff development activities will take place. Some writers suggest, with good reason, that late afternnon or evening sessions are to be avoided if possible. Sessions during school hours are recommended, but are costly because they use staff student-contact time. Saturday and holiday sessions may work out well, particularly if you are in a state where licensure requirements include accumulating continuing education hours.

We recommend that staff development activities be interspersed over the length of the program improvement process. Such activities often are enjoyable and serve as a means to increase morale. Staff development activities need to be planned well in advance so that all involved can participate. Also, staff development should not stop once the major program development efforts have ceased. Professional growth should continue as a means for maintaining continuous individual professional development and program improvement.

Evaluate Staff Development Activities

As we stated, each staff development activity should be evaluated so that its effectiveness can be judged. There are a number of ways to evaluate the impact of activities, including the use of questionnaires, achievement-type tests, observations, and demonstrations. Whatever approach is used, it should be appropriate to the outcomes sought for the staff development activity. For example, observation of new behaviors is a more appropriate evaluation device for experiential staff development activities than it might be for lectures.

In addition, the effectiveness of the overall staff development program needs to be evaluated. Reassessment of the staffs' competencies through use of the original needs assessment instrument provides information as to the staffs' growth. Continued monitoring of the staffs' expressed needs through their professional growth plans also provides evaluative data regarding the effectiveness of the professional growth activities provided.

But, What If . . .

As in all professions there are some individuals in the counseling profession who have either made the wrong career choice or who do not develop their professional promise sufficiently; in short, there are those who are working as school counselors or as school counselor supervisors who are not competent to meet the position requirements. With performance standards outlined as concretely as we have recommended and with a system in place to help staff improve their professional competence, it is possible to terminate those whose performance is detrimental to students' growth and development. Due process rules are in place in most states to protect individuals from arbitrary terminations or reassignments, yet most systems have procedures outlined for helping those who are not in the right career to move. It is important not only for the students we serve but for the profession as a whole to help incompetent counselors find other jobs.

Termination involves legal procedures with important roles for administrators, personnel departments, and school system lawyers. Reassignment to different buildings sometimes helps employees regain their professional commitment. In many instances, clarifying expectations that come from the program improvement process causes individuals to see that they are in the wrong position. Such self-determination is—obviously—preferable, but it also entails work for the administrators.

In any of the above circumstances, the supervisor's role is to base evaluative judgments on the concrete, behavioral criteria established in the writing of the comprehensive guidance program and the position guides. If the less-than-competent staff members have been informed about the criteria, and have been offered the staff development opportunities to acquire the competencies they need, it is professionally appropriate for them to be encouraged to leave the profession.

Guidance Program Leader's Roles and Responsibilities

Ensuring the competency of the school counselors is a primary responsibility of the guidance program leader. The best designed program is meaningless in the hands of insufficiently competent staff. We have said that an effective guidance program leader plays a range of roles to ensure against this. The leader collaborates with the preservice training institution staff as counselor educators develop their programs. Recruitment of qualified applicants provides a pool of talent available for filling jobs that become available. As well as helping select the best person for the job, the program leader has a responsibility to strive to match new counselors' talent with the positions that will use their capabilities to the maximum advantage of the students and the program.

Once school counselors are selected, the leader orients them in the comprehensive guidance program design and goals and ensures their orientation to the buildings they will serve. The roles of the guidance program leader and the campus administrators must be carefully outlined, and an efficient and effective performance improvement system should be designed. As we have said, the resources of supervision, evaluation, and professional development should be focused to assist the school counselors to attain their optimum level of professional competency. In the few cases of incompetence, the guidance administrator must be able to articulate the professional and program standards clearly so that such individuals can seek better use of their particular skills. Clarity of role expectations is critical to ensure the competency of school counselors.

A successful guidance program leader must maintain the vision needed to help the program succeed at its mission, must uphold the basic principles of the profession at large, must keep in touch with the staff and those whom the program serves, must be able to manage change, must select good people as subordinates and trust them to carry out their roles appropriately, and help them when they do not. The program leader must develop appropriate and adequate performance indicators so that problems may be addressed in a timely fashion and opportunities for improvement are allowed to emerge. Finally, with the program and performance standards in place, a district is ready to evaluate its guidance program and the school counseling staff. This is covered in detail in chapter 9.

References

Association for Counselor Education and Supervision. (1986). *Accreditation procedures manual for counseling and related educational programs.* Alexandria, VA: AACD Press.

Barret, R.L., & Schmidt, J. (1986). School counselor certification and supervision: Overlooked professional issues. *Counselor Education and Supervision, 26,* 50–55.

Boyd, J. (Ed.). (1978). *Counselor supervision: Approaches, preparation and practices.* Muncie, IN: Accelerated Development.

Glickman, C.D., & Jones, J.W. (1986). Supervision: Creating the dialogue. *Educational Leadership, 44,* 90–91.

Phillips, L.L. (1979). *Trainer's manual.* Legislative Provisions for the Improvement of Guidance Programs and Personnel Development and Guidance Team Training Program with Emphasis on Guidance for Vocations and Learners with Special Needs. Columbus, OH: National Center for Research in Vocational Education.

PART 4—Evaluating

CHAPTER 9

EVALUATING YOUR COMPREHENSIVE GUIDANCE PROGRAM

Now that the planning and designing phases of the program improvement process have been completed and the implementation phase is under way, we are ready to examine the last phase of the process—evaluation. Because this is the last chapter of the book, evaluation is, of course, the last step in the program improvement process. Right? Wrong! This statement is wrong in the sense that the entire program improvement process is evaluation-based. Evaluation is ongoing, providing continuous feedback during all steps of the process. Evaluation is not something done only at the end of a program in order to see how it came out. The purpose of evaluation is to provide data to make decisions about the structure and impact of the program and the professional personnel involved.

No program is perfect when it is first implemented. Nor do students' needs remain the same over time. A self-monitoring evaluation system can provide information necessary to: (a) prove program effectiveness thereby meeting external demands for accountability; and (b) improve program effectiveness thereby maintaining a guidance program that is dynamically responsive to the changing needs of students and society. (Bleuer-Collet, 1983, p. 1)

The first part of chapter 9 focuses on program evaluation. The use of program standards is described, and attention is directed toward being alert for unanticipated side effects of the program. Then chapter 9 presents discussion of student outcome evaluation issues and procedures. This includes discussing possible evaluation designs, selecting or developing instruments to use, scheduling data collection, and staffing for data collection and processing. Following this chapter 9 offers suggestions for collecting program and student outcome data. Next, ideas about analyzing program and student outcome evaluation data are discussed. Then chapter 9 presents recommendations about reporting program and student outcome evaluation results as well as using these results for staff development and program and administrative decisions. Following that, chapter 9 describes the details of a student competency reporting system. Chapter 9 closes with a detailed discussion of professional personnel evaluation. The focus is on self-evaluation and performance evaluation as well as the assessment of goal attainment. Suggestions for effecting the evaluation process and an example form is provided.

Program Evaluation

Program evaluation is exactly what it says it is. It is an evaluation of the structure and implementation of the program. It involves the collection of data used to make judgments about the structure of the program and how that structure is being implemented.

An Example of the Use of Standards

The use of the concept of standards is one way to accomplish program evaluation. For our purposes, standards are defined as measures of guidance program components against which judgments can be made about the adequacy of the implementation of these program components. To illustrate, Northside Independent School District uses the four guidance program components described in chapter 3 as a basis for its program standards. The degree of compliance is measured using a 5-point scale where 1 = not implemented, 2 = weakly implemented, 3 = average implementation, 4 = strongly implemented, and 5 = fully implemented. The Na category is used when the standard does not apply. The example of standards presented in Figure 9–1 is taken from the document, *Guidance Program Evaluation Self-Study*, Northside Independent School District (1987a).

Possible Unanticipated Side Effects

As program evaluation unfolds, be alert to possible unanticipated side effects. Sometimes activities will create effects unforseen when initially they were put into operation. The program evaluation system should be sensitive enough to pick up these effects so that they can be handled immediately or can be explained when they appear in later program or student outcome evaluation results.

Unanticipated outcomes may be either positive or negative. For instance, student outcomes may be achieved through the curriculum but at an unusually high expense of students' time. The same may be true for the time of some teachers. On the other hand, some of the most valued outcomes of a program may not have been stated in the original design of the program. Attendance may have improved or the dropout rate may have declined.

Figure 9–1
Example of Program Standards

Guidance Curriculum

1. *All* students are assisted in a systematic way to develop knowledge, understanding, and skills identified as necessary to enhance their personal, social, career, and educational development.   na 1 2 3 4 5

2. Developmentally appropriate student outcomes are specified for each grade level.   na 1 2 3 4 5

3. Outcome selection is based on an assessment of student needs for guidance instruction.   na 1 2 3 4 5

4. The guidance curriculum is taught to class-sized groups of students.   na 1 2 3 4 5

5. Teachers are augmenting guidance instruction by infusing guidance curricula into their regular curriculum.   na 1 2 3 4 5

6. Guidance lessons are taught, upon teacher request, in conjunction with the teachers' goals for a particular unit/subject.   na 1 2 3 4 5

7. The facilities and equipment used to conduct guidance curriculum activities are adequate.   na 1 2 3 4 5

8. Sufficient materials are available to support the guidance curriculum.   na 1 2 3 4 5

9. Student learnings from particular lessons/units are assessed systematically.   na 1 2 3 4 5

10. Effectiveness of the guidance curriculum provided for each grade level is evaluated annually.   na 1 2 3 4 5

Individual Planning

1. *All* students are provided information and are assisted in applying the skills necessary to make plans and to take the next appropriate steps toward their established goals.   na 1 2 3 4 5

2. The priority for the component, as indicated by the time spent by the counselor(s) and the activities provided, is to assist students to complete successfully their elementary/middle/high school education.   na 1 2 3 4 5

3. Individual planning activities are preceded by pertinent guidance instruction.   na 1 2 3 4 5

4. There is a systematic approach to helping

Figure 9–1, *continued*

students use their educational opportunities in
school well through an effective orientation
program.   na   1   2   3   4   5

5. There is a systematic approach to helping
students plan/prepare for personally satisfying
and socially useful lives by helping them make
appropriate educational plans.   na   1   2   3   4   5

6. There is a systematic approach to helping
students make wise choices during
preregistration, including helping them be
aware of their possible choices.   na   1   2   3   4   5

7. There is a systematic approach to helping
students understand and respect themselves
through effective interpretation of standardized
and individual test results.   na   1   2   3   4   5

8. There is a systematic approach to helping
students plan/prepare for personally satisfying/
socially useful lives through career/vocational
planning.   na   1   2   3   4   5

9. Individual planning activities are implemented
through effective use of:
    a. Large groups   na   1   2   3   4   5
    b. Medium (class)-sized groups   na   1   2   3   4   5
    c. Small groups   na   1   2   3   4   5
    d. Individual conferences   na   1   2   3   4   5

10. Accurate and attractive printed information is
distributed to support the individual planning
efforts of students and their parents.   na   1   2   3   4   5

11. The facilities and equipment available for
conducting individual planning activities are
adequate.   na   1   2   3   4   5

12. The materials available to support
implementation of the individual planning
activities are effective.   na   1   2   3   4   5

13. Student learnings resulting from individual
planning activities are assessed regularly.   na   1   2   3   4   5

14. The effectiveness of the individual planning
system activities for each grade level is
evaluated annually.   na   1   2   3   4   5

Responsive Services

1. Students in need are assisted in solving
immediate problems that interfere with their

healthy personal, social career, and/or educational development.	na	1	2	3	4	5

2. A balance of service is maintained for students with preventive and remedial level needs. na 1 2 3 4 5

3. There is a systematic provision of responsive services as follows:
   a. Group counseling na 1 2 3 4 5
   b. Individual counseling na 1 2 3 4 5
   c. Staff consultation na 1 2 3 4 5
   d. Parent consultation na 1 2 3 4 5
   e. Referral to other specialists na 1 2 3 4 5

4. Services are provided on the basis of assessed student needs. na 1 2 3 4 5

5. The guidance department maintains an adequate list of referral resources. na 1 2 3 4 5

6. Counselors are readily accessible to students with problems. na 1 2 3 4 5

7. The facilities and equipment available for conducting responsive services are adequate. na 1 2 3 4 5

8. The materials available to support implementation of the responsive service activities are effective. na 1 2 3 4 5

9. Student growth resulting from responsive services activities is assessed regularly. na 1 2 3 4 5

10. The effectiveness of the responsive services activities is evaluated annually. na 1 2 3 4 5

System Support

1. Administrative procedures encourage appropriate use of the counselor(s)' special skills. na 1 2 3 4 5

2. Counselor involvement in nonguidance and counseling activities is streamlined. na 1 2 3 4 5

3. On-campus communication mechanisms are established which facilitate collaboration between the guidance department and administration. na 1 2 3 4 5

4. On-campus communication mechanisms are established which facilitate collaboration between the guidance department and the instructional departments. na 1 2 3 4 5

5. Counselor(s) is/are encouraged to utilize professional growth opportunities. na 1 2 3 4 5

6. Guidance department paraprofessional staff provide needed support to counseling staff. na 1 2 3 4 5

Figure 9–1, *continued*

7. Time is provided for guidance program/activity planning and evaluation.	na	1	2	3	4	5
8. A reasonable budget is appropriated to the guidance department by the campus administration.	na	1	2	3	4	5
9. Facilities and equipment are available and adequate for effective implementation of the program.	na	1	2	3	4	5
10. Counselor(s) is/are provided sufficient access to students so that time is available to implement effective guidance and counseling activities.	na	1	2	3	4	5
11. Opportunities are provided and taken for counselor(s) to explain the guidance and counseling program to the staff.	na	1	2	3	4	5
12. Opportunities are provided and taken for counselor(s) to explain the guidance and counseling program to the community.	na	1	2	3	4	5

Student Outcome Evaluation

Student outcomes, or competencies, as we have chosen to call them, is one of the products of a comprehensive guidance program. Student outcome evaluation "is the measurement of these outcomes both at strategic points during the implementation of the program and at completion of the program" (Upton, Lowrey, Mitchell, Varenhorst, & Benvenuit, 1978, p. 57). Just as program evaluation begins at the start of the program improvement process, so too does student outcome evaluation. Also, just as you developed a plan for program evaluation, so too do you develop a plan for conducting student outcome evaluation.

As you are beginning the process of laying out a student outcome evaluation plan, you should make a number of decisions. You have to decide how you will design the evaluation. You also will need to consider instrumentation, when you will collect data, who will collect data, and how these data will be analyzed.

Evaluation Design

Evaluation Based Upon Predetermined Criterion Standard Comparisons

The process of specifying posttest performance expectations for students is one way to evaluate competency-based programs. This means that you need to establish minimally acceptable performance standards for a competency by indicating the percentage of students in the target population who must attain a particular outcome in order for the program to be considered successful. For example, if it is expected that 95% of the students at a specific grade level will be able to select a course of study consistent with their measured interest and ability, the minimum acceptable performance level has been established at 95%.

The specification of the minimally acceptable level should occur at the same time that the competency is stated initially. There are no hard-and-fast rules for deriving performance standards. Rather, they are usually derived from professional judgment based on the experience of staff members. Performance will vary across competencies rather than be uniform. Factors to consider in setting the minimal performance level of an outcome include the judged importance of the competency, the place of the competency in the developmental sequence, and the probability of attaining the competency.

The next step in the evaluation of competency attainment consists of checking students' posttest performance to determine whether the stated acceptable percentage of students did, in fact, attain each competency. Summary data for making this determination consist of a tally of the number of students attaining the criterion level and the computation of the percentage of the target group achieving the competency. When the sample is small, you can complete this process manually with a check mark in a "yes" or "no" column for each student to indicate attainment or nonattainment of the competency. With larger samples, or where more detailed information is desired, you may wish to use a distribution with means and standard deviations; percentiles can be used as summary data.

Evaluation Based Upon Pretest or Posttest Comparisons

Another method frequently used with a program is pretest-posttest comparison. Before-and-after student data are collected prior to exposure to a guidance activity and upon completion of the activity; these are then compared. The observed differences in the two measures are then interpreted in terms of (a) the statistical significance of the change, (b) the percentage of students attaining a predetermined change standard, or (c) the comparison of change among program and control groups.

Evaluation Based Upon Participant Versus Nonparticipant (Control) Comparisons

The criterion references and pretest-posttest comparisons just discussed provide information that is particularly relevant for program development. The crucial questions regarding the cause of the observed performance or change, however, cannot be answered by these types of comparisons. The cause-effect questions are critical in program continuation or elimination decisions and necessitate comparisons of the performance or gains of participating subjects with those of nonparticipating subjects. These types of comparisons not only provide you with evidence of competency attainment of participating students but also support conclusions that guidance activities were the primary causative factors in the observed outcomes (where significant group differences were observed).

Evaluation Based Upon Responsive Observations

Student outcome evaluation provides information to determine whether specified student competencies have been attained. Evaluation data that provide information about what was not predicted or what was unanticipated are also important as you will recall. Data on unexpected side effects document unintended effects of process operations and dynamics. This type of evaluation not only looks at unanticipated results but also focuses on student and staff responses to their experiences in the program. Attitude surveys, structured reaction sheets, and case-study techniques can be used to collect this type of data.

Another reason for using a responsive type of evaluation is to provide for case studies that portray effects and impact in a natural and direct manner. Case studies can provide a feel for what has happened that cannot be transmitted by examining hard outcome data. Reports of unusual impact on individual students as reported in case illustrations also can be used effectively in communicating more generalized group findings to the public. Take care, however, that this type of evaluation is not interpreted as the collecting of testimonies.

Selecting or Developing Instruments

We recommend the following guidelines in selecting or developing instruments for the collection of student outcome evaluation data.

1. The expected outcome for each student competency should be measured as directly as possible.
2. The instruments for collecting evaluation data should be appropriate for the intended respondent in terms of content, understandability, opportunity to respond, and mechanical simplicity.
3. Directions for the administration, scoring, and reporting for all instruments should be clear, concise, and complete in order to ensure uniformity and accuracy in data collection.
4. The time required for administering, scoring, and reporting evaluation instruments should be kept at a minimum in order to obtain reliable information.
5. Evaluation instruments should meet the tests of validity for the competencies that are measured, reliability in producing consistent results, and feasibility for the operational situation.

Scheduling Data Collection

The data collection schedule for student outcome evaluation should be set up prior to the initial date of the evaluation period and should specify (a) the objective for which data are to be collected; (b) the instrument(s) to be used; (c) the group(s) or individuals from whom data will be collected; (d) the time when data will be collected (pretest, posttest, end of year, and so forth) in relation to the process schedule; and (e) the person(s) to be responsible for data collection. The evaluation design, including the types of comparisons to be made, will dictate most of the decisions relevant to the data collection schedule.

Evaluation data collected for groups to make pretest-posttest comparisons or experimental control-group comparisons need to conform closely to a time schedule related to the process period. Pretest, or baseline data need to be collected prior to the initiation of the activities, and posttest data need to be collected at a specified time after the completion of the activity being evaluated. Some designs also may require the collection of data at specified periods during the activity period or as follow-up some time after the completion of the activity. All such data need to be collected on a predetermined schedule so that all persons involved in the evaluation can make plans and carry out the data collection in accordance with the design.

Staffing for Data Collection and Processing

Adequate staffing to handle the evaluation, including data collection and data processing, is essential. Organize your work groups to (a) plan and coordinate data collection and processing; (b) conduct inservice training of teachers or others who will be responsible for the actual data collection; (c) administer the information-collecting instruments; (d) handle the clerical details of preparing and distributing instruments, collecting and organizing completed instruments, scoring and coding data for processing punching data cards, preparing tables, and preparing evaluation reports; and (e) write and interpret evaluation reports.

The absence of adequate staffing for an evaluation is frequently the underlying cause for the breakdown of the whole evaluation process. Symptoms of inadequate staffing may appear in the form of (a) unmet schedules, (b) resistance from teachers, (c) errors in data processing, and (d) incomplete reports that are not communicated adequately to program and administrative personnel.

The staffing needed for the evaluation cannot be standardized because of the differences in the nature and the size of evaluation projects from school to school. Staffing to conduct a full-scale program evaluation for all grades in a large school system will obviously require more leadership and more person-hours than will the evaluation of one specific activity in one grade. In any case, large or small, comprehensive or specific, the success of evaluation depends on the assignment of specific time to staff for the planning, implementation, and interpretation of the evaluation.

Collecting Program and Student Outcome Data

All data must be collected in accordance with a data collection schedule and with proper administration of evaluation instruments. This process requires careful planning and full cooperation of all persons responsible for collecting or providing the needed information. The following suggestions may be helpful in implementing efficient and accurate data collection.

1. The purposes and details of the evaluation plan should be communicated to all staff members who will be involved in the evaluation process. The threat of evaluation and the added burden of another task can be eased by a full explanation and discussion of all details for implementation before assignments are given to teachers, counselors, and others. Workshops can be used to discuss the data collection schedule and the instruments to be used. A good technique to acquaint teachers and counselors with the evaluation instruments is to let them complete all the instruments they will administer. Emphasis should be given to instructions for the administration of all instruments and the necessity for uniform administration for all respondents. Also, where observers are to be used, it is important that they have had thorough training in making and recording their observations.

2. All instruments and evaluation instructions should be prepared and assembled well in advance of the date for implementing the data collection. Careful planning of the logistics of collecting and processing evaluation data will help avoid delays and ensure compliance with the data collection schedule.

3. All respondents (students, teachers, parents) should be informed of the purposes for collecting information, and confidentiality should be ensured where appropriate. Steps should be taken to motivate students to the task of completing tests or other instruments, as would be done in any other school testing situation. The assumption is made that the responses to evaluation instruments represent the respondents' best effort and an honest response. Any steps, within defined limits, that can be taken to ensure the validity of this assumption will increase the reliability and validity of the data collected.

4. The data collected should be identified properly with respect to target groups, date, and person responsible for their collection. This simple precaution will help prevent lost and mislabeled data and will enable follow-up in case questions arise regarding the data.

5. Evaluation tests and other instruments should be scored and coded for processing as soon as possible after the data are collected. The prearranged coding plan should be followed and then rechecked to ensure accuracy. Many instruments can be scored and cards punched by machine where the appropriate answer sheets have been used and the equipment is available. Planning for the use of machine-scored answer sheets and the related machine-punching of data will result in greater speed and accuracy in processing evaluation data for analysis. (School systems that do not have

their own test-scoring equipment and personnel with expertise in data processing should seek assistance from colleges and universities or commercial agencies that serve their region.)

Analyzing Program and Student Outcome Evaluation Data

The evaluation design is the blueprint for the analysis of evaluation data. The analyses should follow the design in all details; however, additional analyses may be made where the data warrant and where observations of your staff suggest the need for analyses not included in the original design. For example, the original design may have specified the analysis of gains in occupational knowledge between experimental and control subjects, but staff may have observed that the reading ability of students seems to be related to the criterion outcome. In this case, additional analyses are desirable to determine the extent to which the observed outcomes were actually attributable to level of reading ability, and thus how reading ability might be taken into consideration in program planning. This is an example of an unanticipated outcome discussed earlier in this chapter.

The mechanics of completing the analysis of evaluation data are important to ensure speedy and accurate feedback from the evaluation. Computer-assisted analyses are most desirable where a mass of data is involved. Computers, however, depend upon the use of a program appropriate to the analysis and a system of checks for errors or inconsistencies in the raw data input. The services of a computer programmer who understands the data and the desired output is essential. Although these points are mentioned here in the context of data analyses, they are important to consider during the planning for program evaluation.

Some types of evaluation information are not easily adaptable to computer analyses and may in fact be more meaningful when analyzed by you and your staff. For example, subjective counselor reports of guidance activities or certain types of student behaviors may lose meaning if quantified for computer analysis. These subjective analyses may be critical in the interpretation of other outcome data. In addition, small samples of activities or students may not warrant the use of computer analysis and thus will need to be handled manually. In such cases precautions should be taken to reduce human error to a minimum by establishing checks and rechecks.

Reporting Program and Student Outcome Evaluation Results

The reports of evaluation results should be addressed to those persons who have an interest in the basic evaluation questions asked in the evaluation plan. Such persons include district research personnel, program directors, teachers, counselors, the lay public, and funding agencies. The variance in the interests and level of research understanding of these audiences dictates the preparation of separate reports that are appropriate for each group. These diverse interests can be satisfied by preparing (a) a technical report that constitutes a full research report of the design, all statistical data, and evaluative conclusions; and (b) a professional report that focuses on the conclusions regarding the effectiveness of program activities and recommendations for program emphases and modifications. The basic content of these reports is discussed briefly in the following sections.

Technical Reports

A technical report should be a complete description of the program being evaluated, the design of the evaluation, the results, and conclusions and recommendations. The following outline can serve for the content of the technical report of a comprehensive guidance program evaluation.

Program Description

This part of the report should describe the program being evaluated in sufficient detail for the reader to replicate the program as evaluated. The target groups, the specific guidance activities, and the personnel and facilities evaluated should be described in detail.

Evaluation Design

The description of the evaluation design should include a description of procedures used to formulate the evaluation questions and the program objectives. The specific evaluation hypotheses, the comparisons made, the operational definitions or instrumentation, and the types of analyses made for each objective should be described in detail. The case for the design as an adequate approach to answering the evaluation questions should be established in this part of the report.

Evaluation Results

The results of the evaluation should be reported in complete detail in this section. Each goal, objective, or competency evaluated should be presented with the evidence that it was, or was not, achieved. A summary of relevant descriptive statistics, and of the statistical analyses to test outcome hypotheses, should be reported in proper table form. When a large number of statistical tables is needed to report the results, it may be desirable to place some of these tables in an appendix to the report.

Conclusions, Discussion, and Recommendations

This section of the technical report presents the evaluative conclusions regarding the achievement of the stated goals, objectives, or competencies. The discussion of the outcome findings and conclusions can include subjective explanations and additional hypotheses suggested by the evaluative data. Recommendations that are supported by the evaluation, and are relevant to administrative and program decisions, make up one of the most important parts of the evaluation report. This section should provide answers to the basic evaluation questions and discuss the program implications of the findings. The strengths and weaknesses of the program should be identified as indicated by the results. Recommendations for program modifications, and the nature of such modifications, should be presented along with the justifications based on the observed outcomes. Also, this section may include a discussion of the relationship between cost and outcome. Were the results worth the cost?

Appendices to the Technical Report

Materials that illustrate, describe, and support the other sections of the technical report may be included as information for the reader. Forms and unpublished instruments should be included as a matter of record and for readers who may not be acquainted with the details of the methods used. Also, detailed descriptions of activities may be included in an appendix if presentation in the body of the report would distract from clarity and readability.

Professional Reports

Reports of the evaluation for the professional and administrative staff of the school should be short and concise. Those interested in the details that support this report should be referred to the technical report. The professional report should include a brief summary of the findings, conclusions, and recommendations. Often most of this report can be taken directly from the conclusions, discussion, and recommendations section of the technical report. Statistical tables should be used only if absolutely necessary to document the results summarized. However, summary charts that symbolically or graphically show the results may be helpful. Technical language and reference to specific instruments should be avoided whenever possible. For example, it would be better to say "the students had increased career awareness" than to say "the posttest scores on the vocational knowledge inventory were significantly higher than the pretest scores." This report should communicate in straightforward language what happened to students who participated in specific guidance activities. Sometimes uncluttered graphs or charts can be used effectively.

Using Program and Student Outcome Evaluation Reports

Evaluation reports can be used for a variety of purposes. These include (a) conducting staff development, (b) making program decisions, and (c) making administrative decisions. Each of these uses is discussed in the following sections.

Staff Development

Evaluation information can be used for a variety of inservice staff development activities ranging from workshops to research projects and self-assessment. The evaluation reports should help counselors, teachers, and other guidance personnel better understand student needs, the relative effectiveness of guidance activities, and promising new approaches to fulfilling their functions in the educational setting. The following suggestions may be helpful in planning staff development activities using evaluation information:

1. Orient new staff members to the organization and functioning of the guidance program.
2. Provide feedback sessions to develop a fuller staff understanding of the major strengths and weaknesses of the guidance program. Evaluation without feedback to those involved cannot be justified. Reinforcement of successes can be motivating for the staff, whereas the work in doing an evaluation without feedback can be demoralizing.
3. Conduct staff workshops to examine the nature and implications of student needs for the guidance program. This type of activity can be helpful particularly in developing staff understanding of the interrelatedness of student needs and the corresponding contributions of the various guidance activities in responding to those needs. Teachers, counselors, and other school staff may be so involved in their special interests that they have lost sight of the necessity to correlate their activities with those of the rest of the staff. This is particularly true where some staff focus on crisis needs and others on developmental needs.
4. Organize staff-centered program development workshops. Evaluation reports can provide the input to stimulate staff efforts in self-examination and program involvement. The examination of the relevance of the objectives and of process materials and activities can lead to staff interest in creating and initiating program materials and activities supported by the evaluation evidence.

Program Decisions

Evaluation information provides the basis for making program decisions. These decisions vary from broad general issues, such as what activities should be provided, to specific problems, such as what techniques are most effective in facilitating career decision making among minority group 10th-grade students. The value of evaluation results to the program decision making is related to the evaluation questions asked. Here are some to consider: What are the priority student needs that can be served by the guidance program? Which guidance outcome should receive the highest priority in program planning? What is the relative effectiveness of different activities or techniques in achieving specific student outcomes? What is the response of the guidance staff and the students to different guidance procedures and techniques? What are the possible side effects and the procedures and techniques that are not directly related to student outcomes? What crucial professional program questions have not been answered by the evaluation information, and where is there need for further investigation?

Administrative Decisions

Evaluation reports are of value to those responsible for decisions regarding organizational patterns, personnel assignments, and resource management. Most evaluations do not provide direct answers to typical administrative questions but rather provide information from which inferences can be drawn for administrative decision making. Evaluation information may provide input relevant to such administrative questions as: What type of relationship among guidance personnel produces harmonious and efficient operations and the expected outcomes? Where are the personnel strengths and weaknesses in the guidance department? What are the characteristics of the most effective staff members? What was the cost of the outcomes observed? Was the outcome of sufficient significance to justify the cost? Where can shifts in personnel or other resources produce outcomes more effectively? Where should priorities be placed in the allocation of resources for the guidance program?

It is important that your staff be involved in the interpretation of the evaluation results for administrative purposes. Your professional explanations of evaluation results will improve the validity of any inferences that are drawn. Your explanations will contribute to the accurate interpretation of evaluation results.

A Student Competency Reporting System

So far we have discussed program evaluation and student outcome evaluation issues and procedures as well as procedures for collecting, analyzing, and using data gathered from these two types of evaluation. Although these two types of evaluation and the processes involved play a vital role in the overall evaluation of comprehensive guidance programs, we feel an important dimension of evaluation is missing. How can students involved in the guidance program participate in evaluation? How can they join with others to monitor their development that results from their participation in the guidance program? To respond to these questions we recommend establishing a student competency reporting system.

In one way this is not a new idea. Years ago many report cards had an item on it called "conduct." Sometimes the grade for conduct was related to academic subjects, but often it represented a subjective rating of how students behaved in school. As educational philosophies changed, "conduct" changed too. It became "industry" and "attitude." The rating shifted to a judgment of student work habits and how students related to others. Then it became "work habits" and "social growth." Subcategories rated for work habits included "works independently," "follows directions," "listens carefully," "utilizes time appropriately," and "completes daily work." Subcategories rated for social growth included "gets along well with others," "accepts correction," "practices courtesy," "accepts responsibility," "exhibits appropriate school behavior," and "practices self-control."

Though the use of subcategories was an improvement in communicating what was involved in work habits and social growth, it did not keep pace with what was happening in other curriculum areas. Today continuous progress reporting of students' growth regardless of grade placement is common practice. Reading levels and mathematics levels are related from year to year in developmental sequence. Health and physical education reporting systems now describe year-by-year growth in students' ability to perform specified physical activities. Where there was once a single-sheet report card for all instructional areas, there is a trend now toward having each instructional area have its own report card to be included in a report card packet. The newer reporting systems reflect increasing movement toward individual, developmental instructional programs.

We recommend that you consider developing a student competency reporting system for your guidance program that complements systems now being used in some areas of the instruction program. This system would not take the place of process or product evaluation we discussed previously. They are an important part of your evaluation plan. In fact, the student competency reporting system is a type of student outcome evaluation. But it yields much more than do traditional approaches to student outcome evaluation because it becomes a common joining point for students, parents, and staff to take responsibility for the outcomes of the guidance program.

The Basis for the System

The basis for the student competency reporting system is the student competencies you have chosen to assist students to acquire as they are involved in your K–12 guidance program. You will recall that in the guidance curriculum presented in chapter 3, there were 15 goals grouped in three domains. For each goal there were 13 competencies, one for each grade level K–12.

To illustrate the basis for a reporting system more specifically, we selected Goal A from the Self-knowledge and Interpersonal Skills Domain. Goal A contains 13 competencies, one for each grade level. For this example we will use the competency for grade 3 and the competency for grade 12. (See Appendix C.)

> Goal A: Students will develop and incorporate an understanding of the unique personal characteristics and abilities of themselves and others.
> Grade 3 competency: Students will describe themselves accurately to someone who does not know them.

Grade 12 competency: Students will appreciate their uniqueness and encourage that uniqueness.

The next step is to select performance indicators that will show whether or not students have acquired these competencies. Also needed are performance levels. Example performance indicators and suggested performance levels for the grade 3 and grade 12 competencies are presented in Figure 9–2.

Figure 9–2
Example Performance Indicators

Grade 3

Performance indicators	Suggested performance level
Students are able to	Students are able to
1. describe the physical and personality characteristics that they would like others to know about them.	1. describe six (three physical and three personality) characteristics of themselves.
2. recognize any discrepancies in their descriptions and correct them.	2. correct any incorrect descriptions that they gave for #1.
3. describe themselves correctly to someone they are meeting for the first time.	3. describe themselves to one person they do not know well.

Grade 12

Performance indicators	Suggested performance levels
Students are able to	Students are able to
1. describe their uniqueness and why they appreciate that uniqueness.	1. a) describe two ways they are unique. b) describe their appreciation of that uniqueness in respect to benefits for self and others, and the effects upon the feelings of self and others.
2. describe methods they presently use to encourage their uniqueness.	2. describe three methods presently used to encourage uniqueness (for example, time and effort in learning, practicing, evaluation responses, and so on).
3. predict methods they might use in the future to encourage their uniqueness.	3. predict two methods they might use in the future (for example, time and effort in further practice, further learning, further evaluation or responses, and so on).

Possible Formats for a Reporting System

There is a variety of formats you could use to organize competencies for reporting purposes. We suggest two. The first one is a report card format similar to report cards now being used in some instructional areas. The other is a folder format similar to that being used in advisor-advisee systems, particularly in schools where individual planning is featured.

Report Card Format

The report card format suggested is similar to report card formats used in a number of instructional areas, such as reading and physical education. Specific competencies are listed on a report form with some indication as to whether or not students have attained these competencies or if they still are working on them. In this format the ratings are done by teachers or counselors in consultation with students. The report is then shared with parents, as are reports from other instructional areas. Performance indicators and performance levels are used in the rating process. An example of a report card for the 15 competencies for grade 3 is presented in Figure 9–3.

Folder Format

Another format you may wish to consider is a folder. The folder would belong to students. It would be a vehicle for their keeping a record of such things as their academic progress, extracurricular activities, important conferences, and future education and work plans. To help students keep track of the competencies they are acquiring, using a folder format requires developing competency lists that can be made a part of the folder. We suggest that individual sheets of heavy stock paper be used to list the 15 competencies for each grade level included in the folder. The format is illustrated in Figure 9–4.

Competency rating using this format could be done jointly by a student and a counselor or an advisor in an advisor-advisee system. The rating would be done by their initialing a competency on the form when they felt it had been acquired. The performance indicators and performance levels for each competency would be used as a basis for making a judgment.

Booklet Format

Another format that could be used in a student competency reporting system is that of a booklet. An example of this format is the Career Passport that was developed by the National Institute for Work and Learning and published by the National Center for Research in Vocational Education. There is a leader's guide (Charner & Bhaerman, 1986) and a student workbook—the Career Passport (National Institute for Work and Learning, 1987). The Career Passport contains sections for students to present data about themselves, their education and train-

Figure 9–3
Guidance Program
Third-Grade Competencies

Your child can	Quarters			
	1	2	3	4
describe himself or herself accurately.				
describe personal mental health care.				
describe adult responsibilities.				
recognize that actions affect others' feelings.				
talk and listen to close friends and those who are not close friends.				
realize study skills are necessary for learning school subjects.				
define "consumer"; describe how he or she is a consumer.				
recognize that people have varying roles; describe personal roles.				
recognize why work activities are chosen and that choices may change.				
define what "future" means.				
realize that people obtain rewards for their work.				
recognize those accomplishments he or she is proud of.				
describe personal thought processes before making a decision.				
recognize the need to assess possible consequences before making a decision.				
realize that environment influences interests and capabilities.				

The Rating Key
  √ Student has accomplished this competency.
  W Student is still working on this competency.
  ☐ This competency does not apply at this time.
(Blank)

Figure 9–4
Guidance Program
Twelfth-Grade Competencies

Student's Initials	Counselor's Initials	I can
_____	_____	appreciate and encourage my uniqueness.
_____	_____	analyze my personal skills that have contributed to satisfactory physical and mental health.
_____	_____	assess how taking responsibility enhances my life.
_____	_____	understand the value of maintaining effective relationships in today's interdependent society.
_____	_____	evaluate my current communication skills; continually improve those skills.
_____	_____	evaluate ways I presently learn; predict how learning may change.
_____	_____	analyze how I as a citizen and consumer help support the economic system.
_____	_____	assess the interactive effects of life roles, settings, and events and how they lead to a personal life style.
_____	_____	analyze the effects stereotypes have on career identity.
_____	_____	analyze how concerns change as situations and roles change.
_____	_____	speculate what my rights and obligations might be as a producer in the future.
_____	_____	summarize the importance of understanding attitudes and values and how they affect my life.
_____	_____	implement the decision-making process when making a decision.
_____	_____	provide examples and evaluate my present ability to generate alternatives, gather information, and assess consequences in the decisions I make.
_____	_____	assess my ability to achieve past goals; integrate this knowledge for my future.

ing, work experiences, volunteer and community experiences, family-related activities, hobbies, interests, achievements and skills, strengths, and abilities. A section on competencies could be added or incorporated into one of the sections already in the passport.

Suggested Uses of a Student Competency Reporting System

Numerous books have been published in the past few years that provided structured approaches to life career planning. Many of these books contained forms to fill out and exercises to complete. Although the exercises in these books have been helpful to people, they were often limited by time. Once the activities were completed by an individual, there was little or no provision for follow-through. Some books did provide follow-through exercises, but those, too, were limited.

Recently, however, attention has been given to the follow-through issue for special populations by the use of individual education and career development plans and programs. In special education there are individualized education programs (IEPs); in rehabilitation work they are called individual written rehabilitation plans (IWRPs); and in employment and training programs they are called employability development plans (EDPs).

What is needed in schools is a similar vehicle, but for all students. What is needed for each student is an individual life career plan (ILCP) in folder form. The plan could be both an instrument and a process that students could use to create and monitor their own development. As an instrument the plan could provide a way for students to gather, analyze, and synthesize information about themselves and their environment. As a process the plan could become a vehicle through which such information is incorporated into short-range and long-range goal-setting, decision-making, and planning activities. As a process the plan could become a pathway, a guide that students could follow. It would not be a track that would be plotted and followed routinely. Rather, it would be an outline or plan for a quest.

Central to an individual-life-career-plan folder would be the student competency reporting system. The reporting system would provide a mechanism for students to monitor and record their progress in competency acquisition. Lists of competencies from instructional areas could be added easily to the lists of competencies that result from the guidance program.

To implement this idea, we recommend that individual-life-career-planning folders be established for all students, beginning in the elementary school years. The folders would be the property of the students, although they would be maintained in the guidance office. They would be available to students to use in various guidance and instructional activities related to goal setting, decision making, and planning and would be theirs to take with them when they graduated, transferred, or left school. We further recommend that, concurrently, a report card be developed to share with parents the progress of their children in guidance competency acquisition. The use of a report card would be appropriate particularly during the elementary school years and possibly during the middle school or junior high years.

When students leave school, they would take their individual-life-career-plan folder with them. Whether they would go to work or continue with more education, the folder and the accompanying competency lists would be available for additional goal-setting, decision-making, and planning activities. Information in the folder would assist them in a variety of job-seeking and job-keeping activities, including filling out application forms, writing resumes, developing curriculum vitae, or preparing for job advancement. As new experiences are acquired, they would be analyzed and added to the appropriate sections of the folder. Thus the individual-life-career-plan folder with accompanying competency lists could become an ongoing goal-setting and planning vehicle for individuals as long as they would wish to use it.

Professional Personnel Evaluation

As we discussed in chapter 8, a key part of comprehensive guidance program implementation and management is a counselor performance improvement system. The basic purpose of such a system is to assist counselors reach and maintain their professional potential. The system includes counselor supervision, evaluation, and professional development. This section of chapter 9 focuses on personnel evaluation. To illustrate how this can be done we will describe how Northside Independent School District conducts evaluation of its school counselors.

Purposes

The purposes of evaluation are to improve the delivery of the program with its ultimate impact on the students it serves and to provide for communication among school counselors, guidance program leaders, and school administrators. For school counselors, evaluation specifies contract status recommendations and provides summative evaluation as to their effectiveness. For the school system, evaluation defines expectations for counselors' performance and provides a systematic means of measuring their performance relative to these expectations.

Evaluation

There are three facets to the Northside Independent School District counselor evaluation system (1987b): (1) self-evaluation, (2) performance evaluation, and (3) assessment of goal attainment. The self-evaluation and performance evaluation focus on job performance skills and represent data-supported professional judgments as to individuals' proficiency in using the skills required on their job.

The assessment of goal attainment focuses on the individual's program and skill improvement efforts.

Self- and Performance Evaluation

All counselors are evaluated annually. Counselors on probationary status, in the final year of their contract term, and those whose term contracts have not been extended for performance reasons are evaluated twice a year, on or before December 15 and March 1. All others are evaluated on or before May 1.

For elementary school counselors, the primary evaluator is the school principal. For counselors who serve more than one building, the director of guidance designates one principal as the primary evaluator, with the other principal(s) providing relevant data to the primary evaluator. The primary evaluator conducts the evaluation conference or may coordinate a joint evaluation conference. The reviewing officer is the director of guidance, and in this capacity discusses the evaluation results with the primary evaluator before the results are presented to the staff member.

The director of guidance is available to provide data or assist the primary evaluators in making their evaluative judgments. The director *must* be involved in an individual counselor's evaluation when (a) it seems that the contract status recommendation will mean a decrease in contract status, or (b) the overall rating of the counselor will be either "unsatisfactory" or "clearly outstanding," or (c) there is disagreement among the evaluators, including the counselor after his or her self-evaluation. The director of guidance *may* be involved at the request of any of the parties involved in the evaluation process—the counselor, the head counselor, or the principal.

The self- and performance evaluation process consists of (a) data collection, (b) data analysis, (c) evaluation write-up/draft evaluation form completion, (d) evaluation conference, (e) postevaluation conference analysis, and (f) evaluation form completion. The counselor and the evaluator complete steps 1–3 separately. In the evaluation conference, the counselor and the evaluator discuss their evaluations of the counselor's performance. The evaluator then effects steps 5 and 6, obtains the necessary signatures, and distributes the copies of the form as prescribed. The details of how this process works are presented as follows in case you have an interest in instituting a similar process. The form that is used for this process by Northside is shown in Figure 9–5.

Suggestions for Effecting the Various Steps

1. *Data Collection.* Although the nature of evaluation is judgmental, the district believes that effective judgments concerning professional competence should be data-supported. In drawing conclusions about performance, evaluators are asked to rely on data that have been gathered through the supervision system. In clinical supervision, observations and feedback conferences generate relevant

Figure 9–5
Northside Independent School District
Counselor Performance Evaluation Form

NAME _____

SCHOOL _____

REVIEW PERIOD: FROM _____ TO _____ DATE EVALUATION COMPLETED _____

RATINGS SUMMARY:

	POINTS	RATING
1. Guidance curriculum implementation:	_____	_____
2. Individual planning system implementation:	_____	_____
3. Responsive services implementation:	_____	_____
4. System support implementation:	_____	_____
5. Effectiveness of professional relationships:	_____	_____
6. Fulfillment of professional responsibilities:	_____	_____
Total Points	_____	

CRITERIA FOR OVERALL
PERFORMANCE RATING

SCORING RULES: The highest applicable rating applies.

OVERALL
PERFORMANCE
RATING

Clearly Outstanding is earned with at least 27 points and no rating less than Satisfactory (3).　Clearly Outstanding　☐

Exceeding Expectations is earned with at least 21 points and no rating less than Satisfactory (3).　Exceeding Expectations　☐

Satisfactory is earned with at least 16 points, no more than two scores less than Satisfactory (3), and no rating less than Below Expectations (2).　Satisfactory　☐

Below Expectations is earned with at least 14 points and no more than one rating less than Below Expectations (2).

Unsatisfactory is earned in all other cases.

EVALUATION: FALL _____   SPRING _____

CONTRACT STATUS RECOMMENDATION: (Spring Only)

_____ 1-Yr. term contract: Second year
_____ 3-Yr. term contract: First year of 3 years
_____ Nonextension 3-Yr. term contract: Second year of 3 years
_____ Nonextension 3-Yr. term contract: Third year of 3 years
_____ Nonrenewal (term contract)

Signature of Evaluator: _____   Title of Evaluator: _____
Signature of Reviewing Officer: _____
Title of Reviewing Officer: _____
Signature of Employee: _____   Conference Date: _____

Original: Personnel
Copies: Yellow—Counselor   Pink—Principal   Gold—Director of Guidance

2/87

COUNSELOR PERFORMANCE EVALUATION FORM

1. Implements GUIDANCE CURRICULUM through the use of effective INSTRUCTIONAL SKILLS, including
   a. appropriate task analysis
   b. effective use of lesson design
   c. active involvement of students in learning
   d. selection of topics consistent with identified, high priority student needs and district goals

Below
Expectations ☐
Unsatisfactory ☐

Figure 9–5, *continued*

Clearly Outstanding	Exceeding Expectations	Satisfactory	Below Expectations	Unsatisfactory
☐ (5)	☐ (4)	☐ (3)	☐ (2)	☐ (1)

COMMENTS: _____

2. Implements the INDIVIDUAL PLANNING SYSTEM through the effective use of GUIDANCE SKILLS, including
   a. careful planning of sessions
   b. presentation of accurate, relevant, unbiased information
   c. involvement of students in personalized educational and career planning
   d. accurate and appropriate test results interpretation
   e. selection of individual planning activities consistent with identified, high priority student needs and district goals

Clearly Outstanding	Exceeding Expectations	Satisfactory	Below Expectations	Unsatisfactory
☐ (5)	☐ (4)	☐ (3)	☐ (2)	☐ (1)

COMMENTS: _____

3. Implements RESPONSIVE SERVICES through effective use of COUNSELING, CONSULTATION, AND REFERRAL SKILLS, including
   a. proper identification of problems/issues to be resolved
   b. selection of counseling, consulting, and/or referral interventions appropriate to students' problems and circumstances
   c. use of counseling, consulting, and/or referral skills appropriate to students' problems and circumstances
   d. conducting well-planned and goal-oriented sessions

e. use of group and individual techniques that are appropriate to the topic and to students' needs and abilities
f. active involvement of clients in the counseling, consulting, and/or referral process
g. timely follow-up
h. provision of services consistent with high priority, identified student needs and district goals

Clearly Outstanding (5)	Exceeding Expectations (4)	Satisfactory (3)	Below Expectations (2)	Unsatisfactory (1)
☐	☐	☐	☐	☐

COMMENTS: _____

4. Implements SYSTEM SUPPORT through PROVIDING effective SUPPORT for other programs and by effectively ENLISTING SUPPORT for the guidance program, such as

a. providing a comprehensive and balanced guidance program
b. selecting program activities which meet identified, high priority student needs and are consistent with campus and District goals
c. collecting evidence that students achieve meaningful outcomes from program activities
d. operating within established procedures, policies, and priorities
e. contributing to organizational solutions outside of assigned responsibilities
f. working cooperatively with school administrators to garner support for the guidance program
g. implementing programs which explain the school guidance program
h. attending to ideas/concerns expressed regarding the guidance program
i. supporting campus administration policies and goals
j. supporting district policies and goals

Clearly Outstanding (5)	Exceeding Expectations (4)	Satisfactory (3)	Below Expectations (2)	Unsatisfactory (1)
☐	☐	☐	☐	☐

COMMENTS: _____

Figure 9–5, *continued*

5. Establishes effective PROFESSIONAL RELATIONSHIPS by building rapport with
   a. students
   b. staff
   c. parents
   d. other counselors
   e. administrators
   f. other in-school/district specialists
   g. community representatives

Clearly Outstanding	Exceeding Expectations	Satisfactory	Below Expectations	Unsatisfactory
☐ (5)	☐ (4)	☐ (3)	☐ (2)	☐ (1)

COMMENTS: _____

6. Fulfills PROFESSIONAL RESPONSIBILITIES by
   a. seeking professional development
   b. keeping records consistent with ethical and legal guidelines
   c. maintaining professional work habits
   d. practicing according to the profession's ethical standards
   e. demonstrating appropriate personal characteristics
   f. demonstrating effective use of basic skills (e.g., communication, decision-making, problem-solving, educational)

Clearly Outstanding	Exceeding Expectations	Satisfactory	Below Expectations	Unsatisfactory
☐ (5)	☐ (4)	☐ (3)	☐ (2)	☐ (1)

COMMENTS: _____

7. Additional Comments: _____

data. In developmental supervision, program and performance improvement accomplishments generate data, as do the various planning forms utilized by the guidance department such as calendars, goal-setting, and action planning forms. Head counselors keep logs of their supervisory contacts with counselors. It is assumed that performance deficiencies will have been addressed in supervision before they are recorded in the formal evaluation.

2. *Data Analysis.*   The counselor and the evaluator should consider the data as they pertain to the evaluation categories.

3. *Completion of Draft Evaluation Forms.*   Draft evaluations are completed by both the counselor, as the self-evaluation, and the evaluator. The primary evaluator is encouraged to consult with the reviewing officer prior to completing the draft. The cover page should be completed last as it represents the summative judgment and overall rating of the counselor's performance.

The *six areas* for evaluation—instructional skills, guidance skills, counseling, consultation and referral skills, system support implementation, establishment of professional relationships, and fulfillment of professional responsibilities—are considered *separately*. Performance strengths and weaknesses are identified; both are supported by specific, behavioral examples. (Descriptors as well as example observation forms are provided in Appendices F and G.) Suggestions for improvement are made for incorporation in the counselor's professional development plan.

Each area is *scored holistically*; that is, the rating for that area reflects a summative judgment of the counselor's performance of the various tasks that contribute to the delivery of the skills identified. "In most instances, the counselor performs most of these subskills _____ly." To be judged as "clearly outstanding," performance of the listed indicators as well as many of the discretionary items should be *consistently* outstanding, exemplary, excellent. To be judged as "exceeding expectations," performance of the listed indicators as well as discretionary items should be at an observably high level. In rating a counselor's performance as "clearly outstanding" or "exceeding expectations," the evaluator should consider how the counselor handles not only required duties but also discretionary tasks. Northside's expectations for counselors are high. To be judged "satisfactory," performance of at least the listed indicators is judged as meeting standard expectations, that is, as being consistently good most of the time. To be judged "below expectations," performance on the listed indicators is in need of specifically identifiable improvement, and be judged as consistently poor most of the time. To be judged "unsatisfactory," performance on the listed indicators is either not done or done in a clearly unacceptable manner. "Satisfactory" is the rating earned by counselors who perform their job skills with proficiency. Performance that is rated below or above that needs to be supported by documentation.

The *overall performance rating* is a reflection of the summary of ratings for each of the six skill areas plus consideration of the rating levels. To arrive at the overall performance rating, the ratings for each area and the related points are transferred to the cover page and the points totaled. The criteria for overall performance rating should be studied and the appropriate overall rating applied and recorded.

The *Contract Status Recommendation* is completed in the spring evaluation only, although an indication of probable/possible contract status recommendation may be discussed in the fall evaluation, especially for those counselors for whom a decrease in contract status is envisioned.

4. *Evaluation Conference.*   The counselor and the evaluator bring their drafts of the evaluation form to the conference to facilitate mutual discussion. The evaluation conferences are scheduled by the primary evaluator with sufficient advance notice provided so that the drafts and related data are available at the time of the conference. The counselor's strengths as well as weaknesses are discussed. Discrepancies between the two evaluation drafts also are discussed. Because the purpose of evaluation is to help each counselor attain his or her professional potential, suggestions for performance improvement are offered for *all* counselors.

5. *Postevaluation Conference Analysis.*   The primary evaluator is responsible for developing the formal evaluation. The evaluator is encouraged to consider the counselor's input in arriving at his or her final performance evaluation and may seek the advice of the director of guidance, other campus administrators, or may gather other relevant data in resolving discrepancies between the two opinions.

6. *Evaluation Form Completion.*   The primary evaluator completes the district-approved Counselor Performance Evaluation Form. It should be typed by the principal's secretary, not the counselor's secretary. The signature of the reviewing officer should be obtained prior to obtaining the counselor's signature. The counselor's signature verifies that the evaluation has been discussed, and does not necessarily indicate agreement with the information. The counselor and the primary evaluator have the right to attach additional statements to the formal evaluation form, provided the statements are signed and dated by both parties and the reviewing officer; again, the signatures verify discussion, not agreement.

Assessment of Goal Attainment

The program improvement and professional growth plans are the means for implementing the comprehensive guidance program as defined by the district. The purpose of this evaluation is to assess the level of the counselors' contribution to the improvement of the guidance program on the campus and in the district, and the level of their efforts to upgrade their professional skills/knowledge. The judgment assesses the counselors' efforts to reach goals they have set for themselves under the supervision of the head counselor (at the secondary level), the director of guidance, and the principal. It also reflects, where appropriate, the effectiveness of the individual counselor's efforts as reflected in the guidance program evaluation.

The data for this evaluation grow out of the developmental supervision component. It is a summative judgment as to the counselors' level of effort in attaining the goals established at the beginning of the school year and recorded on the "Guidance Program Improvement Planning Form" (see Figure 7–7 in chapter 7) and on the "Counselor Professional Growth Plan" (see Figure 8–2 in chapter 8). A performance report is submitted to the director of guidance at the end of the school year recording the primary evaluator's assessment of the level of accomplishment. Documentation includes student outcome data gathered in activity and program evaluation and skill improvement data gathered in clinical supervision.

Concluding Thoughts

In the opening words of this chapter, we stated that although evaluation is the last phase of the program improvement process, the entire improvement process is evaluation-based. This means that as the planning, designing, and implementing phases get under way, and during the time they are under way, the activities involved and the program structures and content that evolve need to be constructed and implemented based on sound evaluation principles and procedures so that they can be evaluated. Thus the work completed in the first three phases of the improvement process must be done well so that the work involved in the evaluation phase can be completed in a similar manner. Demonstrating accountability through the measured effectiveness of the delivery of the guidance program and the performance of the guidance staff helps ensure that students, parents, teachers, administrators, and the general public will continue to benefit from quality comprehensive guidance programs.

References

Bleuer-Collet, J. (1983). *Comprehensive guidance program design.* Ann Arbor, MI: Counseling and Personnel Services Clearinghouse Fact Sheet.

Charner, I., & Bhaerman, R. (1986). *Career passport leader's guide.* Columbus, OH: National Center for Research in Vocational Education.

National Institute for Work and Learning. (1987). *Career passport student workbook.* Columbus, OH: National Center for Research in Vocational Education.

Northside Independent School District. (1987a). *Guidance program evaluation self study.* San Antonio, TX: Author.

Northside Independent School District. (1987b). *Guide to counselor performance improvement through supervision, evaluation, and professional development.* San Antonio, TX: Author.

Upton, A.L., Lowrey, B., Mitchell, A.M., Varenhorst, B., & Benvenuit, J. (1978). *A planning model for developing a career guidance curriculum.* Fullerton, CA: California Personnel and Guidance Association.

APPENDICES

APPENDIX A

Time and Task Analysis Log
(Partial Log Shown)

Time	Curriculum	Individual Planning	Responsive Services	System Support	Nonguidance Administrative Activities
			Examples of Activities		
	Classroom Activities, Group Activities	Individual Advisement, Individual Assessment, Placement, Vocational/Occupational Exploration, Missouri Scholars Academy, Four-Year Plan Development	Consultation, Personal Counseling, Small Groups, Individual Counseling, Crisis Counseling, Referral	Research, Staff/Community Development, Curriculum Development, Professional Development, Committee/Advisory Boards, Community Involvement/PR, Program Management/Operation	Bus Duty, Lunchroom Duty, Playground Duty, Balancing Class Sizes, Building Master Schedule, Substitute Teaching, Figuring GPA's, Figuring Class Rank, Lunch Break
7:00–7:15					

7:15– 7:30		7:30– 7:45		7:45– 8:00		8:00– 8:15		8:15– 8:30		8:30– 8:45		8:45– 9:00		9:00– 9:15			

APPENDIX B

PROGRAM COMPONENT DESCRIPTIONS

NORTHSIDE INDEPENDENT SCHOOL DISTRICT
COMPREHENSIVE GUIDANCE PROGRAM FRAMEWORK

Framework of the Guidance Curriculum

I. *Definition*

The guidance curriculum component is that through which all students are assisted in a systematic way to develop knowledge, and to understand skills identified as necessary to enhance their personal, social, career, and educational development.

The guidance curriculum should be developed and taught to assist students to reach specific outcomes by acquiring developmentally appropriate competencies.

Teaching to facilitate students' learning the guidance curriculum entails five steps:

1. Introducing (preteaching, readiness development)
2. Teaching (develop, emphasize)
3. Reinforcing (review, refine)
4. Expanding/Reteaching
5. Applying (under supervision of counselor)

II. *Content Overview*

Fifteen curriculum strands have been identified for guidance. Students should:

1. Understand and respect themselves
2. Understand and respect others
3. Behave responsibly in school
4. Behave responsibly in the family
5. Behave responsibly in the community
6. Make wise choices

7. Manage change successfully
8. Solve problems
9. Use well their educational opportunities in the classroom
10. Use well their educational opportunities in the school
11. Use well their educational opportunities in the community
12. Plan to use their future educational opportunities well
13. Communicate effectively
14. Plan and prepare for personally satisfying lives
15. Plan and prepare for socially useful lives

III. *Implementation Methods*
The guidance curriculum is taught to groups of students. Although the preferred size of groups varies with the content of the particular strand, unit, or lesson, the generally preferred delivery modes are, first, class-sized groups; second, small groups of approximately 10 students; and, third, large groups of no more than 35.

Framework of the Individual Planning System

I. *Definition*
The individual planning system is the component of the comprehensive guidance program through which each student is provided the information available and is assisted in applying the skills needed to make plans and to take the next appropriate steps towards his or her established goals.

II. *Content*
Eight major activities have been identified for assisting students to make and implement plans:
1. Orientation
2. Educational planning
3. Preregistration
4. Registration
5. Dissemination/interpretation of standardized test results
6. Interpretation of specialized individual/group tests
7. Career/vocational planning
8. Application of other skills taught in guidance curriculum

III. *Implementation Methods*
Although the objective of the activities is to help students make personalized plans, it is recommended that the activities be conducted with groups of students or parents in lieu of individual conferences. Dissemination of printed information, such as senior handbooks and course catalogs, is an integral part of this system.

Individuals are seen as part of the Responsive Services component to receive help for atypical problems or special needs. It is recommended that individuals with academic difficulties (i.e., class failures) be counseled in a structured and systematic way.

Assisting students to successfully complete their elementary and secondary education is the priority for this component of the guidance program. College and other postsecondary education planning are primarily the responsibility of the students and their parents.

Although individual planning activities are important at all grade levels, the grade levels with highest priority are the 9th, 8th, 6th, and 5th grades.

Framework of the Responsive Services Component

I. *Definition*

The responsive services component is that through which some students are assisted in solving immediate problems that interfere with their healthy personal, social, career, and educational development.

II. *Content*

Thirteen topics have been identified as those most frequently presented by students, their teachers or parents for response by the counselors. Most of these recur regardless of the school level of the student. They are listed below in priority order.

1. Academic failures
2. Child abuse
3. Divorce/single parents
4. Grief/death/loss
5. Suicide threats
6. Sexuality issues
7. Tardiness/absences/truancy/schoolphobia/dropping out
8. Discipline/behavior problems
9. Peer problems
10. Alcohol/drug/inhalant abuse
11. Family situations
12. Information seekers
13. Application of other skills taught in guidance curriculum

III. *Implementation Methods*

In responding to special needs identified by students, teachers, and parents, counselors may counsel small groups with similar problems, or individuals; consult with teachers, parents, or administrators; refer individuals to other in-district or community specialists; or provide mechanisms for information dissemination.

Counselors' case loads in providing responsive services at each school level vary depending on the topic, the number of students presenting the problem, and the response procedure recommended as most effective for problem resolution.

Elementary and middle school students with needs for preventive counseling should receive approximately 60% of the time allocated to this component, and those with needs for remediation services should receive approximately 40% of the time allocated.

High school students with needs for preventive services should receive approximately 50% of the time allocated to this component, and those with needs for remediation services should receive approximately 50% of the time allocated.

Framework of the System Support Component

I. *Definition*

This component describes (a) the support the guidance program needs from the educational system to ensure effective implementation of the other three components; and (b) the support the guidance program provides to facilitate the implementation of other facets of the total educational system.

II. *Content*

A. *Framework for Support From the Educational System to the Guidance Department*

Support to the guidance program is implemented through provision of

1. Appropriate policy/administrative procedures
2. Staff development
3. Program development
4. Budget
5. Facilities and equipment
6. Adequate staff allocations
7. Scheduled time to access students
8. Public relations

B. *Framework of Guidance Department Support to Other Educational Programs*

The guidance department coordinates, conducts, or participates in activities that support eight other programs in NISD's educational system:

1. Regular education (elementary & secondary)
2. Testing program
3. Career education
4. Special education
5. Gifted education
6. Vocational education

      7. Discipline management program

      8. Compensatory education

III. *Implementation Methods*

Recommendations as to the level of support needed for the guidance program to operate effectively are made by the guidance steering committee, the director of guidance, or other administrators at the time of implementing various districtwide activities.

Priorities for allocation of counselors' time to support other programs have been established and disseminated in administrative procedures. Clarification of the counselors' and others' roles in the various relevant activities is being specified in procedural regulations.

APPENDIX C

LIFE CAREER DEVELOPMENT: STUDENT COMPETENCIES BY DOMAINS AND GOALS

I. Self-knowledge and Interpersonal Skills
  A. Students will develop and incorporate an understanding of the unique personal characteristics and abilities of themselves and others.
    1. Students will be aware of the unique personal characteristics of themselves and others.
    Students will
      a. describe their appearance and their favorite activities. (Kindergarten)
      b. recognize special or unusual characteristics about themselves. (first grade)
      c. recognize special or unusual characteristics about others. (second grade)
      d. describe themselves accurately to someone who does not know them. (third grade)
    2. Students will demonstrate an understanding of the importance of unique personal characteristics and abilities in themselves and others.
    Students will
      a. analyze how people are different and how they have different skills and abilities. **(fourth grade)**
      b. specify personal characteristics and abilities that they value. (fifth grade)
      c. analyze how characteristics and abilities change and how they can be expanded. (sixth grade)
      d. compare their characteristics and abilities with those of others and accept the differences. (seventh grade)
      e. describe their present skills and predict future skills. (eight grade)

     f. value their unique characteristics and abilities. (ninth grade)

     g. analyze how characteristics and abilities develop. (tenth grade)

  3. Students will appreciate and encourage the unique personal characteristics and abilities of themselves and others.

    Students will

     a. specify characteristics and abilities they appreciate most in themselves and others. (eleventh grade)

     b. appreciate their uniqueness and encourage that uniqueness. (twelfth grade)

B. Students will develop and incorporate personal skills that will lead to satisfactory physical and mental health.

  1. Students will be aware of personal skills necessary for satisfactory physical and mental health.

    Students will

     a. describe ways they care for themselves. (Kindergarten)

     b. describe how exercise and nutrition affect their mental health. (first grade)

     c. describe how they care for their physical health. (second grade)

     d. describe how they care for their mental health. (third grade)

     e. recognize that they are important to themselves and others. (fourth grade)

     f. determine situations that produce unhappy or angry feelings and how they deal with those feelings. (fifth grade)

     g. understand what "stress" means and describe methods of relaxation of handling stress. (sixth grade)

  2. Students will demonstrate personal skills that will lead to satisfactory physical and mental health.

    Students will

     a. distinguish between things helpful and harmful to physical health. (seventh grade)

     b. distinguish between things helpful and harmful to mental health. (eighth grade)

     c. predict methods they may use in caring for medical emergencies. (ninth grade)

  3. Students will demonstrate satisfactory physical and mental health.

    Students will

     a. effectively reduce their stress during tension-producing situations. (tenth grade)

     b. continually evaluate the effects their leisure-time activities have on their physical and mental health. (eleventh grade)

     c. analyze their own personal skills that have contributed to satisfactory physical and mental health. (twelfth grade)

C. Students will develop and incorporate an ability to assume responsibility for themselves and to manage their environment.
1. Students will be aware of their responsibilities in their environment. Students will
   a. describe areas where they are self-sufficient. (Kindergarten)
   b. describe responsibilities they have in their environment. (first grade)
   c. give such examples of their environment as their address and the way from school to home. (second grade)
   d. describe the responsibilities of adults they know. (third grade)
2. Students will understand the importance of assuming responsibility for themselves and for managing their environment. Students will
   a. know their responsibilities and can be trusted to do them. (fourth grade)
   b. analyze how growing up requires more self-control. (fifth grade)
   c. know their responsibilities and evaluate their effect on others. (sixth grade)
   d. compare and contrast the responsibilities of others in their environment. (seventh grade)
   e. evaluate how responsibility helps manage their lives. (eighth grade)
   f. analyze when they take responsibility for themselves and when they do not. (ninth grade)
3. Students will assume responsibility for themselves and manage their environment. Students will
   a. show how they manage their environment. (tenth grade)
   b. assess how avoiding responsibility hinders their ability to manage their environment effectively. (eleventh grade)
   c. assess how taking responsibility enhances their lives. (twelfth grade)
D. Students will develop and incorporate the ability to maintain effective relationships with peers and adults.
1. Students will be aware of their relationships with peers and adults. Students will
   a. describe their work and play relationships with others. (Kindergarten)
   b. describe the process of making a friend. (first grade)
   c. describe the process of making and keeping a friend. (second grade)
   d. recognize the actions they take that affect others' feelings. (third grade)

      e. indicate methods that lead to effective cooperation with children and adults. (fourth grade)

      f. describe their relationships with family members. (fifth grade)

  2. Students will demonstrate a growing ability to create and maintain effective relationships with peers and adults.

    Students will

      a. analyze the skills needed to make and keep friends. (sixth grade)

      b. evaluate ways peers and adults interact. (seventh grade)

      c. analyze effective family relationships, their importance, and how they are formed. (eighth grade)

      d. evaluate the importance of having friendships with peers and adults. (ninth grade)

      e. describe situations where their behaviors affect others' behaviors toward them. (tenth grade)

      f. assess their current social and family relationships and evaluate their effectiveness. (eleventh grade)

  3. Students will maintain effective relationships with peers and adults.

    Students will

      a. understand the value of maintaining effective relationships throughout life in today's interdependent society. (twelfth grade)

E. Students will develop and incorporate listening and expression skills that allow for involvement with others in problem-solving and helping relationships.

  1. Students will be aware of listening and expression skills that allow for involvement with others.

    Students will

      a. recognize that they listen to and speak with a variety of people. (Kindergarten)

      b. describe methods that enable them to speak so they can be understood by others. (first grade)

      c. describe listening and expression skills that allow them to understand others and others to understand them. (second grade)

  2. Students will use listening and expression skills that allow for involvement with others.

    Students will

      a. listen to and speak with friends and others that are not close friends. (third grade)

      b. evaluate how what they say affects others' actions and how what others say affects their actions. (fourth grade)

      c. evaluate ways others listen and express thoughts and feelings to them. (fifth grade)

      d. use effective nonverbal communication. (sixth grade)

      e. evaluate how listening and talking help to solve problems. (seventh grade)

      f. analyze how communications skills improve their relationships with others. (eighth grade)

      g. analyze how communications skills contribute toward work within a group. (ninth grade)

  3. Students will use listening and expression skills that allow for involvement with others in problem-solving and helping relationships. Students will

      a. use communications skills to help others. (tenth grade)

      b. analyze how their communications skills encourage problem solving. (eleventh grade)

      c. evaluate their current communication skills and continually improve those skills. (twelfth grade)

II. Life Roles, Settings, and Events

  A. Students will develop and incorporate skills that lead to an effective role as a learner.

    1. Students will be aware of themselves as learners. Students will

      a. describe things they learn at school. (Kindergarten)

      b. relate learning experiences at school to situations in the home. (first grade)

      c. recognize some benefits of learning. (second grade)

      d. realize that certain study skills are necessary for learning each school subject. (third grade)

      e. describe the various methods they use to learn in school. (fourth grade)

    2. Students will use skills that lead to an effective role as a learner. Students will

      a. analyze how their basic study skills relate to desired work skills. (fifth grade)

      b. analyze how school learning experiences relate to their leisure activities. (sixth grade)

      c. predict how they will use knowledge from certain subjects in future life and work experiences. (seventh grade)

      d. learn both in and out of the school setting. (eighth grade)

      e. describe personal learning and study skills and explain their importance. (ninth grade)

      f. evaluate personal learning and study skills and explain how they can be improved. (tenth grade)

    3. Students will be effective in their roles as learners.

Students will

a. predict how their developed learning and study skills can contribute to work habits in the future. (eleventh grade)

b. evaluate ways they presently learn and predict how learning may change in the future. (twelfth grade)

B. Students will develop and incorporate an understanding of the legal and economic principles and practices that lead to responsible daily living.

1. Students will be aware of legal and economic principles and practices. Students will

a. recognize the town, state, and country in which they reside. (Kindergarten)

b. understand why people use money in our economic system. (first grade)

c. describe rules they follow in their environment and why those rules are necessary. (second grade)

d. understand what a consumer is and how they are consumers. (third grade)

e. describe how people depend on each other to fulfill their needs. (fourth grade)

f. recognize that a wage earner is required to pay taxes. (fifth grade)

g. describe how the government uses tax money. (sixth grade)

2. Students will demonstrate a growing ability to use legal and economic principles and practices that lead to responsible daily living. Students will

a. describe the rights and responsibilities they have as citizens of their towns and states. (seventh grade)

b. describe the rights and responsibilities they have as U.S. citizens. (eighth grade)

c. evaluate the purposes of taxes and how taxes support the government. (ninth grade)

d. evaluate their roles as consumers. (tenth grade)

e. analyze their legal rights and responsibilities as consumers. (eleventh grade)

3. Students will use responsible legal and economic principles and practices in their daily lives. Students will

a. analyze how they, as citizens and consumers, help to support the economic system. (twelfth grade)

C. Students will develop and incorporate an understanding of the interactive effects of life styles, life roles, settings, and events.

1. Students will be aware of life styles, life roles, settings, and events. Students will

      a. describe their daily activities at school. (Kindergarten)

      b. realize how they have changed during the past year. (first grade)

      c. describe necessary daily activities carried out by self and others. (second grade)

      d. recognize that people have varying roles and describe their own roles. (third grade)

      e. understand what important events affect the lives of self and others. (fourth grade)

      f. recognize what a life style is and what influences their life styles. (fifth grade)

  2. Students will acknowledge the interactive effects of life styles, life roles, settings, and events in their lives.
Students will

      a. analyze ways they have control over themselves and their life styles. (sixth grade)

      b. evaluate their feelings in a variety of settings. (seventh grade)

      c. predict their feelings in a variety of potential settings. (eighth grade)

      d. analyze how life roles, settings, and events determine preferred life styles. (ninth grade)

      e. compare how life styles differ depending on life roles, settings, and events. (tenth grade)

  3. Students will understand the interactive effects of life styles, life roles, settings, and events.
Students will

      a. determine how life roles, settings, and events have influenced their present life styles. (eleventh grade)

      b. assess the interactive effects of life roles, settings, and events and how these lead to a preferred life style. (twelfth grade)

D. Students will develop and incorporate an understanding of sterotypes and how stereotypes affect career identity.

  1. Students will be aware of stereotypes and some of their effects.
Students will

      a. mentally project adults into work activities other than those they do presently. (Kindergarten)

      b. recognize how peers differ from themselves. (first grade)

      c. distinguish which work activities in their environment are done by certain people. (second grade)

      d. recognize why people choose certain work activities and that those choices may change. (third grade)

      e. define the meaning of "stereotypes" and indicate how sterotypes affect them. (fourth grade)

   f. describe stereotypes that correspond with certain jobs. (fifth grade)
2. Students will demonstrate a growing ability to understand stereotypes and how stereotypes affect career identity.
   Students will
   a. predict how stereotypes might affect them in work activities. (sixth grade)
   b. describe occupations that have stereotypes and will analyze how those stereotypes are reinforced. (seventh grade)
   c. evaluate the ways in which certain groups (men, women, minorities, and so on) are stereotyped. (eighth grade)
   d. analyze stereotypes that exist for them and how those stereotypes limit their choices. (ninth grade)
   e. analyze stereotypes others hold and how those stereotypes can limit choices. (tenth grade)
3. Students will understand stereotypes in their lives and environment and how stereotypes affect career identity.
   Students will
   a. evaluate their stereotypes and explain those they have changed. (eleventh grade)
   b. analyze the effect stereotypes have on career identity. (twelfth grade)
E. Students will develop and incorporate the ability to express futuristic concerns and the ability to imagine themselves in these situations.
   1. Students will be aware of the future and what situations might occur in the future.
      Students will
      a. describe situations that are going to happen in the future. (Kindergarten)
      b. describe situations desired for the future and when they would like those situations to happen. (first grade)
      c. recognize what they would like to accomplish when they are three years older. (second grade)
      d. define what "future" means. (third grade)
   2. Students will demonstrate a growing ability to express futuristic concerns and to imagine themselves in such situations.
      Students will
      a. imagine what their lives might be like in the future. (fourth grade)
      b. imagine what the world will be like in twenty years. (fifth grade)
      c. predict what they will be like in twenty years. (sixth grade)
      d. predict ways in which some present careers may be different in the future. (seventh grade)
      e. predict how they may have to change to fit into a career in the future. (eighth grade)

      f. analyze how choices they are making now will affect their lives in the future. (ninth grade)

      g. predict some of the concerns they will have as they get older. (tenth grade)

   3. Students will express futuristic concerns and will imagine themselves in these situations.

   Students will

      a. evaluate the need for flexibility in their roles and in their choices. (eleventh grade)

      b. analyze how concerns change as situations and roles change. (twelfth grade)

III. Life Career Planning

   A. Students will develop and incorporate an understanding of producer rights and responsibilities.

      1. Students will be aware of what a producer is and that producers have rights and responsibilities.

      Students will

         a. describe the work activities of family members. (Kindergarten)

         b. describe different work activities and their importance. (first grade)

         c. define "work" and recognize that all people work. (second grade)

         d. realize that people obtain rewards for their work. (third grade)

         e. recognize that a producer can have many different roles. (fourth grade)

         f. recognize how they depend on different producers. (fifth grade)

      2. Students will demonstrate an understanding of what a producer is and producer rights and responsibilities.

      Students will

         a. demonstrate steps they follow in producing a product or task they take pride in. (sixth grade)

         b. show appreciation when others successfully complete a difficult task. (seventh grade)

         c. analyze the relationship between interests and producer satisfaction. (eighth grade)

         d. analyze how producers may have to cooperate with each other to accomplish a large or difficult task. (ninth grade)

         e. evaluate the importance of having laws and contracts to protect producers. (tenth grade)

      3. Students will understand and exemplify producer rights and responsibilities.

      Students will

         a. specify their rights and responsibilities as producers. (eleventh grade)

    b. speculate what their rights and obligations might be as producers in the future. (twelfth grade)

B. Students will develop and incorporate an understanding of how attitudes and values affect decisions, actions, and life styles.

  1. Students will be aware of attitudes and values and their effects. Students will

    a. describe people and activities they enjoy. (Kindergarten)

    b. describe actions of others that they do not appreciate. (first grade)

    c. describe things they have learned that aid in making choices. (second grade)

    d. recognize accomplishments they are proud of. (third grade)

    e. define "attitudes" and "beliefs" and describe the effects attitudes and beliefs have on decisions. (fourth grade)

    f. define "values" and describe their own values. (fifth grade)

  2. Students will demonstrate a growing understanding of how attitudes and values affect decisions, actions, and life styles. Students will

    a. analyze how their attitudes and values influence what they do. (sixth grade)

    b. compare and contrast others' values. (seventh grade)

    c. predict how their values will influence their life styles. (eighth grade)

    d. describe and set priorities for their values. (ninth grade)

    e. describe decisions they have made that were based on their attitudes and values. (tenth grade)

  3. Students will understand how attitudes and values affect decisions, actions, and life styles. Students will

    a. analyze how values affect their decisions, actions, and life styles. (eleventh grade)

    b. summarize the importance of understanding their attitudes and values and how those attitudes and values affect their lives. (twelfth grade)

C. Students will develop and incorporate an understanding of the decision-making process and how the decisions they make are influenced by previous decisions made by themselves and others.

  1. Students will be aware of decisions and the decision-making process. Students will

    a. describe choices they make. (Kindergarten)

    b. describe decisions they make by themselves. (first grade)

    c. recognize why some choices are made for them; they can accept those choices and make their own decisions when appropriate. (second grade)

  d. describe their thought processes before a decision is made. (third grade)
  e. describe why they might want to change a decision and recognize when it is or is not possible to make that change. (fourth grade)
  f. describe the decision-making process. (fifth grade)
  g. recognize how school decisions influence them. (sixth grade)
2. Students will understand the decision-making process and factors that influence the decisions they make.
  Students will
  a. provide examples of how past decisions they have made influence their present actions. (seventh grade)
  b. analyze how past decisions made by their families influence their present decisions. (eighth grade)
  c. evaluate the influence that past legal decisions have on their present decisions. (ninth grade)
  d. analyze the decision-making process used by others. (tenth grade)
3. Students will effectively use the decision-making process and understand how the decisions they make are influenced by previous decisions made by themselves and others.
  Students will
  a. identify decisions they have made and analyze how those decisions will affect their future decisions. (eleventh grade)
  b. implement the decision-making process when making a decision. (twelfth grade)
D. Students will develop and incorporate the ability to generate decision-making alternatives, gather necessary information, and assess the risks and consequences of alternatives.
  1. Students will be aware of methods of generating decision-making alternatives, gather necessary information, and assess the risks and consequences of alternatives.
    Students will
    a. realize the difficulty of making choices between two desirable alternatives. (Kindergarten)
    b. recognize those decisions that are difficult for them. (first grade)
    c. realize that they go through a decision-making process each time they make a choice. (second grade)
    d. recognize that they are able to assess possible consequences of a decision before actually making the choice. (third grade)
  2. Students will demonstrate a growing ability to generate decision-making alternatives, gather necessary information, and assess the risks and consequences of alternatives.
    Students will
    a. generate alternatives to a specific decision. (fourth grade)

   b. evaluate some of the risks involved in choosing one alternative over another. (fifth grade)
   c. consider the results of various alternatives and then make their choice. (sixth grade)
   d. provide examples of some consequences of a decision. (seventh grade)
   e. demonstrate how gaining more information increases their alternatives. (eighth grade)
   f. analyze the importance of generating alternatives and assessing the consequences of each before making a decision. (ninth grade)
   g. distinguish between alternatives that involve varying degrees of risk. (tenth grade)
   h. analyze the consequences of decisions that others make. (eleventh grade)
   3. Students will generate decision-making alternatives, gather necessary information, and assess the risks and consequences of alternatives. Students will
      a. provide examples and evaluate their present ability to generate alternatives, gather information, and assess the consequences in the decisions they make. (twelfth grade)
E. Students will develop and incorporate skill in clarifying values, expanding interests and capabilities, and evaluating progress toward goals.
   1. Students will be aware of values, interests and capabilities, and methods of evaluation.
      Students will
      a. describe growing capabilities. (Kindergarten)
      b. identify capabilities they wish to develop. (first grade)
      c. recognize activities that interest them and those that do not. (second grade)
      d. realize that environment influences interests and capabilities. (third grade)
      e. recognize different methods of evaluating task progress. (fourth grade)
      f. describe the meaning of "value" and how values contribute toward goal decisions. (fifth grade)
   2. Students will gain skill in clarifying values, expanding interests and capabilities, and evaluating progress toward goals.
      Students will
      a. predict five goals (based on their interests and capabilities) they would like to achieve within five years. (sixth grade)
      b. analyze various methods of evaluating their progress toward a goal. (seventh grade)

    c. contrast goals they desire to complete with goals they expect to complete. (eighth grade)

    d. define their unique values, interests, and capabilities. (ninth grade)

    e. evaluate the importance of setting realistic goals and striving toward them. (tenth grade)

3. Students will clarify their values, expand their interests and capabilities, and evaluate their progress toward goals.

    Students will

    a. analyze how their values, interests, and capabilities have changed and are changing. (eleventh grade)

    b. assess their ability to achieve past goals and integrate this knowledge for the future. (twelfth grade)

APPENDIX D

SAMPLE POSITION GUIDE

NORTHSIDE INDEPENDENT SCHOOL DISTRICT

Title: *High School Counselor*

Primary Function: to provide, as a member of the guidance department staff, a comprehensive guidance and counseling program for students in grades 9–12 and specifically to provide services to meet the special needs of his/her assigned case load (500); to consult with teachers, staff, and parents to enhance their effectiveness in helping students' educational, career, personal, and social development; and to provide support to other high school educational programs.

Major Job Responsibilities: (1) teach the high school guidance curriculum; (2) guide groups of students and individual students through the development of educational and career plans; (3) counsel small groups and individual students through the development of educational and career plans; (4) counsel small groups and individual students with problems; (5) consult with teachers, staff, and parents regarding meeting the developmental needs of adolescents and regarding specific information about the youths for whom they have responsibility; (6) refer students or their parents with problems to specialists or special programs; (7) participate in, coordinate, or conduct activities that contribute to the effective operation of the school; (8) plan and evaluate the campus guidance program; and (9) pursue continuous professional growth.

*Illustrative
Key Duties*:

(1) *teach the high school guidance curriculum*: conduct developmental guidance lessons in classroom settings as planned in conjunction with the instructional departments, or through the advisory system or study halls, or as otherwise devised in conjunction with the school administration; consult with or be a resource person to teachers to facilitate the infusion of guidance content into the regular education curriculum.

(2) *guide groups and individual students through the development of educational and career plans*: provide orientation activities for students new to the school such as "brown bag" lunch sessions; participate in orientation programs for incoming 9th graders; guide 9th and 10th graders in the updating of their "High School 4–Year Plans"; guide 11th and 12th graders to evaluate their current status and plan their achievement of high school graduation; guide 12th graders to develop and take appropriate steps toward implementing their post-high school educational or career plans; plan/coordinate/assist in preregistration of 9th, 10th, and 11th graders for 10th, 11th, and 12th grades, respectively; collaborate with middle school counselors to effect the preregistration of 8th graders for 9th grade; assist students new to the district with course selection at the time of registration; interpret standardized test (TEAMS, TAP, DAT, OVIS) results information to students, parents, and teachers; guide groups and individual students in applying the test results information to their educational and career plans; interpret results of college entrance tests or career assessments to groups of students; guide all students to develop tentative career/vocational plans through the conduct or supervision of career education activities such as career center orientations and utilization of the GIS system and other career center resources; provide a mechanism for the systematic and efficient dissemination of current, accurate information needed by individual students or parents as they develop their educational or career plans.

(3) *counsel small groups and individual students with problems*: conduct structured, goal-oriented counseling sessions in systematic response to identified needs

of individuals or groups of students—recurrent topics at the high school level include academic failure, attendance and behavior problems, peer problems, family issues, child abuse, substance abuse, suicide threats and attempts, and sexuality issues.

(4) *consult with teachers, staff, and parents regarding meeting the developmental needs of adolescents and regarding specific information about the youths for whom they have responsibility*: participate in staffings; conduct inservice programs for faculty as a whole or by departments; conduct/facilitate conferences with teachers, students, or parents; conduct or provide opportunities for parent education programs; write articles for parent newsletters; assist families with school-related problems.

(5) *refer students or their parents with problems to specialists or special programs*: consult and coordinate with in-district and community specialists such as school nurses, administrators, and psychologists and community-based psychologists, service agencies, and physicians.

(6) *participate in, coordinate, or conduct activities that contribute to the effective operation of the school*: cooperate with administration in planning and implementing preregistration and PREP days; interpret group test results to faculty and staff; contribute to the principal's goals for enhancing education on the campus; cooperate with instructional staff in implementing the ''Placement Recommendation Guidelines''; establish effective liaisons with the various instructional departments; provide input to administration as the master schedule is built; act as an advocate for groups or individual students as system decisions are made; supervise the changing of student schedules in accordance with district policies; cooperate with other school staff in placing students with special needs in appropriate programs, including other regular education, special education and vocational education opportunities; cooperate with administration/coordinate campuswide administration of the district testing program (TEAMS, TAP, DAT, OVIS): supervise administration of special group testing (e.g., PSAT, SAT, ACT,

CEEB:AP; ASVAB); cooperate with administration/ supervise the teacher advisory system.

(7) *plan and evaluate the campus guidance program*: annually design, with the other members of the guidance department staff, the campus guidance program based on needs by clearly stating program goals and objectives, establishing the guidance department calendar, and completing the Annual Guidance Program Plan—High School; evaluate strategies as they are implemented; complete the annual Guidance Program Evaluation Report—High School.

(8) *pursue continuous professional growth*: attend district-sponsored staff development offerings; join associations (e.g., NCA, STACD, TACD, AACD); read professional journals; attend relevant workshops and conferences sponsored by professionally appropriate organizations (e.g., Region 20, TEA, and associations); take postgraduate courses.

Organizational Relationships: is supervised by the head counselor, the principal, and the director of guidance; works collaboratively with other counselors and guidance department staff; and works cooperatively with other campus or district staff.

Performance Standards: A high school counselor's performance is considered satisfactory when (1) The head counselor, principal, and director of guidance concur and the counselor's level of competence is reflected as such on the NISD Counselor Evaluation Form; and (2) evaluation of the Annual Guidance Program Plan—High School indicates overall effectiveness of the program.

APPENDIX E

IDEAS FOR DISCREPANCY REPAIR

NORTHSIDE INDEPENDENT SCHOOL DISTRICT

RESULTS OF BRAINSTORMING WAYS TO REDUCE DISCREPANCIES BETWEEN THE CURRENT AND THE DESIRED GUIDANCE PROGRAM

Steering Committee Ideas

Elementary Level

Increase time spent in curriculum role.

- Develop and teach baseline curriculum.
- Establish systematic schedule (weekly, monthly).

Decrease time spent in system support.

- Establish other staff responsibilities for tasks.
- Clarify our own responsibilities and communicate them to faculty and administration.
- Reduce clerical work.
- Reduce support to special education system.
- Help principals understand appropriate assignments for counselors; eliminate time-consuming, inappropriate tasks.

Middle School Level

Increase time spent in curriculum.

- Assign three counselors to every middle school to ensure a counselor for each grade level.
- Assign counselors by grade level rather than by alphabet to enhance the developmental part of the program.

- Establish a schedule of operation and have it endorsed by the principal.
- Schedule students for guidance by taking them from two academic classes per year (one per semester); i.e., every teacher gives up only two class periods a year.
- Provide inservice to teachers on guidance curriculum purposes and "tasks" for students.

Decrease time spent in system support.

- Hire "technical assistants" to relieve counselors of
  1. schedule changes.
  2. registration of new students during the school year.
  3. test coordination.
- Assign education office students to counseling office to help file, etc.

High School Level

Increase time spent in curriculum.

- Work with groups (vs. individuals) to disseminate information, e.g., junior and senior credit checks, test score interpretation.
- Involve with clubs, organizations, and other extracurricular activities through assignment if necessary.
- Increase time spent in group activities.
- Set yearly calendar that will facilitate counselors' keeping on task for group activities.
- Get into the classroom to be a visible part of the educational team.

Decrease time spent in system support.

- Spend less time in offices.
- Add clerical help or computerized resources to accomplish clerical tasks.
- Remove counseling case load from head counselors to allow them to be program administrators and to manage major tasks (e.g., test program co-ordination).
- Review utilization of vocational counselors.

All Levels

Increase time spent in curriculum.

- Define program expectations, monitor implementation.
- Develop curriculum resources.
- Provide staff development for counselors.
- Communicate program to and enlist support of administration and faculty.
- Design systematic delivery system (calendar, timeline, individual vs. group).

Decrease time spent in system support.

- Evaluate specific paperwork responsibilities.
- Review activities to determine if they can be accomplished through data processing.
- Move some responsibility to students and parents.
- Evaluate clerical staff in counseling departments.
- Evaluate adequacy of staffing in counseling departments (professional and clerical).
- Study reduced student load for head counselors to allow more coordination.
- Move administrative duties to administration; increase administrative staff if necessary.
- Use and evaluate new streamlined procedures for ARD participation.

High School Principals' Ideas

Increase time spent in curriculum.

- Times to conduct curriculum activities:
  —advisories.
  —4th period study hall.
  —on-campus suspension class.
  —coverage for teachers at conventions.
  —club schedule.
  —identify and work with classes that have needs, e.g., lower level academic classes.
- Different methods of assigning counselors to case load/job responsibilities.
- Priority: students on campus now, not for their future.
- Inservice for teachers on such topics as behavior management, listening skills.
- Planned for the year, consistent.
- Calendar.

Decrease time spent in system support.

- Program computer to do credit checks.
  —mainframe, data base.
  —microcomputer programs.
- Shift philosophy from the counselor back to the student and parent(s) as the responsible person for seeing that graduation is achieved.
- Lengthen yearly contracts (beyond student days).
- Head counselor do system support activities, lessen their student case load.
- "Run" for classes in August.
- Teacher advisor program.

High School Counselors' Ideas

Increase time spent in curriculum.

- Group guidance to teach decision-making skills, self-esteem.
- Do away with parent notes on schedule changes.
- More inservice with teachers, e.g., with freshmen teachers to help freshmen become successfully involved in school.
- More time in 9th-grade advisories.
- Freshmen advisory: guidance in the first month of school; orientation to high school, study skills, attendance, 4–Year Plan revision, involvement.
- 9th graders' orientation to career center.
- More time interpreting OVIS.
- Need facilities to do group guidance.
- More use of advisory to have small groups with all students.
- "Brown bag" sessions.
- Make "official time" for counselors to go into classrooms; ideas: restructure school day periodically, more faculty involvement with credits, clubs, etc.; get principals' verbal support; sell ideas to key teachers or department heads.
- Counselors need planning time.
- Priorities: feeling good about themselves, decision-making and study skills.

Decrease time spent in system support.

- Follow-up studies should not be done by counselors.
- Reduce testing coordination time.
- Campus-based testing specialist to coordinate and administer all district and state testing.
- Administration should coordinate responsibility for state mandated, minimum competency testing.
- System analysis to evaluate feasibility of computer support for counselors.
- Computer terminal for each counselor.
- Hire professional registrar.
- Work with state/national college admissions counselors and associations to eliminate undue college admissions paperwork, e.g., letters of recommendation; develop standard checklist to accomplish this.
- Work with scholarship agencies to develop standardized form.
- Close adherence to district guidelines to reduce number of schedule changes.
- Functions to be streamlined: hand-scheduling new students; paperwork required for special ed referrals; master schedule adjustments—balancing classes, forming new classes, master schedule errors; credit checks; planning senior assembly; TEAMS failures; retention paperwork; making lists for potential school projects; test coordination; hand tallying of master schedule; ARDs.

- Need input to new course offerings and master schedule development.
- Need principals' verbal support for the program.
- Reduce miscellaneous paperwork: teacher lists, testing procedures, preregistration bulletin, premature scheduling, athletic schedule changes, elective changes, teacher prejudgments, leveling, college day forms.
- Structure staff consultation, calendar, and agenda.
- Reduce time spent in personal support to teachers; could handle recurrent issues through inservice.
- Support personnel register new students.
- Restructure curriculum information dissemination.

Middle School Principals' Ideas

Increase time spent in guidance curriculum.

- Calendar classroom visits—develop with and share with administrators.
- Short blocks of time.
- Advisory time.
- "Essential elements"—teachers/departments identify topics and times of year (counselors too).
- Teachers work with counselors in classrooms.
  —team efforts.
  —roles of each will be clarified.
- Need principal's support.
- Inservice for teachers by counselors regarding the guidance curriculum.
- Inservice for counselors (e.g., group skills).
- Change slowly.

Decrease time spent in system support.

- Time management.
- Teacher inservice regarding guidance program and services (what is and is not done).
- Referral of teachers for private counseling when needed.
- Referral of teachers to administrators for school-related problems.
- Increase clerical help, e.g., testing schedules, new student enrollment shared between main office and counseling office.
- A-V aids for orientation (e.g., videotape for new students, especially at schools with large numbers and constant flow of new students.
- Brochure.
- Administrative staffings.
- Improved communication methods.
- Registration: forms have little to do with "guidance."

- Implement a teacher-advisor program.
- Counselors should have input into master schedule development.

Middle School Counselors' Ideas

Increase time spent in guidance curriculum.

- Need administrative support for classroom guidance.
- Develop *Curriculum Guide*, lesson plans.
- Need teacher support and cooperation.
- Need structured and organized time.
- Relieve counselors of system support duties to provide time for classroom guidance.
- Counselors be assigned to do classroom guidance by grade level, not alphabetically.
- Have one counselor for each grade level.
- Occupational Investigation teachers implement Career Day.
- Work through "OI" to meet with 8th-grade students.
- Use 2 days from each subject to effect classroom guidance and not take an undue amount of time from one department.

Decrease time spent in system support.

- Special education handle referral paperwork.
- Hire "technical assistant"/technician to handle those duties, e.g., registration of new students, all preregistration and scheduling, plan and coordinate standardized testing, schedule changes.
- Use administrative specialists (teacher level) to do administrivia, e.g., lockers, books, master schedule.
- Have computer terminal in counselors' offices and train staff to use it.
- 8th to 9th grade registration done completely by high school staff.
- Counselors should not do the 5–Year Plan.
- Counselors should not sponsor extracurricular activities, clubs, etc.
- Eliminate building responsibility for master schedule, but continue to have input.
- Reduce paperwork, clerical work.
- Attendance office or main office handle new student initial registration procedure.
- Counselor secretaries are needed to work more days because their duties involve being registrar and data processing.
- Streamline counselor involvement with special programs, e.g., TIPS, LPAC, Special Ed, CVAE.
- Counselors post schedule/calendar of activities and availabilities.

- Define counselor job role to minimize "other duties as assigned. . ."
- Need separate guidance department telephone line.
- More assistance from student aides.

Elementary Principals' Ideas

Increase time spent in guidance curriculum.

- Individual home study packets—a home program.
- Encourage self-viewing of media available.
- Increase counselor time in classroom on self-esteem.
- Assist teachers with motivational techniques.
- Peer counseling to help those in need—counselors used as support for peer counselors.
- Schedule classes for each 6 weeks; topics: study skills, citizenship, test awareness.
- Support recommendation; recognize following concerns: educational curriculum reform, part-time counselors, campuses with heavy load of special education of federal programs.

Decrease time spent in system support.

- Draw up a time-saving recorder of information for referring students for help.
- Common planning time would help.
- Support the recommendation, but each campus's needs should be considered.

Elementary Counselors' Ideas

Increase time spent in guidance curriculum.

- Schedule classes regularly.
- Develop districtwide curriculum.
- Make classrooms available for guidance.
- Allocate a percentage of time each week.
- Expand teachers' involvement.
- Individual campus teams for planning.
- Standardize district procedures.
- Assess student needs.
- Need principals' support.
- Need teachers' support.
- Need materials.
- Need lesson plans and units for specific topics.

- Fewer interruptions.
- Problem of availability of students.
- Curriculum needs to be seen as having priority.
- Curtail special education responsibilities.

Decrease time spent in system support.

- Eliminate special ed paperwork.
- Limit participation in admission, review & dismissal committee meetings.
- Secretarial help.
- Limit Promise testing.
- Eliminate make-up testing.
- Drop CAP West referral work.
- Eliminate Early Childhood referrals.
- Eliminate the ''go f'r'' syndrome—principals to counselors, e.g., So. Association Accreditation Study Chair.
- Eliminate responsibility for before and after school and lunch duty.
- Stop doing newsletter articles.
- Stop being parents' ''tour guide.''
- Stop driving students to PAC/physicals.

APPENDIX F

DESCRIPTORS RELATED TO EVALUATION CATEGORIES

These descriptors are provided to counselors, their supervisors, and administrators as a means of enhancing communication about the nature of guidance and counseling and the specifics upon which to base sound evaluative judgments as to the proficiency of the school counselor. The specific items were generated by and large by Northside counselors, with some reaffirmation and augmentation from the guidance and counseling literature. They are offered to assist new counselors, experienced counselors, non-guidance-trained administrators, and guidance-trained-administrators have similar definitions for the skills and knowledge expected of our school counselors.

Specifically, the items provide more concrete descriptions for the performance indicators suggested for the areas that counselors are evaluated on. If it were laid out in one document, the format would be as follows:

Category	Performance Indicator	Descriptors
1. implements guidance curriculum through the use of effective instructional skills	a. appropriate task analysis	1. selection of terminal objective 2. specification of learning increments 3. weeding out of nonessentials 4. instruction at appropriate level of difficulty 5. selection of learning sequence 6. explanation of unfamiliar or specially used terms
	b. effective use of lesson design	1. focus 2. explanation

. . . etc. . . .

Still, this list is not all-inclusive nor are all items necessarily mutually exclusive. It is not meant to be used as a checklist, but rather it is intended to make the school counselor's role more tangible.

1. **Implements guidance curriculum through the use of effective instructional skills, including**
   a. appropriate task analysis
      1) selects terminal objective
      2) specifies learning increments
      3) weeds out nonessentials
      4) instructs at an appropriate level of difficulty
      5) selects learning sequence
      6) explains unfamiliar or specially used terms
   b. effective use of lesson design
      1) focus
      2) explanation
      3) checking for understanding
      4) monitoring and adjusting
      5) modeling
      6) guided practice
      7) closure
      8) independent practice
      9) extensions
      10) corrections
      11) evaluation
   c. active involvement of students in the learning process
      1) varies activities
      2) interacts with students in appropriate group formats
      3) solicits student participation
      4) extends students' responses/contributions
      5) provides "wait time"
      6) secures and maintains students' attention
      7) gives clear directions
      8) manages students' behavior
      9) uses effective teaching practices
      10) uses strategies to motivate students for learning
      11) maintains supportive environment
      12) provides materials and equipment needed for lessons ready for use at appropriate time
   d. selection of topics consistent with identified, high priority student needs and district goals
      1) implements instruction at appropriate level of difficulty

2) assesses student needs formally and informally

3) adheres to district guidance scope and sequence and curriculum

2. Implements the individual planning system through the effective use of guidance skills, including

 a. careful planning of sessions

1) performs appropriate task analysis

2) effectively uses lesson design, with expanded use of guided practice

3) guided practice

4) uses variety of guidance techniques

5) has materials, audiovisual aids, and facilities ready for use

6) understands/applies theories of vocational choice

 b. presentation of accurate, relevant, unbiased information

1) makes no significant errors

2) presents information so that students can process/internalize it

 a. uses vocabulary appropriate to the students

 b. explains content clearly

 c. presents appropriate amounts of information

3) stresses important points

4) clarifies students' misunderstanding

5) uses accurate language

6) identifies, selects, organizes, and makes accessible educational and career information systems; makes information resources available to students

7) utilizes materials effectively

8) is knowledgeable about the range of educational and career alternatives and the value of each of these

 c. involvement of students in personalized educational and career planning

1) helps students establish goals and use planning skills

2) knows students' abilities, achievements, interests, and goals

3) effectively uses consultation skills as needed

4) encourages parental input into student planning

5) correctly assesses students' educational and career aspiration and information needs

6) makes appropriate and appropriately presented recommendations

7) conducts activities with groups of sizes conducive to ensure effectiveness and efficiency

 d. accurate and appropriate test results interpretation

1) provides appropriate information to students, parents, and school staff in timely manner

2) ensures that individuals know how to read reports of interest/use to them

3) strives to guard against the overinterpretation or other inappropriate use of test results data
4) in presenting test results interpretation, attends to the confidential and private nature of individual test information
5) (reference: item 2b. above regarding accuracy of information)
6) understands/applies basic statistical concepts essential in the use of appraisal instruments and data
7) understand/applies basic concepts and principles of measurement and evaluation
8) processes appraisal data appropriately for use in guidance and counseling
9) makes effective use of appraisal data in counseling and guidance
  e. selection of individual planning activities consistent with identified, high priority student needs and district goals
1) assesses student needs for planning assistance formally and informally
2) presents needs-identification data to reflect data from follow-up studies of former students' actual educational and career progress
3) provides information about important dates and tasks to be accomplished
4) adheres to *District Guidance Program Framework* timeframe and priorities

3. **Implements responsive services through effective use of counseling, consultation, and referral skills, including**
  a. proper identification of problems/issues to be resolved
1) uses effective intake procedures to properly discern problems/issues
2) in counseling, assists students to define their problems
3) in consultation, collaborates with consultee in problem definition
4) in referral, understands and articulates the basis for referral
  b. selection of counseling, consulting or referral interventions appropriate to students' problems and circumstances
1) recognizes own personal/professional limitations and organizes case load appropriately
2) accepts referrals in a competent and professional manner
3) responds appropriately to requests for information
  c. uses counseling, consulting, or referral skills effectively
  Counseling:
1) utilizes a variety of techniques and procedures
2) operates from a consistently applied and conscious awareness of own theoretical base
3) is nonjudgmental of students

4) understands the dynamics of individual behavior in the counseling relationship or in a group

Consulting:

1) has expertise to share
2) shares information
3) in problem specification, gathers as much information as needed to consult effectively and efficiently
4) in goal setting, understands consultees' responsibilities and goals
5) establishes credibility by being able to suggest a variety of options, alternatives, resources, or strategies
6) coordinates the development and implementation of the consultees' behavioral plan of action

Referral: (process: problem specification, evaluation of need for referral, resource identification, referral and follow-up)

1) is knowledgeable about sources for referral
2) seeks out referral sources
3) conducts adequate research about referral sources
4) refers at appropriate time in helping process
5) is able to explain the need for referral and the referral process
6) provides minimum of three referral options to client

d. conducts well-planned and goal-oriented sessions

1) sessions are effective: objectives are established and attained
2) sessions are efficient: objectives are the focus of the sessions; however, sensitivity to divergent needs of the group/individual is imperative also
3) materials, aids, and facilities are ready for use

e. use of group and individual techniques that are appropriate to the topic and to students' needs and abilities

1) discerns when individual or group counseling would be most facilitative to the problem presented by the counselees
2) uses group counseling when it is determined to be more or as effective as individual counseling
3) structures specialized groups as to topic and purpose as well as membership composition
4) displays working knowledge of developmental tasks and coping behaviors of different age levels and the skills to use group techniques appropriate for client level

f. actively involves counselees/consultees/refer-ees in the process

Counseling:

1) counseling results in students' acting to solve problems
2) holds student-oriented sessions

3) allows students to speak freely about problems
4) assists students in exploration of affect
5) assists students in goal setting
6) assists students in establishing a concrete, behavioral plan aimed at problem resolution
7) ensures that plan is developed at an appropriate level of specificity
8) avoids premature advice or superficial reassurance
9) listens effectively

Consulting:
1) consulting results in consultee acting to solve problem
2) encourages input from consultee
3) facilitates communication between participants
4) avoids premature, superficial advice or reassurance
5) handles expressions of conflict in a constructive manner
6) is appreciative of ideas expressed by others
7) promotes a spirit of compromise and cooperation
8) listens effectively

Referral:
1) exhibits skill in the art of referral such that person needing referral feels comfortable
2) assistance results in client going to referral source
3) initiates contacts between referral sources and individuals who have been referred

g. timely follow-up
1) follows up with students and other clients as to their progress in implementation of the problem-solving action plan
2) communicates with referral sources
3) ensures communication between appropriate people
4) prepares/maintains appropriate documentation, forms, records, etc. relevant to cases
5) implements follow-up activities as recommended for clients by referral sources

h. provision of services consistent with high priority, identified student needs and district goals
1) conducts formal and informal needs assessments
2) determines needs and priorities as perceived by students, parents, staff, and administration
3) recognizes situations that need attention
4) attends to priorities established in the *Guidance Program Framework* and in other district memos

4. Implements system support through providing effective support for other programs and by effectively enlisting support for the guidance program, such as

   a. providing a comprehensive and balanced guidance program
   1. uses effective planning skills
      a) assesses program needs and priorities accurately
      b) establishes realistic program goals
      c) uses results of evaluation to improve program
      d) plans program and activities
      e) provides alternative plans
      f) determines suitable and workable time schedule
      g) plans an overview of the year
      h) writes program plan
   2. uses effective organizational skills
      a) establishes meaningful objectives
      b) sequences activities in a meaninful design
      c) sets timelines and follows them
      d) operates from a program calendar
      e) provides an appropriately balanced and comprehensive program
   3. uses resources effectively
      a) resources = materials, human dollars, equipment, facilities
      b) selects and creates sound materials
      c) manages equipment and facilities and budget effectively
      d) takes proper care/makes proper use of equipment
      e) assigns tasks or duties appropriately/delegates effectively
      f) considers strengths of human talent available
      g) seeks assistance if does not have adequate answers
      h) utilizes administration and other staff as appropriate
      i) utilizes available resources
      j) provides resource materials and information to students, staff, parents
      k) determines what personal and natural resources are available/ needed
   4. evaluates program effectively
      a) systematically evaluates overall program effectiveness
      b) uses results of evaluation to improve program

   b. selecting program activities that meet identified, high priority student needs and are consistent with campus and district goals
   1. bases campus program on student and community needs
   2. bases campus program on the district framework

   c. collecting evidence that students achieve meaningful outcomes from program activities
1. evaluates effectiveness of activities
2. evaluates quantity and quality of student growth in guidance and counseling activities
3. provides for a system of evaluating programs and activities
4. plans, implements, and accesses systematic evaluation tools
5. uses results of evaluation tools to reassess program goals, objectives, and strategies
6. consistently evaluates program activities

   d. operating within established procedures, policies, and priorities
1. complies with letter and intent of regulations, directives, and instructions from superiors
2. administers activities in accordance with district guidelines

   e. contributing to organizational solutions outside of assigned responsibilities
1. works as member of team in working to solve organizational problems
2. accepts responsibility for helping others learn their responsibilities and is able to do this without taking over others' roles

   f. working cooperatively with school administrators to garner support for the guidance program
1. collaborates with administration in developing the campus guidance program goals and objectives
2. seeks their support on matters of concern

   g. implementing programs that explain the school guidance program
1. explains the philosophy, priorities, and practices of the guidance program effectively and articulately
2. has a campus PR plan for helping the parents as well as the students and staff understand the guidance program and its variety of activities
3. uses a variety of strategies to communicate to parents, e.g., newsletters, columns, parent education sessions, open houses

   h. attending to ideas/concerns expressed regarding the guidance program
1. listens with an open mind
2. accepts suggestions gracefully
3. is not unnecessarily defensive with parents or community representatives; works to understand their concerns
4. maintains professional detachment in circumstances where patrons are misinformed, mistrusting, (JER's 5 categories)

   i. supporting campus administration policies and goals
1. establishes objectives that contribute to the goals of the campus administration
2. complies with letter and intent of regulations, directives, and instructions from superiors

3. supports administrative directives
4. cooperates with campus administration in addressing campus goals
j. supporting district policies and goals
1. supports administrative directives, school board goals, and organizational policies
2. adheres to *Guidance Program Framework*
3. cooperates with district administration in guidance program improvement efforts.

5. **Establishes effective professional relationships by building rapport with**
   a. Students
   1. demonstrates knowledge of, interest in, and understanding of the roles and responsibilities of the student
   2. acts as student advocate appropriately and effectively
   3. communicates effectively with and about students
   4. exhibits sensitivity, empathy, and acceptance necessary for establishing rapport
   5. encourages students to have respect for the rights, property, and opinions of others
   6. primary commitment is to the student, yet keeps communications open with others
   7. is student advocate and liaison for students/administration/faculty/parents
   8. knows the students' backgrounds
   9. encourages students to assume responsibility for own behaviors, choices, and relationships
   b. Staff
   1. demonstrates knowledge of, interest in, and understanding of the roles and responsibilities of the teacher and other staff members
   2. works cooperatively as a team member with staff
   3. communicates effectively with and about staff
   4. exhibits sensitivity, empathy, and acceptance necessary for establishing rapport
   5. works as a team member—educator, consultant
   6. respects professional judgments of staff
   7. seeks and respects ideas of others
   8. is receptive to teachers' comments and suggestions
   9. encourages teachers to adjust their programs to individual needs of students
   c. Parents
   1. demonstrates knowledge of, interest in, and understanding of the roles, responsibilities, and circumstances of the parent

    2. cooperates with parents in problem solving

    3. communicates effectively with and about parents

    4. exhibits sensitivity, empathy, and acceptance necessary for establishing rapport

    5. encourages parents to practice effective parenting skills

    6. communicates effectively with parents regarding students' progress and areas of difficulty and success

d. Other Counselors

    1. where there is more than one counselor on a campus: operates as a team member; works collaboratively in the development of goals and the implementation of the campus guidance program

    2. cooperates with counselors from other campuses in the interest of serving students and the program better

e. Administrators

    1. demonstrates knowledge of, interest in, and understanding of the roles and responsibilities of the administrator

    2. work cooperatively as a team member with administrators

    3. communicates effectively with and about administrators

    4. understands and responds appropriately to the different roles/responsibilities of the campus and district administrators

    5. exhibits sensitivity, empathy, and acceptance necessary for establishing rapport

    6. plays the child advocate role appropriately

f. Other In-school/District Specialists

    1. demonstrates knowledge and understanding of the roles and responsibilities of other specialists

    2. communicates effectively with and about other specialists

    3. maintains positive working relationships with other specialists

    4. exhibits sensitivity

    5. seeks specialists' assistance when needed/beneficial to the student or other clients

    6. initiates communication when needed/beneficial to the student

    7. does not overrely on other specialists

g. Community Representatives

    1. communicates effectively with referral agency staff

    2. maintains positive working relationships with PTA and other patron groups

    3. is interested in and understands roles/responsibilities of community agency representatives

    4. exhibits sensitivity, warmth, and openness for establishing rapport

    5. establishes harmonious relationships with referral sources commonly used

    6. informs community about total school and guidance programs

6. Fulfills professional responsibilities by

a. seeking professional development

1. has adequate knowledge to be an effective counselor
   a) understands, applies, and can articulate own theoretical framework
   b) understands the organization and operation of the school and the district
   c) is knowledgeable of developmental characteristics of age group served
   d) has basic knowledge of
      1) guidance content and theory
      2) program model
      3) school system organization and operation
   e) can articulate own theoretical framework with respect to guidance and counseling, psychology, and human dynamics
   f) understands and applies basic concepts of psychological theory, measurement and evaluation, group and individual techniques of counseling and guidance
   g) has an internally consistent approach to guidance and counseling

2. plans for and engages in professional development
   a) monitors and evaluates own professional performance
   b) implements his or her Professional Growth Plan
   c) makes use of opportunities for improving skills and acquiring new and relevant knowledge
   d) has developed and is implementing a personal, professional growth plan
   e) attends professional workshops, conferences, and courses
   f) belongs to professional organization(s)
   g) invests personal time
   h) is selective in choosing programs
   i) participates actively in in-district inservice offerings
   j) assumes responsibility for own professional growth
   k) seeks opportunities to improve skills and to acquire new knowledge
   l) maintains contact with current research and practice
   m) combines information from various sources to solve problems/ to innovate
   n) attempts sound innovative and creative approaches to problems
   o) is open to new learning/is willing to learn

3. demonstrates commitment to the counseling and education professions
   a) invests own resources in professional development—time and money

      b) volunteers to serve on committees or accepts other leadership opportunities as offered

      c) accepts leadership roles in professional associations

      d) shares, joins, serves

      e) encourages others to use new ideas

      f) takes pride in being a member of the counseling profession

      g) understands roles/responsibilities of the school counselor at own and at other levels

      h) applies research knowledge and skills to further the field of guidance and counseling

b. keeping records consistent with ethical and legal guidelines

    1. keeps organized, accurate, legal, and ethically appropriate records

    2. interprets records to others as is consistent with ethical and legal guidelines

    3. keeps records in an organized and consistent fashion

    4. communicates and interprets accurately and openly

    5. monitors overall records procedure

    6. delegates appropriately

    7. supervises paraprofessional staff effectively

    8. ensures security, confidentiality, and legality

    9. is knowledgeable of proper procedures

    10. maintains adequate, differentiated records

    11. documents consultations, referrals, and other guidance and counseling events

    12. completes paperwork in a timely and efficient manner

c. maintaining professional work habits

    1. performs responsibilities in an organized, timely, and dependable manner

    2. complies with district's standards for attendance

    3. is considerate of others' time

    4. completes required forms and reports

    5. attends/participates in required staff meetings

    6. exercises professional judgment in absences from work

    7. plans and utilizes time to best advantage

    8. complies with established district work hours

    9. is task-oriented

    10. maintains a positive atmosphere for learning and growing

    11. attends to detail

d. practicing according to the profession's ethical standards

    1. observes ethical standards of the American School Counselor Association and the American Association of Counseling and Development

    2. implements counselor's role as defined in the *Northside Comprehensive Guidance Program Framework* and other district guidelines

    3. adheres to district policies and legal guidelines
    4. refrains from revealing confidential information inappropriately
    5. does not impose personal value judgments on students, their families, or on school staff
    6. demonstrates impartiality with respect to sex, ethnicity, or ability of students
    7. is aware of own personal/emotional and professional limitations
    8. maintains confidentiality within established parameters
e. demonstrating appropriate personal characteristics
    1. demonstrates attitudes conducive to effective guidance and counseling; is:

positive	persevering	accessible/available
pleasant	genuine	supportive
cheerful	open-minded	receptive to change
accepting	future-minded	willing to share
enthusiastic	realistic	information and ideas
cooperative	optimistic	flexible
helpful	personally	has vision
	courageous	

    2. demonstrates attributes conducive to effective guidance and counseling:
        a) takes initiative
        b) is caring, kind, warm
        c) has a sense of humor
        d) demonstrates patience
        e) is sensitive to others; has empathy
        f) uses intelligence and creativity
    3. holds values conducive to effective guidance and counseling
        a) demonstrates self-acceptance, -understanding and -confidence
        b) holds positive regard for the worth, dignity, and uniqueness of each individual
        c) demonstrates belief in ability of others to change, grow, and accept responsibility for own actions
        d) demonstrates honesty and loyalty
        e) values own role as model to others
        f) demonstrates belief in the value of learning and schooling
        g) respects individual differences
        h) resists imposing conforming behaviors on individuals
        i) makes a commitment of primary responsibility to students while providing adequate communication to teachers, parents, administrators, and other referral sources without violating confidentiality of the counseling relationship
    4. has high professional standards

a) accepts constructive criticism
b) adapts to unusual circumstances
c) tolerates ambiguity
d) maintains objectivity/professional detachment in problem situations
e) seems informed and confident in expression
f) has professional image with students, staff, and parents
g) models expected social behavior, grooming, and courtesy
h) maintains poise and emotional stability
i) strives for excellence
j) is motivated to achieve
k) maintains good physical health
l) provides a good moral example for students
m) handles decisions of superiors appropriately
n) recognizes own leadership role on campus and accepts the responsibilities of leadership on the campus

f. demonstrating effective use of basic skills, e.g., communication, problem-solving, decision-making, educational

1. uses communication skills
   a) listens actively
   b) builds rapport
   c) is interested in others' messages
   d) uses appropriate vocabulary
   e) maintains a supportive environment
   f) speaks and writes professionally
   g) uses both verbal and nonverbal communication behaviors appropriately
   h) uses appropriate attending behaviors
   i) uses open-ended questions and prompts
   j) reflects feelings of communicator
   k) accurately paraphrases content of communicator's message
   l) uses interpretation skills effectively
   m) responds to verbal and nonverbal communications in meaningful ways

2. problem solving
   a) diagnoses problems accurately
   b) prescribes appropriate remedies
   c) approaches problems with impartiality
   d) is able to think of multiple options for problem solution
   e) is able to envision consequences of various options
   f) handles dissenting individuals and groups

3. decision making

a) recognizes the need for a decision
b) explores alternative choices
c) predicts accurately the probable outcome of each choice
d) assigns personal values to each choice
e) determines the costs/risks attendant to each choice
f) applies a variety of decision strategies
g) makes a plan for decision implementation
h) evaluates the outcome of decisions

4. educational skills
   a) imparts information effectively
   b) strengthens students' capacity to cope with life situations
   c) allows "wait time"
   d) maintains physical environment appropriate to the session conducted
   e) has materials, aids, and facilities ready for use for various activities
   f) maximizes use of time available for guidance and counseling
   g) manages student behavior, e.g.,
      1) specifies expectations
      2) uses techniques to prevent, redirect, or stop off-task, inappropriate, or disruptive behavior
      3) applies rules consistently and fairly
      4) uses reinforcement techniques effectively
   h) uses effective strategies to motivate students to respond to guidance and counseling
   i) displays a working knowledge of group dynamics, e.g.,
      1) content and process variables
      2) typical stages of group development
      3) various leadership styles and their effective use
      4) conditions for promoting healthy groups

APPENDIX G

OBSERVATION FORMS

GUIDANCE DEPARTMENT
NORTHSIDE INDEPENDENT SCHOOL DISTRICT

SUMMARY OF COUNSELOR OBSERVATION AND FEEDBACK
COUNSELING SKILLS

Counselor _____ Date of Observation _____

School _____ Observation: From _____ to _____

General Information—(theme, screening criteria, etc.)

Grade level: _____ No. of students _____

Session #: _____

Goal of group: _____

Objective(s) of session: _____

Client(s)' descriptions: _____

	Observed? (Circle)	Indicators/ Comments:
I. *Results of program Plans and Preparation*		
a. Selects group/individual needs appropriately for efficiency and effectiveness	Yes No	_____
b. Uses appropriate procedures for group member selection	Yes No	_____
c. Clearly articulates purpose and strategies of session	Yes No	_____
d. Responds appropriately to requests for information	Yes No	_____

e. Length of session is appropriate to
   plans   Yes   No   _____

f. Has materials, etc., ready for use   Yes   No   _____

g. Establishes environment conducive
   to counseling   Yes   No   _____

h. Selects strategies that are student-
   centered and appropriate to stu-
   dents' age level and problems   Yes   No   _____

i. Provides services consistent with
   high priority student needs and dis-
   trict goals   Yes   No   _____

Comments:

II. *The Counseling Process*

a. Provides focus for group   Yes   No   _____

b. Keeps group on task   Yes   No   _____

c. Facilitates students' problem defini-
   tion and goal setting   Yes   No   _____

d. Gently encourages participation of
   each member   Yes   No   _____

e. Provides opportunity for student in-
   teraction   Yes   No   _____

f. Facilitates communication between
   participants   Yes   No   _____

g. Listens effectively   Yes   No   _____

h. Avoids premature of superficial ad-
   vice or reassurance   Yes   No   _____

i. Handles expressions of hostility in a
   constructive manner   Yes   No   _____

j. Checks for understanding   Yes   No   _____

k. Facilitates "guided practice" (if
   appropriate)   Yes   No   _____

l. Clearly states follow-up plans   Yes   No   _____

m. States independent practice/"chal-
   lenges"   Yes   No   _____

Comments:

III. *Personal/Professional*
   a. Protects confidentiality   Yes No   _____
   b. Leads without dominating   Yes No   _____
   c. Explains clearly and concisely   Yes No   _____
   d. Is genuine as opposed to "phony"   Yes No   _____
   e. Interrupts destructive interaction ap-
      propriately   Yes No   _____
   f. Discloses own feelings and beliefs
      in a constructive manner   Yes No   _____
   g. Is tolerant of ideas others express   Yes No   _____
   h. Treats individuals with respect   Yes No   _____
   i. Recognizes individuals within group   Yes No   _____
   j. Uses appropriate vocabulary   Yes No   _____
   k. Applies a sound theoretical base   Yes No   _____
   l. Operates within realistic limitations
      of school counseling services   Yes No   _____
   Comments:

SUMMARY COMMENTS AND RECOMMENDATIONS:

FEEDBACK CONFERENCE DATE: _____ TIME: _____
OBSERVER: _____ COUNSELOR: _____
(Signatures are for the sole purpose of documenting the conference.)

GUIDANCE DEPARTMENT
NORTHSIDE INDEPENDENT SCHOOL DISTRICT

SUMMARY OF COUNSELOR OBSERVATION
CONSULTATION SKILLS

Counselor _____ Date of Observation _____

School _____ Observation: From _____ to _____

General Information—(context, participants, objectives, etc.)
    Student grade level:
    People involved in session:
    Topic:

	Observed? (Circle)	Indicators/ Comments:
I. *Planning and Preparation*		
a. Makes objectives of session clear	Yes No	_____
b. Is prepared for conference (e.g. has relevant information, knows students' background, is focused on the problem/issue)	Yes No	_____
c. Prepares appropriate documentation, forms, records, etc.	Yes No	_____
d. Has knowledge of community resources and referral sources	Yes No	_____
e. Demonstrates knowledge of school district policy	Yes No	_____
f. Has established that consultation is an appropriate intervention	Yes No	_____
Comments:		
II. *The Consultative Process*		
a. Uses effective intake procedures to properly discern problem/issue	Yes No	_____
b. Collaborates with consultee in definition of problem and goal setting	Yes No	_____

c. Coordinates a specific behavioral plan
    of action   Yes   No   _____

d. Listens effectively   Yes   No   _____

e. Facilitates communication between
    participants   Yes   No   _____

f. Suggests various options for problem
    resolution   Yes   No   _____

g. Avoids premature, superficial advice
    or reassurance   Yes   No   _____

h. Handles expressions of conflict in a
    constructive manner   Yes   No   _____

i. Conducts session efficiently and ef-
    fectively   Yes   No   _____

j. States plan for follow-up   Yes   No   _____

k. Summarizes conference results ac-
    curately   Yes   No   _____

Comments:

III. *Personal/Professional*

a. Protects confidentiality   Yes   No   _____

b. Is genuine as opposed to "phony"   Yes   No   _____

c. Is appreciative of ideas others express Yes   No   _____

d. Recognizes diversity of individuals'
    perspectives   Yes   No   _____

e. Promotes a spirit of compromise and
    cooperation   Yes   No   _____

f. Establishes professional credibility   Yes   No   _____

g. Applies a sound theoretical base   Yes   No   _____

SUMMARY COMMENTS AND RECOMMENDATIONS:

FEEDBACK CONFERENCE DATE: _____ TIME: _____
OBSERVER: _____ COUNSELOR: _____
(Signatures are for the sole purpose of documenting the conference.)

GUIDANCE DEPARTMENT
NORTHSIDE INDEPENDENT SCHOOL DISTRICT

SUMMARY OF COUNSELOR OBSERVATION
REFERRAL SKILLS

Counselor _____ Date of Observation _____

School _____ Observation: From _____ to _____

General Information—(context, participants, objectives, etc.)
  Student grade level:
  People involved in session:
  Topic:

	Observed? (Circle)	Indicators/ Comments:
I. *Plans and Preparation*		
a. Understands and articulates reason(s) for referral	Yes No	_____
b. Is prepared for conference (e.g. has relevant information, knows students' background, is focused on the problem/issue)	Yes No	_____
c. Prepares appropriate documentation, forms, records, etc.	Yes No	_____
d. Has knowledge of community resources and referral sources	Yes No	_____
e. Demonstrates knowledge of school district policy	Yes No	_____
f. Has established that referral is an appropriate intervention	Yes No	_____
Comments:		
II. *Referral Conference*		
a. Uses effective intake procedures to properly discern problem/issue	Yes No	_____
b. Defines problem clearly	Yes No	_____

c. Expresses rationale for referral
   clearly   Yes   No   _____

d. Outlines action steps for referral
   process   Yes   No   _____

e. Listens effectively   Yes   No   _____

f. Provides minimum of three referral
   options to client (if referral is non-
   district, program/specialists)   Yes   No   _____

g. Helps individuals referred to have
   realistic expectations of services
   available from referral source   Yes   No   _____

h. Helps individuals referred to understand their responsibilities and to
   make plans for action   Yes   No   _____

i. States own follow-up/coordination
   plans   Yes   No   _____

j. Summarizes conference results   Yes   No   _____

Comments:

III. *Personal/Professional*

a. Promotes confidentiality   Yes   No   _____

b. Is genuine as opposed to "phony"   Yes   No   _____

c. Recognizes feelings and thoughts of
   client(s)   Yes   No   _____

d. Promotes a spirit of cooperation
   and problem-solving   Yes   No   _____

e. Establishes professional credibility   Yes   No   _____

f. Assists individual(s) referred to feel
   comfortable about referral   Yes   No   _____

SUMMARY COMMENTS AND RECOMMENDATIONS:

FEEDBACK CONFERENCE DATE: _____ TIME: _____

OBSERVER: _____ COUNSELOR: _____

(Signatures are for the sole purpose of documenting the conference.)

NOTES

INDEX

NOTES

NOTES

NOTES

NOTES

NOTES

NOTES